Multilingual Education

THE CAMBRIDGE APPLIED LINGUISTICS SERIES

The authority on cutting-edge Applied Linguistics research

Series Editors   2007–present: Carol A. Chapelle and Susan Hunston
                       1988–2007: Michael H. Long and Jack C. Richards

For a complete list of titles please visit: www.cambridge.org/elt/cal

Recent titles in this series:

Narrative Research in Applied Linguistics
Edited by Gary Barkhuizen

Teacher Research in Language Teaching
A Critical Analysis
Simon Borg

Figurative Language, Genre and Register
Alice Deignan, Jeannette Littlemore and Elena Semino

Exploring ELF
Academic English Shaped by Non-native Speakers
Anna Mauranen

Genres across the Disciplines
Student Writing in Higher Education
Hilary Nesi and Sheena Gardner

Disciplinary Identities
Individuality and Community in Academic Discourse
Ken Hyland

Replication Research in Applied Linguistics
Edited by Graeme Porte

The Language of Business Meetings
Michael Handford

Reading in a Second Language
Moving from Theory to Practice
William Grabe

Modelling and Assessing Vocabulary Knowledge
Edited by Helmut Daller, James Milton and Jeanine Treffers-Daller

Practice in a Second Language
Perspectives from Applied Linguistics and Cognitive Psychology
Edited by Robert M. DeKeyser

Feedback in Second Language Writing
Edited by Ken Hyland and Fiona Hyland

Task-Based Language Education
From Theory to Practice
Edited by Kris van den Branden

Second Language Needs Analysis
Edited by Michael H. Long

Insights into Second Language Reading
A Cross-Linguistic Approach
Keiko Koda

Research Genres
Exploration and Applications
John M. Swales

Critical Pedagogies and Language Learning
Edited by Bonny Norton and Kelleen Toohey

Exploring the Dynamics of Second Language Writing
Edited by Barbara Kroll

Understanding Expertise in Teaching
Case Studies of Second Language Teachers
Amy B. M. Tsui

Criterion-Referenced Language Testing
James Dean Brown and Thom Hudson

Corpora in Applied Linguistics
Susan Hunston

Pragmatics in Language Teaching
Edited by Kenneth R. Rose and Gabriele Kasper

Cognition and Second Language Instruction
Edited by Peter Robinson

Research Perspectives on English for Academic Purposes
Edited by John Flowerdew and Matthew Peacock

Computer Applications in Second Language Acquisition
Foundations for Teaching, Testing and Research
Carol A. Chapelle

Multilingual Education
Between language learning and translanguaging

Edited by

Jasone Cenoz

University of the Basque Country, UPV/EHU, Spain

and

Durk Gorter

University of the Basque Country, UPV/EHU, Spain

CAMBRIDGE
UNIVERSITY PRESS

CAMBRIDGE
UNIVERSITY PRESS

University Printing House, Cambridge CB2 8BS, United Kingdom

Cambridge University Press is part of the University of Cambridge.

It furthers the University's mission by disseminating knowledge in the pursuit of education, learning and research at the highest international levels of excellence.

www.cambridge.org
Information on this title: www.cambridge.org/9781107477513

© Cambridge University Press 2015

First published 2015

A catalogue record for this publication is available from the British Library

Library of Congress Cataloguing in Publication data
Multilingual education : between language learning and translanguaging / edited by Jasone Cenoz, University of the Basque Country, UPV/EHU, Spain and Durk Gorter, University of the Basque Country, UPV/EHU, Spain.
  p. cm. – (The Cambridge Applied Linguistics Series)
  ISBN 978-1-107-47751-3 (pbk.)
1. Multilingualism.   2. Bilingual, Education.   3. Language and languages – Study and teaching.   4. Language acquisition.   5. Language transfer (Language learning)   6. Languages in contact.   I. Cenoz, Jasone, editor. II. Gorter, D. (Durk) editor.

P115.2.M85   2015
404'.2–dc23

2014032589

ISBN   978-1-107-47751-3   Paperback

Contents

List of contributors

Igone Arteagoitia is a research scientist at the Center for Applied Linguistics in Washington, DC, USA. She is currently Associate Director of the National Clearinghouse for English Language Acquisition of the US Department of Education. Her research focuses on the language and literacy development of Spanish–English bilingual children, cross-linguistic influence and language assessment. She has recently served as principal investigator in a research project funded by the US Department of Education examining the effects of a cognate-based vocabulary intervention on the development of language and literacy skills in Spanish–English bilingual students. Her work has been published in the *Bilingual Research Journal* and *TESOL Quarterly* and presented at international conferences such as the International Symposium on Bilingualism and the Society for the Scientific Study of Reading.

Susan Ballinger received her PhD from McGill University, Montreal, Canada, in 2013. Her research has focused on peer interaction and language learning in bilingual and immersion contexts in the USA and Québec. Specifically, her research topics have included investigations of Spanish and English language use in US two-way immersion, cross-linguistic teaching interventions in Québec French immersion and ESL contexts, and peer interaction for L2 learning. She has published in *Language Teaching Research*, *Language Awareness* and the *Journal for Immersion and Content-Based Language Education*. In addition, she has co-edited a special issue of *Language Teaching Research* with Roy Lyster (2011), and is currently co-editing a book with Masatoshi Sato entitled *Peer Interaction and Second Language Learning* (Language Learning & Language Teaching series, John Benjamins). She is the editor of ESL publications for Scolaire Québec at Chenelière Education.

Adrian Blackledge is Professor of Bilingualism and Director of the MOSAIC Centre for Research on Multilingualism, School of Education, University of Birmingham, UK. His research interests include translanguaging, and the practice and politics of multilingualism. His recent publications include *Heteroglossia as Practice and Pedagogy* (with Angela Creese; Springer, 2014), *The Routledge*

Handbook of Multilingualism (with Marilyn Martin-Jones and Angela Creese, 2012) and *Multilingualism: A Critical Perspective* (with Angela Creese; Continuum, 2010).

David Block is ICREA Research Professor in Sociolinguistics at the Universitat de Lleida. Over the past 25 years, he has published articles and chapters on a variety of topics, including second language learning and teaching, migration, multiculturalism, multilingualism, language and identity and, most recently, political economy and social class. He is author of *Social Class in Applied Linguistics* (Routledge, 2014), *Second Language Identities* (Continuum, 2007), *Multilingual Identities in a Global City: London Stories* (Palgrave, 2006) and *The Social Turn in Second Language Acquisition* (Edinburgh University Press, 2003). He co-authored, with John Gray and Marnie Holborow, *Neoliberalism and Applied Linguistics* (Routledge, 2012) and co-edited, with Deborah Cameron, *Globalization and Language Teaching* (Routledge, 2002). He is assistant editor of the journal *Applied Linguistics Review* and editor of the Routledge book series Language, Society and Political Economy.

Jasone Cenoz is Professor of Research Methods in Education at the University of the Basque Country, UPV/EHU, Spain. Her research focuses on multilingual education, third language acquisition, bilingualism and multilingualism. Specific topics Jasone Cenoz has investigated in her research include the multilingual lexicon, translanguaging in written production, Basque multilingual education and cross-linguistic influence. She has published articles on multilingual education in the *Modern Language Journal, Applied Linguistics, Language Culture and Curriculum, TESOL Quarterly, Language Teaching* and the *International Journal of Bilingual Education and Bilingualism* among others. She is also the author of several book chapters and books, including the award-winning monograph *Towards Multilingual Education* (Multilingual Matters, 2009). She has served as AILA publications coordinator for eight years and has been a member of the Executive Committee of IASCL and the International Association of Multilingualism.

Angela Creese is Professor of Educational Linguistics and Deputy Director of the MOSAIC Centre for Research on Multilingualism, School of Education, University of Birmingham, UK. Her research interests are in linguistic ethnography, language ecologies, multilingualism in society and multilingual classroom pedagogy. Her publications include *Heteroglossia as Practice and Pedagogy* (with Adrian

Blackledge; Springer, 2014), *The Routledge Handbook of Multilingualism* (with Marilyn Martin-Jones and Adrian Blackledge, 2012), *Multilingualism: A Critical Perspective* (with Adrian Blackledge; Continuum, 2010), *Ecology of Language, Encyclopedia of Language and Education*, Volume IX (Springer, 2009), *Teacher Collaboration and Talk in Multilingual Classrooms* (Multilingual Matters, 2005) and *Multilingual Classroom Ecologies* (co-edited with Peter Martin; Multilingual Matters, 2003).

Nelson Flores is Assistant Professor of Educational Linguistics at the University of Pennsylvania Graduate School of Education, USA. His research critically examines the historical origins of modern language ideologies and their continued role in producing educational policies and practices that marginalize the language practices of language minoritized students. His work also seeks to theorize new approaches to educational policy and practice that are more responsive to the needs of these students. He has published articles on a range of topics related to language ideologies in education in *TESOL Quarterly*, *Linguistics and Education* and *Critical Inquiry in Language Studies* among others. He has also authored several book chapters pertaining to this topic.

Janet M. Fuller is Professor of Anthropology at Southern Illinois University at Carbondale, USA. Her research interests lie in the area of social identities and language ideologies in multilingual contexts, especially educational contexts. She has recently published a monograph looking at these issues in bilingual classrooms with a particular focus on how socioeconomic class plays a role in language and education (*Bilingual Pre-Teens: Competing Ideologies and Multiple Identities in the U.S. and Germany*; Routledge, 2012). Her textbook entitled *Spanish Speakers in the USA* (Multilingual Matters, 2013) addresses issues of race and ethnicity along with language, identities and ideologies. She is also co-author (with Ron Wardhaugh) of the forthcoming seventh edition of *An Introduction to Sociolinguistics*.

Ofelia García is professor in the PhD programs of Urban Education at the Graduate Center of the City University of New York, USA. She has been Professor of Bilingual Education at Columbia University's Teachers College, and Dean of the School of Education at the Brooklyn Campus of Long Island University. She is the associate general editor of the *International Journal of the Sociology of Language* and has published widely in the areas of sociolinguistics, bilingualism and bilingual education.

Durk Gorter is Ikerbasque Research Professor at the University of the Basque Country, UPV-EHU, Spain. He does research on different aspects of multilingual education, comparing language education policies on European minority languages, in particular Basque and Frisian, and diversity in linguistic landscapes. Among his publications are *Minority Languages and Multilingual Education* (co-edited with Vicky Zenotz, Xabier Etxague and Jasone Cenoz; Springer, 2014), *Minority Languages in the Linguistic Landscape* (co-edited with Heiko Marten and Luk Van Mensel; Palgrave Macmillan, 2012), *Focus on Multilingualism in School Contexts* (co-edited with Jasone Cenoz as a special issue of the *Modern Language Journal*, 2011), *Linguistic Landscape: Expanding the Scenery* (co-edited with Elana Shohamy; Routledge, 2009) and *Multilingual Europe: Facts and Policies* (co-edited with Guus Extra; De Gruyter, 2008). He is the editor in chief of *Language, Culture and Curriculum*.

Elizabeth R. Howard is an associate professor of Bilingual Education in the Neag School of Education at the University of Connecticut, USA, where she teaches graduate courses on linguistic and cultural diversity and conducts research focusing on dual language education, biliteracy development and the preparation of teachers to work with multilingual learners. She has recently served as a principal investigator of two federally funded research studies focusing on the literacy attainment of Spanish–English bilingual students, as well as co-director of a faculty learning community designed to improve the capacity of teacher education faculty to help preservice teachers work effectively with English language learners. She is a co-author of *Realizing the Vision of Two-Way Immersion: Fostering Effective Programs and Classrooms* (with Julie Sugarman; Delta, 2006) and co-editor of *Preparing Classroom Teachers to Succeed with Second Language Learners* (with David Moss, forthcoming).

Michael Huffmaster is Assistant Professor of German at the University of Puerto Rico, Mayagüez. His current book project, *Reading Kafka's Mind: The Cognitive Poetics of a Multilingual Imagination*, employs cognitive theory to explain the Kafkaesque. In addition to German language, literature and culture, he has taught translation theory and practice and has published (with Claire Kramsch) on the benefits of literary translation in the foreign language classroom. His research focuses on the ways in which adult foreign language learning and the study of literature in a foreign language foster critical and creative cognitive skills as well as on how these disciplines promote the core democratic values of a liberal arts education.

Claire Kramsch is Professor of German and Affiliate Professor of Education at the University of California at Berkeley, USA. Her research focuses on foreign/second language education, second language acquisition and social approaches to multilingualism. She has explored in particular the relation of language and culture, the role of discourse in language learning and language use, and what it means to be multilingual. She is the author of numerous articles, book chapters and books. Her more well-known publications include *The Multilingual Subject* (Oxford University Press, 2009), *Language Acquisition and Language Socialization: Ecological Perspectives* (Continuum, 2002), *Language and Culture* (Oxford University Press, 1998), *Context and Culture in Language Teaching* (Oxford University Press, 1993) and *Discourse Analysis and Second Language teaching* (Centre for Applied Linguistics, 1981). She is the past co-editor of *Applied Linguistics* and past president of AAAL, and is the current vice-president of AILA.

Glenn S. Levine is Professor of German and German Language Program Director in the Department of European Languages and Studies at the University of California, Irvine, USA. His areas of research include second language acquisition and socialization, and curriculum design and teaching. His publications address code choice in second language learning; constructivist, ecological and critical approaches to curriculum design and teaching; language and digital media use during study abroad; and issues of language programme direction. His books are *Code Choice in the Language Classroom* (Multilingual Matters, 2011) and *Incomplete First-Language Acquisition in the Immigrant Situation: Yiddish in the United States* (Max Niemeyer Verlag, 2000). He also co-edited (with Alison Phipps) *Critical and Intercultural Theory and Language Pedagogy* (Cengage Heinle, 2012).

Li Wei is Professor of Applied Linguistics at Birkbeck College, University of London, UK, where he is also Pro-Vice-Master and Director of the Birkbeck Graduate Research School. His research covers various aspects of bilingualism and multilingualism, including bilingual and multilingual acquisition, bilingual education, and language policy. Amongst his numerous publications are *Applied Linguistics* (Wiley-Blackwell, 2014), *The Bilingualism Reader* (Routledge, 2nd edition 2007), the award-winning *Blackwell Guide to Research Methods in Bilingualism and Multilingualism* (with Melissa Moyer; Wiley-Blackwell, 2008) and *Translanguaging: Language, Bilingualism and Education* (with Ofelia García; Palgrave

Macmillan, 2014). He is principal editor of the *International Journal of Bilingualism*.

Angel M. Y. Lin is an associate professor at the Faculty of Education, University of Hong Kong. She received her PhD from the Ontario Institute for Studies in Education, University of Toronto, Canada, in 1996. Since then her research and teaching have focused on classroom discourse analysis, bilingual education, and language policy and planning in postcolonial contexts. She has published six research books and over eighty research articles, and sits on the editorial boards of leading international research journals including *Applied Linguistics*, the *International Journal of Bilingual Education and Bilingualism*, *British Educational Research Journal*, *Journal of Critical Discourse Studies*, *Language and Education* and *Pragmatics and Society*.

Gladys N. Y. Luk is Assistant Lecturer at the School of Education and Languages of the Open University of Hong Kong. She is pursuing her EdD degree at the University of Hong Kong under the supervision of Dr Angel Lin. Her research interests mainly lie within the area of medium of instruction and bilingual education. She is also interested in discourse analysis and teacher language awareness. Her publications include full paper proceedings in the fields of pragmatics and translation study, and conference papers in the areas of code-switching and language attitudes towards Cantonese, English and Putonghua in Hong Kong society.

Jaspreet Kaur Takhi joined the School of Education, University of Birmingham, UK, in June 2010, as Bilingual Research Fellow on the HERA JRP funded project 'Investigating discourses of inheritance and identity in four multilingual European settings' with Adrian Blackledge and Angela Creese. She investigated linguistic repertoires and notions of inheritance and identity among young people living in Birmingham and attending a Panjabi complementary school. She has published (with Adrian Blackledge and Angela Creese) on aspects of multilingualism and superdiversity in: *Multilingual Urban Sites: Structure, Activity, Ideology* (Cambridge University Press, forthcoming), *The Multilingual Turn: Implications for SLA, TESOL and Bilingual Education* (Routledge, 2013) and *NALDIC Quarterly* among others. Her research interests include code-switching, conflict between migrant generations and negotiating identity through language and popular culture.

Heather Homonoff Woodley is Clinical Assistant Professor of Multilingual-Multicultural Studies in the Department of Teaching and

Learning at the Steinhardt School of Culture, Education, and Human Development, New York University, USA. She is a recent graduate of the PhD program in Urban Education at the CUNY Graduate Center and has taught in schools in New York City and Washington, DC. Her research focuses on culturally relevant teaching and classroom empowerment for linguistic and religious minority youth in schools.

Series editors' preface

The title of this volume, *Multilingual Education: Between language learning and translanguaging*, reflects its focus on an area of study in transition. As the first chapter explains, the study of multilingualism in educational contexts has taken on a new character and significance in the current era because of globalization. Never before has the world experienced such dramatic levels of language contact, which results in the need for people to use a language other than their own to learn, make friends and conduct business. The editors point out that this situation, which has arisen because of the growth in connections among people that has been made possible through increased mobility and technology, requires new perspectives for applied linguists to study meaningfully the acquisition and use of more than one language in contexts where multiple languages are in use.

The editors define multilingualism as the use of languages that are not originally from nearby geographical areas. Multilingualism can be studied both as a social phenomenon and at the individual level. The former perspective investigates who uses what language for what purposes. In other words, research on societal multilingualism stems from a sociolinguistic orientation to the study of language use. The study of individual multilingualism intersects with research on language acquisition, including an individual's choice of language in social use as well. The study of multilingualism as reported in the 11 chapters of the volume demonstrates the intersection of the social and individual perspectives as multilingualism is taught and enacted in educational settings around the world.

The global dimensions of multilingual education are evident in the range of languages that appear in the research on various multilingual configurations: Chinese–English in Hong Kong and the UK, English–French in Canada, English–German in the USA and Germany, English–Panjabi in the UK and Spanish–English in the USA. In each of the contexts under investigation, the goal of multilingual education is for students to develop, use and value more than one language. Multilingual education as defined in this volume rejects the educational goals of transitioning students towards monolingualism, for example the use of the home language as a temporary stepping stone to help students while they learn to function in the majority language.

By excluding certain uses of bilingual education from the definition of multilingualism, the editors explicitly present an ideological orientation to the volume that has implications for the research. Perhaps most important is the fact that, in a framework where multilingualism is valued, the implicit norm for educational goals cannot be the monolingual native speaker of one of the languages. The need to adopt the multilingual as norm has been evident to many applied linguists for some time, but in this volume, readers can see how this ideological position plays out in real educational settings. We are therefore pleased to add this volume to the Cambridge Applied Linguistics series.

Carol A. Chapelle and Susan Hunston

Acknowledgements

The authors and publishers are grateful to the following contributors:

Aptara: text design and page make-up
Jacqueline French: freelance editorial services

The authors and publishers acknowledge the following sources of copyright material and are grateful for the permissions granted. While every effort has been made, it has not always been possible to identify the sources of all the material used, or to trace all copyright holders. If any omissions are brought to our notice, we will be happy to include the appropriate acknowledgements on reprinting.

Fig 11.1 on p. 226 taken from Apples and Oranges: Or, Why Apples are Not Orange and Don't Need to Be. *Modern Language Journal*, 82,1. 83–90. Used with permission of Sue Gass.

1 Towards a holistic approach in the study of multilingual education

Jasone Cenoz and Durk Gorter

1.1 Multilingualism at school as a global phenomenon

Although multilingualism is not a recent phenomenon, it has become more common in recent years due to globalization, transnational mobility of the population and the spread of ICT. According to Aronin and Hufeisen (2009), contemporary multilingualism has spread geographically and socially and is characterized by the use of languages that are not originally from neighbouring areas. Furthermore, technology has contributed to instantaneous communication among multilingual speakers in different parts of the world. The statistics on the use of English and other languages on the Internet show that multilingualism is increasing. English is still the most widely used language on the Internet. It was used by 51.3% of internet users in the year 2000 (Graddol, 2006), but this figure dropped to 26.8% in 2011 (Internet World Stats, 2011). Meanwhile, the use of other languages such as Arabic, Chinese and Russian is growing much faster than the use of English on the Web (Internet World Stats, 2011). Globalization has given multilingualism not only visibility but also an added value associated with the ability to speak several languages (Edwards, 2004).

Multilingualism at the individual level (also referred to as plurilingualism) brings together the process of acquiring second or foreign languages and the use of these languages. Individuals may learn and use languages of wider communication such as English or Mandarin, but they may also learn languages used in their sociolinguistic environment. Multilingualism can give better opportunities, particularly in the job market, but it is also linked to identity and belonging to one or more speech communities. The latter is often the case with less spread languages, such as Maori in New Zealand, Basque in the Basque Country or Welsh in the UK. Speakers of these languages are usually fluent in international languages (English in the case of Maori and Welsh, French and/or Spanish in the case of Basque), but they go on using their own languages.

1

Multilingualism has spread in education and nowadays it has more visibility in school settings. Many schools in different parts of the world have second or foreign languages as part of the curriculum. English is the most common second/foreign language taught at schools, but other national and minority languages are taught as well. Languages have traditionally been part of the education of the elite, but now that education is more accessible to all sectors of the population, multilingualism has become more widespread in education. Another reason for this spread is the mobility of the population. Today it is common to find schoolchildren in the same class who speak different languages at home, and these languages can be part of the school curriculum or not (Candelier, 2008; Extra & Gorter, 2008; Hélot, 2012).

Multilingual education refers to the use of two or more languages in education, provided that schools aim at multilingualism and multi-literacy. The processes of learning and teaching languages may take place at school as part of the official curriculum but also in complementary or community schools that teach the home language and culture. Most research on multilingual education has been carried out in Europe and North America, but there is an increasing number of research studies on multilingualism in educational settings in Africa, Latin America and Asia (Feng, 2007; Hélot & De Mejía, 2008; Skutnabb-Kangas & Heugh, 2012). There is a great diversity of types of multilingual education. This diversity is associated with the characteristics of the languages involved, their use in society and educational factors (Cenoz, 2009). The typological distance between the languages already known by the speaker (the first language/s or others) and the target language(s) can have an influence on the acquisition process. When languages are closer to each other, individuals have more resources at their disposal and can use many elements from the languages they already know when learning an additional language. For a Dutch L1 student, for example, learning English (or German) is not the same as learning Japanese (or Arabic).

The sociolinguistic environment in which the school is placed also needs to be taken into account. Factors such as the number of multilingual speakers, the status of the different languages or their use in the media and the linguistic landscape can affect motivation to learn languages. The languages used by schoolchildren at home with their parents and siblings or the extended family, their neighbours and peers can be influential as well. The educational factors that should be considered include the languages of instruction used at school, the intensity of language instruction, the age of introduction of the languages, teachers' multilingual abilities and teaching methodology.

When multilingualism is an educational aim, students are expected to become competent speakers of different languages. One of the most important issues in this process is to identify the best possible conditions and approaches to teach second and foreign languages, that is, the most efficient ways of 'becoming multilingual'. These strategies necessarily include using the languages, and therefore 'being multilingual'. Some schoolchildren have already developed communicative skills in two or more languages because they use different home languages or they live in multilingual areas. They have experienced what 'being multilingual' means to a larger extent, and the school can develop such children's competencies further so that multilingualism is an enriching experience. In this volume we look both at 'becoming multilingual' and at 'being multilingual'. These situations cannot be considered as a dichotomy because multilinguals use their languages in the process of expanding their multilingual competence.

1.2 New trends in the study of multilingual education

The study of multilingual education cannot separate language acquisition, 'becoming multilingual', from language use, 'being multilingual'. In the last 15 years, there has been a shift from a cognitive to a social perspective in the fields of both second language acquisition (SLA) and bilingualism (Firth & Wagner, 1997; Block 2007; Canagarajah, 2007). Besides this 'social turn' in recent years, there has also been a 'multilingual turn' (Cenoz & Gorter, 2011; Kramsch, 2012; May, 2014; Ortega, 2014). These social and multilingual turns have brought studies on second language acquisition and multilingualism closer and have challenged previous ideas about the use of the monolingual native speaker as a reference and the isolation of languages in educational contexts.

The native speaker has traditionally been the reference when teaching and learning languages in school contexts. Learners are expected to achieve some level of communicative competence that could get them progressively closer to the native speaker of the target language. The native speaker is identified with a total command of the target language, a goal that is usually unreachable. As a consequence, this impossible goal produces a sense of failure and lack of self-confidence when learning languages. When the curriculum includes several languages, the possibility of becoming 'an ideal multilingual' with native competence in several languages is even more remote. Apart from being an unreachable goal, the idea of using the native speaker as a reference has been challenged for other reasons. According to Cook (1992, 1995), multilinguals have a qualitatively different type of competence, a complex type of competence that he calls 'multicompetence'. If this is the case, the comparison with the monolingual native speaker of each language does not seem to be sustainable any longer (see also Ortega, 2014). Research on the use of English as a lingua franca (ELF) also calls into question the idea of the monolingual native speaker because the competence of ELF speakers 'derives from their multilingual life' (Canagarajah, 2007: 925).

There is an increasing interest in analysing the way in which multilingual speakers communicate, by looking at language practices both in and out of school (Rampton, 2006; Auer, 2007; Creese & Blackledge, 2010, 2011; Cenoz & Gorter, 2014). The analysis of multilingual discourse practices shows that these practices are quite different from the speech associated with monolingual native speakers. Multilingual speakers are creative, using elements from different languages, and their practices reflect a type of competence that multilingual speakers need to be accepted as members of a community of practice (Kramsch & Whiteside, 2008). As Kramsch (2010) points out, multilingual speakers shape their communicative context while engaging in language practices (see also Canagarajah, 2007).

There is a trend towards adopting a holistic approach when looking at multilingual students and their languages. Many years ago, Grosjean (1985) had already rejected the idea that the bilingual should be expected to be like two monolinguals and proposed a holistic view that includes the bilingual's whole linguistic repertoire. Some theoretical proposals on the acquisition of several languages, such as the 'Dynamic Model of Multilingualism', adopt a holistic view (Herdina & Jessner, 2002). In the field of education, a holistic view of the linguistic repertoire is adopted in 'Focus on Multilingualism', an approach to research and teaching in multilingual education proposed by Cenoz and Gorter (2011). This holistic approach aims at integrating the curricula of the different languages so as to activate the resources multilingual speakers have. In this way, multilingual students can use their resources cross-linguistically and become more efficient language learners than when languages are taught separately.

A related trend that goes against well-established traditions is the idea of softening boundaries between languages. The ideology of language separation is well rooted in education and the teaching practices that date from the Direct Method and avoids translation and interaction between languages. There is a strong idea of separating the target language from the student's L1 or from other languages in the curriculum. Thus, only the target language is expected to be used so as to avoid interference from the other languages. The idea that languages have to be kept as separate containers has been referred to as 'parallel monolingualism' (Heller, 1999: 271), 'two solitudes' (Cummins, 2005: 588) or 'separate bilingualism' (Blackledge & Creese, 2010). In contrast to this traditional view, there are proposals for pedagogies that soften hard boundaries between languages (Cummins, 2007; Lin, 2008; Coste & Simon, 2009; Lyster et al., 2009; Macaro, 2009; Moore & Gajo, 2009; Levine, 2011). One of the strategies is to use the L1 as a resource when acquiring a second or additional language, particularly when the target language is used as the language of instruction and the learning tasks are complex (Cummins, 2007; Turnbull & Dailey-O'Cain, 2009; Levine, 2011).

Some other scholars look at mixed language practices in the classroom as indicators of the development of multilingual identities (García, 2009; Blackledge & Creese, 2010). Blackledge and Creese (2010) refer to 'flexible bilingualism' as an approach that places the speaker at the heart of the interaction and views languages as a social resource without clear boundaries. García (2009) uses the term 'translanguaging' to refer to multiple discursive practices (see also Li Wei, 2010). Research on translanguaging generally focuses on the analysis of multilingual practices which are hybrid and without clear boundaries. Some scholars consider that the hybridity of multilingual communication can be better explained by focusing on language features and multimodal resources than by referring to languages (Makoni & Pennycook, 2007; Jørgensen, 2008; García, 2009; Rampton & Charalambous, 2012). Apart from translanguaging, terms such as 'metrolingualism' (Otsuji & Pennycook, 2009), 'heteroglossia' (Bailey, 2012; Creese & Blackledge, 2014) or 'polylingualism' (Jørgensen, 2008) have been proposed in recent years.

1.3 Becoming multilingual and being multilingual

The new trends in the study of multilingual education have influenced research focusing both on 'becoming multilingual' and on 'being multilingual'. In this section we look at both situations but would like to highlight that they can be represented as a continuum rather than a dichotomy, as in Figure 1.1.

Figure 1.1 represents a continuum between 'becoming multilingual' and 'being multilingual'. This continuum refers to the approaches taken by researchers when studying the interaction between languages or language features in the context of multilingual education. Research in multilingual education is linked to areas of research that study multilingualism and multilingual education from different perspectives and pose different research questions. This continuum shows the positions that

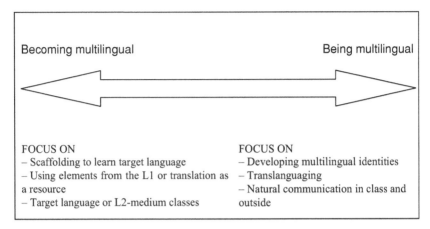

Figure 1.1 Focus of the research study: becoming and being multilingual

represent the crossing over of applied linguistics and second language acquisition theory to sociolinguistic theory and a social approach to language.

Researchers can adopt positions along the continuum, and these can be positions that are either close to the ends or intermediate. Research that focuses on 'becoming multilingual' looks at the process of acquiring communicative competence in a second or additional language and is closely related to second language acquisition studies. Research at this end of the continuum looks at the linguistic goals to be achieved in the school context. It usually observes classes where the target language is learned either as a subject or as the language of instruction, and these studies aim at learning more about the acquisition of multilingual competence in school contexts. This end of the continuum looks at studies focusing on the acquisition of second and additional languages in school contexts. These languages can be classical languages such as Latin, Sanskrit or Greek, second languages used in the sociolinguistic context (national languages or minority languages) and foreign languages of international communication. In contrast to the traditional isolation of languages for teaching, the new trends in the study of multilingual education suggest that the L1 (or other languages) can be used in the target language classroom. This does not mean that the target language is not the medium of instruction, but it allows the use of other languages when necessary. Swain (2012) advocates the use of the L1 as a cognitive tool when the learning tasks are complex, particularly in the case of content-based instruction (see also Turnbull & Dailey-O'Cain, 2009). The position at the 'becoming multilingual' end of the continuum shares many characteristics with traditional SLA research, but there are also important differences. Most SLA researchers still see the use of resources of other languages in the linguistic repertoire as negative transfer. In contrast, researchers who have taken a multilingual turn consider that the languages learners have in their linguistic repertoire can be used as a resource when learning additional languages. Language is still seen as a code, but its boundaries are permeable. In many cases researchers also question the idea of the native speaker as a reference and look at second language learners as emergent multilinguals. This position, which focuses on the process of becoming multilingual from a multilingual perspective, still needs conceptual and methodological development because it is still work in progress (see also Ortega, 2014).

Research that can be placed at the other end of the continuum, 'being multilingual', comes mainly from sociolinguistics. Research on some areas of multilingualism such as code-switching has received a lot of attention in studies on bilingualism and multilingualism for many years. However, the traditional linguistic approaches were challenged by social approaches (Heller, 2007). The idea is not how multilinguals learn or mix codes, but how they use their linguistic resources in their multilingual practices. Studies on 'being bilingual' focus on the way multilingual speakers navigate between languages and examine this intersection, often referred to as multilingual practices or translanguaging (Creese & Blackledge, 2010, 2011; Li Wei, 2010, 2011; García & Sylvan, 2011). In these studies multilingual practices are analysed inside and outside the classroom as related to identities and ideologies.

The continuum reflects the crossing over of ideas from sociolinguistics to second language acquisition in the context of multilingual education. The multilingual turn implies that languages are no longer isolated entities, as their boundaries are becoming softer. At the same time, the fields of second language acquisition and sociolinguistics are also becoming more open and permeable. It is difficult to foresee how these different traditions will interact in the future, but it is clear that we are at a different stage compared to the interest in isolating disciplines and areas of research. The interest of researchers in using a specific perspective can place their research closer to one or the other end of the continuum but also in the middle of the continuum. It is possible, as Block (this volume) points out, to find 'becoming multilingual' and 'being multilingual' in the same context. It is the focus of the research that changes. 'Becoming multilingual' and 'being multilingual' are dynamic concepts because they are processes that interact and develop over time.

As we have already said, the best way to represent the positions of 'being multilingual' and 'becoming multilingual' is a continuum, because becoming and being multilingual are obviously interlinked in practice. The two ends of the continuum are also necessarily interlinked in research studies that focus on multilingual contexts where more than one language is used in everyday life and students are learning these and other languages at school at the same time. Learners in these contexts are in the process of expanding their multilingual competence, and they are already multilingual. This is the case for schoolchildren in areas where a minority language is spoken, such as Catalonia or the Basque Country in Europe. Students can 'be multilingual' because they are fluent in both the minority and the national language (Catalan/Basque and Spanish) and at the same time 'becoming multilingual' because they go on learning these languages and additional languages such as English. The concurrency between 'becoming multilingual' and 'being multilingual' exists in many other situations (see also Block, this volume). Some research approaches highlight one of the ends of the continuum, while others look at both.

'Focus on multilingualism' is a holistic approach for teaching and conducting research in multilingual education that combines 'becoming multilingual' and 'being multilingual' (Cenoz & Gorter, 2011, 2014). This approach proposes soft boundaries between languages and relates the way multilingual students use their communicative resources in spontaneous conversation to the way languages are learned and taught at school. It explores the possibility of establishing bridges between second/foreign language teaching at school and multilingualism in real-life communication, involving all the languages and multilingual discursive practices of speakers. Therefore, it is not the idea of students using the L1 or other languages only when facing difficulties but of them using their competence in different languages as a resource in communication both in the classroom and outside school. 'Focus on multilingualism' considers that the metalinguistic awareness and communicative competence acquired in previously learned languages can be actively used to learn the target language in a more efficient way. In this way, the cognitive advantages that learners have developed as a result of their bilingualism (Bialystok, 2010) and the specific advantages that bilinguals have over monolinguals in the acquisition of a third or additional language (Cenoz, 2013) can be activated when learning second or additional languages. 'Focus on multilingualism' also looks at multilingual practices as examples of real communicative language use that can be employed as a resource in the classroom so as to raise awareness of different types of communicative contexts (Cenoz & Gorter, 2014).

1.4 Multilingual education: new perspectives

This volume explores some holistic trends in the study of multilingual education by putting together research studies that analyse the processes of 'becoming multilingual' and 'being multilingual' in educational contexts. The chapters report studies on the acquisition and use of Chinese, English, French, German, Panjabi and Spanish in the following combinations: Chinese–English in Hong Kong and the UK, English–French in Canada, English–German in the USA and Germany, English–Panjabi in the UK and Spanish–English in the USA.

As the title suggests, this volume focuses on multilingualism in school contexts and brings together the fields of second language acquisition and multilingualism. It links concepts such as translanguaging or the whole multilingual repertoire to language learning in school contexts. The connections between ideas from sociolinguistics and linguistic anthropology and the process of second or additional languages open new possibilities but also shake the foundations of traditional perspectives.

The contributions to this volume reflect different theoretical frameworks and research methodologies, but the coherence of the volume is achieved by sharing a perspective of multilingual education that does not draw hard boundaries between languages. All the chapters in this volume pay particular attention to the interaction between the different languages being learned and used, highlighting to a different extent the use of the L1 or other languages as a scaffold in language learning, code-switching and translanguaging. The chapters in this volume can be placed on the continuum which we discussed before, ranging from 'becoming multilingual' to 'being multilingual'.

This chapter ('Towards a Holistic Approach in the Study of Multilingual Education' by Jasone Cenoz & Durk Gorter) discusses new trends in multilingual education teaching and research. These trends not only reveal the fact that multilingual speakers have a type of competence that is different from that of monolingual speakers but also highlight the need to use multilingualism as a resource when learning and using languages. This chapter also distinguishes between 'becoming multilingual' and 'being multilingual' as the two ends of a continuum that also allows for intermediate positions.

Chapters 2, 3 and 4 focus on using the learner's linguistic resources when learning an additional language. They could be placed on the 'becoming multilingual' end of the continuum because the studies reported here analyse the way the L1 is used as a scaffold for facilitating the acquisition of a second language. However, the multilingual practices also show the link to the other end of the continuum because students are 'being multilingual' as well. In Chapter 2, 'L1 as a Pedagogical Resource in Building Students' L2 Academic Literacy', Gladys N. Y. Luk and Angel M. Y. Lin report on a study conducted in a Hong Kong school. They analyse how science teachers provide the necessary linguistic and cognitive scaffolding when using the students' L1 (Chinese) along with the L2 (English). The results of this case study indicate that the use of the two languages as a pedagogical resource is associated with confidence and interest in the subject as well as with good academic outcomes. Susan Ballinger analyses the results of an intervention in two French immersion classes in Montreal, Canada, in Chapter 3, 'Linking Content, Linking Students: A Cross-linguistic Pedagogical Intervention'. The intervention includes a project to develop biliteracy and a reciprocal language learning strategy, and uses students' existing linguistic resources to build bridges across the two languages, French and English. In Chapter 4, 'The Role of the Native Language in the Literacy Development of Latino Students in the USA', Igone Arteagoitia and Liz Howard look at the possible advantages that Spanish-speaking students may have in the acquisition of vocabulary when they use their knowledge of the L1. They report a study conducted with 230 middle-school students in the USA on the effect of English and Spanish cognate knowledge on reading comprehension in English. The results indicate that using the students' knowledge of the L1 as a resource can facilitate second language development.

The next three chapters (5, 6 and 7) are on English–German multilingualism in school settings. These chapters could be placed somewhere between the two ends of the continuum because they combine 'becoming multilingual' as a language learning process with the experience of 'being multilingual' and the development of multilingual identities. In Chapter 5, 'A Nexus Analysis of Code Choice during Study Abroad and Implications for Language Pedagogy', Glen S. Levine reports on the code-choice practices in their social networks, both face-to-face and digital, of a group of US students studying abroad in Germany. The analysis of these practices is based on Scollon and Scollon's (2004) nexus analysis. Among other teaching implications, the author considers that the principled use of the L1 in the L2 class would be more realistic and closer to the experience of studying abroad than the reference of the monolingual native speaker of the L2. Claire Kramsch and Michael Huffmaster examine an alternative to the extended monolingual static pedagogies in Chapter 6, 'Multilingual Practices in Foreign Language Study'. They do so by looking at the multiple semiotic resources that are used in multilingual practices. Kramsch and Huffmaster highlight the need to raise students' awareness of the meaning-making processes when constructing a cultural and social experience that can be achieved by using teaching techniques such as translation and transposition. In Chapter 7, 'Language Choices and Ideologies in the Bilingual Classroom', Janet M. Fuller looks at the language choices made by children in a German–English bilingual school in Berlin. The theoretical framework for the analysis is social constructionist, and students' identities are shown to be part of a framework of language ideologies constructed in a bilingual school. The findings indicate that students challenge monolingual ideologies by using bilingual discourse.

Chapters 8, 9 and 10 look at the role of translanguaging in the classroom as linked to the development of multilingual identities. These chapters could be placed towards the 'being multilingual' end of the continuum because the aim of the studies is not to see how the students' linguistic repertoire can be used as a scaffold to learn the target language. The studies focus on multilingual practices and try to explain their meaning. Obviously these practices can also contribute to becoming more multilingual. In Chapter 8, 'Communicative Repertoires in the Community Language Classroom: Resources for Negotiating Authenticity', Angela Creese, Adrian Blackledge and Jaspreet Kaur Takhi investigate multilingual practices in a Panjabi complementary school in Birmingham (UK). They found that the teacher's use of signs across language boundaries links the classroom to domains of language use and identity positions beyond the classroom. Another important finding of this study is that identities are not fixed. Li Wei examines the translanguaging practices of Chinese ethnic origin children in complementary schools in Britain in Chapter 9, 'Complementary Classrooms for Multilingual Minority Ethnic Children as a Translanguaging Space'. He discusses the concept of 'translanguaging space', a space where translanguaging takes place and at the same time a space created through translanguaging. The analysis of translanguaging practices reflects multilingual children's multicompetence, creativity and criticality. Furthermore, through translanguaging children become aware of their own sociocultural identity in a globalized world. In Chapter 10, 'Constructing In-between Spaces to "Do" Bilingualism: A Tale of Two High Schools in One City', Ofelia García, Nelson Flores and Heather Homonoff Woodley look at translanguaging in two schools in New York. They explain how multilingual practices are still stigmatized, but the data presented in this chapter show that they are needed in this context. In fact, it is through translanguaging spaces that Latino emergent bilinguals can succeed in an American high school because it makes the students' cognitive and linguistic repertoire more complex.

In the final chapter of the book, 'Becoming Multilingual and Being Multilingual: Some Thoughts' (Chapter 11), David Block discusses the 'becoming multilingual'/'being multilingual' continuum and highlights how they are interrelated and interlinked.

Note

This chapter was written with the assistance of the research grant EDU2012-32191 from the Spanish Ministry of Science and Technology and the Basque Government funding for the research group *Donostia Research on Education and Multilingualism* (DREAM), UFI 11/54.

References

Aronin, L. and Hufeisen, B. (eds.) (2009). *The Exploration of Multilingualism*. Amsterdam: John Benjamins.

Auer, P. (2007). The monolingual bias in bilingualism research, or: why bilingual talk is (still) a challenge for linguistics. In M. Heller (ed.), *Bilingualism: A Social Approach* (pp. 319–39). London: Palgrave Macmillan.

Bailey, B. (2012). Heteroglossia. In M. Martin-Jones, A. Blackledge and A. Creese (eds.), *The Routledge Handbook of Multilingualism* (pp. 499–507). London: Routledge.

Bialystok, E. (2010). Global-local and trail-making tasks by monolingual and bilingual children: beyond inhibition. *Developmental Psychology*, 46, 93–105.

Blackledge, A. and Creese, A. (2010). *Multilingualism: A Critical Perspective*. London: Continuum.

Block, D. (2007). Bilingualism: four assumptions and four responses. *Innovation in Language Learning and Teaching*, 1, 66–82.

Canagarajah, S. (2007). Lingua franca English, multilingual communities and language acquisition. *The Modern Language Journal*, 91, 923–39.

Candelier, M. (2008). Awakening to languages and Language policy. In J. Cenoz and N. Hornberger (eds.), *Encyclopedia of Language and Education* (2nd edn), Vol. VI: *Knowledge about Language* (pp. 219–32). Berlin: Springer.

Cenoz, J. (2009). *Towards Multilingual Education*. Bristol: Multilingual Matters.

Cenoz, J. (2013). The influence of bilingualism on third language acquisition: focus on multilingualism. *Language Teaching*, 46, 71–86.

Cenoz, J. and Gorter, D. (2011). Focus on multilingualism: a study of trilingual writing. *The Modern Language Journal*, 95(3), 356–69.

Cenoz, J. and Gorter, D. (2014). Focus on multilingualism as an approach in educational contexts. In A. Creese and A. Blackledge (eds.), *Heteroglossia as Practice and Pedagogy* (pp. 239–54). Berlin: Springer.

Cook, V. (1992). Evidence for multicompetence. *Language Learning*, 42, 557–91. doi: 10.1111/j.1467-1770.1992.tb01044.x

Cook, V. (1995). Multi-competence and the learning of many languages. *Language, Culture and Curriculum*, 8, 93–8.

Coste, D. and Simon, D. L. (2009). The plurilingual social actor: language, citizenship and education. *International Journal of Multilingualism*, **6**, 168–85. doi: 10.1080/14790710902846723

Creese, A. and Blackledge, A. (2010). Translanguaging in the bilingual classroom: a pedagogy for learning and teaching? *The Modern Language Journal*, **94**, 103–15.

Creese, A. and Blackledge, A. (2011). A flexible and separate bilingualism in complementary schools. *Journal of Pragmatics*, **43**, 1196–208.

Creese, A. and Blackledge, A. (eds.) (2014). *Heteroglossia as Practice and Pedagogy*. Berlin: Springer.

Cummins, J. (2005). A proposal for action: strategies for recognizing heritage language competence as a learning resource within the mainstream classroom. *The Modern Language Journal*, **89**, 585–92.

Cummins, J. (2007). Rethinking monolingual instructional strategies in multilingual classrooms. *Canadian Journal of Applied Linguistics*, **10**, 221–41.

Edwards, V. (2004) *Multilingualism in the English-Speaking World*. Oxford: Blackwell.

Extra, G. and Gorter, D. (eds.) (2008). *Multilingual Europe: Facts and Policies*. Berlin: Mouton de Gruyter.

Feng, A. (ed.) (2007). *Bilingual Education in China*. Clevedon: Multilingual Matters.

Firth, A. and Wagner, J. (1997). On discourse, communication and (some) fundamental concepts in SLA research. *The Modern Language Journal*, **81**, 285–300.

García, O. (2009). *Bilingual Education in the 21st Century: A Global Perspective*. Malden, MA and Oxford: Blackwell-Wiley.

García, O. and Sylvan, C. E. (2011). Pedagogies and practices in multilingual classrooms: singularities in pluralities. *The Modern Language Journal*, **95**, 385–400.

Graddol, D. (2006). *English Next: Why Global English May Mean the End of English as a Foreign Language*. London: British Council.

Grosjean, F. (1985). The bilingual as a competent but specific speaker-hearer. *Journal of Multilingual and Multicultural Development*, **6**, 467–77. doi: 10.1080/01434632.1985.9994221

Heller, M. (1999). *Linguistic Minorities and Modernity: A Sociolinguistic Ethnography*. London: Longman.

Heller, M. (ed.) (2007). *Bilingualism: A Social Approach*. London: Palgrave Macmillan.

Hélot, C. (2012). Linguistic diversity and education. In M. Martin-Jones, A. Blackledge and A. Creese (eds.), *Routledge Handbook of Multilingualism* (pp. 214–31). New York / London: Taylor and Francis.

Hélot, C. and De Mejía, A. M. (2008). *Forging Multilingual Spaces: Integrated Perspectives on Majority and Minority Bilingual Education*. Bristol: Multilingual Matters.

Herdina, P. and Jessner, U. (2002). *A Dynamic Model of Multilingualism*. Clevedon: Multilingual Matters.

Internet World Stats (2011). Internet world users by language. Retrieved from www.internetworldstats.com/stats7.htm

Jørgensen, J. N. (2008). Polylingual languaging around and among children and adolescents. *International Journal of Multilingualism*, 5, 161–76. doi: 10.1080/14790710802387562

Kramsch, C. (2010). *The Multilingual Subject*. Oxford: Oxford University Press.

Kramsch, C. (2012). Authenticity and legitimacy in multilingual SLA. *Critical Multilingualism Studies*, 1, 107–28.

Kramsch, C. and Whiteside, A. (2008). Language ecology in multilingual settings: towards a theory of symbolic competence. *Applied Linguistics*, 29, 645–71.

Levine, G. S. (2011). *Code Choice in the Language Classroom*. Bristol: Multilingual Matters.

Li, Wei (2010). Moment analysis and translanguaging space: discursive construction of identities by multilingual Chinese youth in Britain. *Journal of Pragmatics*, 43, 1222–35. doi:10.1016/j.pragma.2010.07.035

Li, Wei (2011). Multilinguality, multimodality, and multicompetence: code- and modeswitching by minority ethnic children in complementary schools. *The Modern Language Journal*, 95, 370–84.

Lin, A. M. Y. (2008). Code-switching in the classroom: research paradigms and approaches. In K. A. King and N. H. Hornberger (eds.), *Encyclopedia of Language and Education* (2nd edn), Vol. X: *Research Methods in Language and Education* (pp. 273–86). New York: Springer Science.

Lyster, R., Collins, L. and Ballinger, S. (2009). Linking languages through a bilingual read-aloud project. *Language Awareness*, 18, 366–83. doi:10.1080/09658410903197322

Macaro, E. (2009). Teacher use of code-switching in the L2 classroom: exploring 'optimal' use. In M. Turnbull and J. Dailey-O'Cain (eds.), *First Language Use in Second and Foreign Language Learning* (pp. 35–49). Bristol: Multilingual Matters.

Makoni, S. and Pennycook, A. (2007). *Disinventing and Reconstituting Languages*. Clevedon: Multilingual Matters.

May, S. (ed.) (2014). *The Multilingual Turn: Implications for SLA, TESOL and Bilingual Education*. New York: Routledge.

Moore, D. and Gajo, L. (2009). Introduction: French voices on plurilingualism and pluriculturalism – theory, significance, and perspectives. *International Journal of Multilingualism*, 6, 137–53. doi:10.1080/14790710902846707

Ortega, L. (2014). Ways forward for a bi/multilingual turn in SLA. In S. May (ed.), *The Multilingual Turn: Implications for SLA, TESOL and Bilingual Education* (pp. 32–53). New York: Routledge.

Otsuji, E. and Pennycook, A. (2009). Metrolingualism: fixity, fluidity and language in flux. *International Journal of Multilingualism*, 7, 240–54. doi: 10.1080/14790710903414331

Rampton, B. (2006). *Language in Late Modernity: Interaction in an Urban School*. Cambridge: Cambridge University Press.

Rampton, B. and Charalambous, C. (2012). Crossing. In M. Martin-Jones, A. Blackledge and A. Creese (eds.), *The Routledge Handbook of Multilingualism* (pp. 482–98). London: Routledge.

Scollon, R. and Scollon, S. W. (2004). *Nexus Analysis: Discourse and the Emerging Internet*. London: Routledge.

Skutnabb-Kangas, T. and Heugh, K. (2012). *Multilingual Education and Sustainable Diversity Work: From Periphery to Center*. London: Routledge.

Swain, M. (2012). A Vygotskian sociocultural perspective on immersion education. Keynote address at the Fourth International Conference on Immersion Education. Minneapolis–Saint Paul, MN, 18–20 October 2012.

Turnbull, M. and Dailey-O'Cain, J. (eds.) (2009). *First Language Use in Second and Foreign Language Learning: Intersection of Theory, Practice, Curriculum and Policy*. Clevedon: Multilingual Matters.

2 L1 as a pedagogical resource in building students' L2 academic literacy: pedagogical innovation in a science classroom in a Hong Kong school

Gladys N. Y. Luk and Angel M. Y. Lin

2.1 Introduction

The topic of medium of instruction (MOI) has long been an important site of contestation in Hong Kong. Owing to its high socioeconomic status and its gate-keeping function in higher education, English-medium instruction (EMI) has been keenly sought after by parents for their children since the 1980s. Indeed, English was widely adopted as the medium of instruction in secondary schools despite the fact that Chinese was granted the status of an official language in 1974. In 1960, for example, only 57.9% of the secondary schools in Hong Kong were English-medium schools, but by 1980, 87.7% of them had adopted English as their MOI (Bray & Koo, 2004).

In 1978, the introduction of compulsory nine-year education in Hong Kong meant that many students who formerly could not enter secondary schools were receiving their education in EMI schools. In these EMI schools many teachers adopted a bilingual approach in which they switched between Chinese (practised as spoken Cantonese and written Standard Chinese), the home languages of the students, and English, their L2, because many students were not capable of learning through English alone. This approach was regarded by the Hong Kong government as unproductive, and in 1998 the government adopted a linguistic streaming policy which allowed only 114 secondary schools to use EMI in their junior forms (Forms 1–3; equivalent to Grades 7–9), whereas the rest of the schools (about 70%) had to change to Chinese-medium instruction (CMI) in their junior forms (schools still retain their autonomy to choose the medium of instruction for senior forms). This policy, however, met with a great deal of opposition, mainly from parents who believed that this practice only deepened the stigmatization of Chinese-medium schools by suggesting that they were for the less competent, and who wanted access to EMI for the sake of their children's future jobs and the higher educational opportunities it afforded them. Amidst political pressure, a fine-tuned MOI policy was implemented by the government in September 2010.

2.2 The fine-tuned MOI policy for secondary schools

Since September 2010, many CMI schools have chosen to change the medium of instruction of one or two of their academic subjects (usually science or mathematics), or some percentage of the lessons of each of their academic subjects, from CMI to EMI, also because of strong parental demand for English for their children. One pressing question, however, remains: what kind of bridging curriculum and pedagogy will help former CMI students to cope with learning in the English medium?

If we take science as an example, does it mean that using an English textbook and adopting English as the MOI will enable students to learn the subject in English? As can be predicted, it is not easy for students, especially junior secondary students, to study science in English, not only because the concepts are difficult to grasp but also because the scientific language is too complicated for students to handle. According to Fang (2005), the science register, with its feature of packing knowledge into highly condensed and abstract language, often creates extreme difficulty for learners, and especially foreign language learners.

Therefore, if students are to study solely in English, they may have to overcome two hurdles: the language of science and the English language. Although the Hong Kong government has blamed 'mixed code teaching' as the main factor contributing to falling standards, many researchers have found that a principled bilingual approach, when carried out systematically and judiciously, is beneficial to both teaching and learning (Cook, 1995, 2001; Cummins, 2007; Cenoz, 2009; Turnbull & Dailey-O'Cain, 2009; Swain et al., 2011; Ballinger, this volume).

In this chapter we document the curriculum and pedagogical innovation of a team of science teachers in a Hong Kong secondary school in providing the necessary linguistic and cognitive scaffolding for their students to develop L2 English academic literacy. Through developing Chinese–English bilingual science texts that are systematically laid out side by side on the same page, and through flexible bilingual classroom language use, the science teachers mobilized their students' L1 resources to help them develop both the confidence and the interest in learning science in English and enhance their English academic literacy. We also discuss the implications of this case study for building a possible model for flexible yet principled bilingual language use as a pedagogical resource in bilingual education classrooms.

2.3 A case study of a former CMI secondary school

2.3.1 Background of the school and its language policy and practice

The school is situated in a new town outside the urban areas of Hong Kong. Secondary schools in Hong Kong are generally divided into three bands, with band 1 having the highest academic standards and band 3 the lowest. This school is a band 2 school.

When the school was first founded two decades ago, English was adopted as the medium of instruction. However, after the implementation of the government's linguistic streaming policy in 1998, it had to change to CMI for its junior-form students, while senior-form students learned either in Chinese or in English depending on the English proficiency level of the class. As a result, a gap between Form 3 and Form 4 was created. Under the fine-tuned MOI policy implemented in 2010, at junior levels, Integrated Science and Integrated Humanities are taught in English in preparation for the learning of these subjects in English at senior levels. In order to help students, especially those who have only very basic English proficiency, bilingual materials have been designed. It is hoped that students will gradually acquire the confidence and ability to tackle Integrated Science exams in English. This is particularly important if they choose to study science subjects, including physics, chemistry and biology, in senior forms in preparation for higher education, as almost all universities in Hong Kong officially use English as the MOI.

2.3.2 Rationale for switching the medium of instruction for Integrated Science

In fact, the school may use CMI for both junior and senior forms, but the team of science teachers believe that it is better for students to learn science in English. A report produced by the team of science teachers at the school in 2008 pointed out that in order to prepare students for learning advanced science through the medium of English a basic level of competence in using English is needed. At the same time, the effectiveness of using the mother tongue as an instructional medium for promoting interest was also recognized.

While the teachers seemed to be under the ideological influence of the global discourse of English for science, the most pragmatic reason was probably the school's need to maintain a positive image in order to attract good students to the school. As a consequence of the report, a decision was taken to design a bridging programme. The bridging programme that was designed, with Chinese as the cornerstone of learning and English as the tool for further development in science, was two-dimensional. The two dimensions were bridging in language and bridging in subject knowledge. Bridging in language means the mastery of a second language on the basis of the mother tongue. The bridging in language as a tool of learning is a pressing need, and especially so for secondary schools where the junior-form subjects are largely offered in CMI and the senior-form subjects are offered in EMI. The bridging in subject knowledge is crucial for junior-level students, for whom, of course, knowledge of science and its concepts may be limited. Even if they have encountered some scientific concepts at primary school, these will have been explained using Chinese, their first language. What's more, the language of science is often considered a challenge to secondary students, especially those in junior forms, because of its abstraction and complex nature.

This was also argued by Fang (2005) who has examined several secondary coursebooks and analysed the texts using the systemic functional linguistics approach. She found that the language of science is extremely complex because sentences tend to be densely packed with information. Moreover, the use of nominalization and the abstraction of action processes into nominal entities create further ambiguity and difficulty for novice students.

FUNCTIONS OF L1 USE

The role of students' L1 as the cornerstone of learning is a topic of great interest to educators and linguists, and research on the topic has been done in many parts of the world, including the USA and Europe. Some research has tried to measure the amount of L1 use between teachers and students, and among students themselves, during interaction in language classrooms; other research has tried to determine the functions of L1 in such circumstances. The studies of Duff and Polio (1990) and Polio and Duff (1994), for example, have revealed that students' L1 has an important role to play in the acquisition of a second language, while the work of Turnbull (2001) has pointed to the fact that efforts to maximize the use of the target language (TL) do not, in fact, and should not, lead to the avoidance of L1. Indeed, both L1 and TL can exist side by side.

In their studies, Polio and Duff (1994: 317) identified the following eight functions for L1 use.

1. For administrative vocabulary items – the amount of L1 is generally restricted to a single word or phrase
2. For grammar instruction – L1 use may be found at the lexical level, within a partial utterance, or over a sequence of utterances
3. For classroom management
4. To index a stance of empathy or solidarity
5. For L1 practice by the teacher with tutoring from the students
6. To provide translations for unknown TL (Target Language) vocabulary
7. To remedy students' apparent lack of comprehension
8. Interactive effect involving students' use of L1

Another model for L1 functions comes from Macaro and Franklin (cited in Cook, 2002: 340), which highlights the following five functions for L1 use.

1. Giving instructions about tasks
2. Translating and checking comprehension
3. Giving feedback to pupils
4. Using the first language to maintain discipline
5. Explaining grammar

These two models clearly have some categories in common. Both regard students' L1 as a useful resource for classroom management and maintaining discipline. Neither have any doubts about the effectiveness of using students' L1 in enhancing target language vocabulary learning and comprehension, nor about its role in empowering students in their learning.

Indeed, the above lists of functions sound familiar, and many other studies have produced similar lists of functions that can be categorized into three basic types: (1) functions related to unpacking the field (i.e. making the content of the subject comprehensible to students), (2) functions related to negotiating different kinds of role-relationships and (3) functions related to providing signposts or transition markers for different topics, tasks or stages of the lesson (Lin, 2008, 2013). These three major types of functions can help researchers categorize the diverse range of functions found in the literature under a few key principles inspired by Halliday's functional linguistics. Using Halliday's framework, we may reduce or summarize the range of functions under each category as follows:

1. Functions related to unpacking the field:
   • Giving grammar instruction – L1 use may occur at the lexical level, within a partial utterance or during a sequence of utterances
   • Providing translations for unknown target language vocabulary
   • Remedying students' apparent lack of comprehension

- Translating and checking comprehension
- Explaining grammar

2. Functions related to negotiating relationships:
   - Indexing a stance of empathy or solidarity
   - Managing the classroom environment or maintaining discipline
   - Motivating students to interact in class

3. Functions related to marking shifts of focus, topic, task or stage of the lesson:
   - Giving instructions about a task to be carried out
   - Highlighting topic change or task transition

It should be stressed that teachers may use the L1 for multiple functions at any moment with any single utterance: for example, when the teacher in the extracts below is trying to convince the students that English is not really too difficult (and he switches to L1 to do this), the teacher may be seen to be at once trying to unpack the discipline for students (e.g. helping students to work out the meaning of a technical term such as 'condensation' by breaking it down into its root and its word end) and also trying to negotiate a closer relationship with the students (e.g. playing the role of both instructor and encouraging parent figure).

In the following two sections, we will describe how the major actors in the school have used L1 strategically to help their students access L2 science learning and also look at the way in which they went about innovating their teaching materials in order to provide their students with L1 scaffolding. We will also describe how our present study of their innovative teaching efforts was conducted.

THE SCIENCE TEAM

For schoolteachers in Hong Kong, Integrated Science lessons are generally supplementary to their total number of teaching periods. In other words, no science teacher teaches only Integrated Science. In the school which is the focus of our study, the Science team consists of four teachers. These include the head of the team, the vice-principal of the school and two other science teachers. Some of these teachers also teach senior-form science subjects in English.

TEACHING MATERIALS

An English science coursebook was adopted along with supplementary materials designed by the team of teachers. The supplementary materials were in both languages, with English and Chinese placed side by side or

V.2010.1   (2011/2/17)

4.1 寫出一件物件 (儲有／擁有／發出／使用／獲取／失去／減少) 的**能量**。

題目常以 What (甚麼) 的形式提出。

常見詞彙：   [store   儲有]
              [has / have   擁有／儲有]
              [gain   獲取(更多)]
              [lose / lost   失去／減少]
              [give out   發出]
              [use   使用]

- What energy does   a cell   store ?
- 甚麼   能量   蓄電池 儲有 ?

⇒   蓄電池   儲有   甚麼   能量 ?

Figure 2.1 Example of a page taken from the supplementary materials

with Chinese appearing immediately below the English, as shown in Figure 2.1, for students' easy reference. Exercises in the supplementary materials provided drills on sentence patterns that enabled students to answer questions in English.

2.3.3 The classroom study

The present classroom study explores whether and how the flexible use of classroom language can benefit the teaching and learning of science in English. The study was carried out in two Form 1 Integrated Science classes taught by the same teacher, and this, to a certain extent, helped to eliminate the possibility of having two teachers with different teaching styles and attitudes.

THE METHODOLOGY

The school was chosen because of its innovative bilingual practice. The team of science teachers was invited to take part in the study, and the lessons of the head of the team were observed. The aim was to investigate the adoption of bilingual strategies and whether and how they might be beneficial to the school, the teachers and the students.

The study adopted both qualitative and quantitative research approaches. Regarding the qualitative approach, data were collected through classroom observation and semi-structured interviews with students. As for the quantitative part, pre- and post-tests, which contained multiple-choice questions and short questions, were given to students. Questions were set on materials taken from Chapter 1:

Introducing science, Chapter 4: *Energy*, Chapter 5: *The wonderful solvent – water* and Chapter 6: *Matter as particles*. The pre-test was given before classroom observation and the post-test was given after it. The results were used to investigate the effectiveness of using flexible bilingual classroom strategies.

To ensure that English did not have adverse effects on the performance of the students, the pre-tests were designed in both English and Chinese. Half of the students did the English version first and then the Chinese version next, whereas the others did the tests in the reverse order. The post-test, which was the same as the pre-test, was then given to students after the observations had been carried out. This time they took the test in English only.

Classroom observation was carried out in two Form 1 classes: 1A and 1D. The students in this school are streamed according to their academic performance. Form 1A consisted of students of mixed ability, while 1D was an elite class, elite in the sense that the students have higher motivation and language proficiency. Form 1A was a smaller class with 35 students, while 1D had 41 students. They were taught by the same science teacher who is the head of the Science team.

There are eight periods of Integrated Science for each class in a ten-day cycle. Each period lasts 35 minutes. Most of the classes were conducted in the science laboratory and some in the classroom. All eight periods were observed and video-taped. The observation lasted for nine weeks with a total of 28 school days.

Interviews were conducted by the first author after observation had been finished to find out about students' responses to this bilingual classroom practice; 11 students from the class were interviewed. They were chosen according to the result of the pre- and post-tests. They were divided into four groups. One group consisted of students who performed the best in both tests. One group consisted of students who performed the worst in both tests. The other groups included students who made the greatest improvement and those who made the greatest regression. This selection criterion was not made known to the students to avoid the risk of it having a labelling effect on them or affecting their self-concepts. Pseudo-names were used.

The interviews were conducted in Cantonese, the students' L1. Questions related to the study of science were asked. (For details of the questions, please refer to the Appendix.)

THE FINDINGS

The following paragraphs present the findings of the case study, including both qualitative and quantitative findings. Special features found in the lessons – as well as the functions of L1 used by the teacher whose lessons were observed – will be discussed, and then the student interview data, followed by the pre- and post-test results, will be presented.

The following features were observed during the science lessons of the two classes. Most of the time, the teacher dominated the lessons. He spoke throughout the lessons, and there were only a few instances when students themselves responded. This was usually when students were called upon to answer the teacher's questions or on a few occasions when one or two of the more proficient students asked a question. He tried to speak in English during the whole lesson, following the explicit language policy of the school. Not only did he teach concepts and procedures related to the science syllabus, but he also tried to convince the students that English is not difficult by helping them to analyse the words and terms and suggesting ways to understand the materials better.

The teacher's code-switching practice can be regarded as inter-sentential switching. He used this practice on many occasions. For instance, on one occasion the teacher asked students to guess the meaning of the word *expect*. When students almost got the answer, he said, 'Ok. Close. 接近喇' (接近 is the Chinese equivalent of 'close' and 喇 is a conversation particle with the pragmatic function of confirming). On the next occasion, after the teacher has finished explaining a term he asked the students to keep it in mind. He said, 'Keep that in mind. 要記住佢添喎 !' (要記住佢添喎 ! is the Cantonese translation of 'keep that in mind'). This was clearly to encourage students to be aware of and try to remember important information. There were also a few instances of intra-sentential switching. For example, 'Condensation 都係 tion' (都係 means 'also is'; the teacher was here highlighting for the students the fact that the word ending '-tion' is common to several technical terms).

When talking about rules and regulations, the science teacher appeared to be a stern teacher. However, when explaining some effective ways to handle spelling and tackle examinations, he demonstrated a sense of humour as well as a sound understanding of the relationship between spelling and pronunciation. He also seemed to show a sound foundation in the English language.

To encourage students not to be afraid of using English, he kept emphasizing the view that English is not as difficult as they think. He pointed out that there are many similarities between English and Chinese and that they can have a better understanding when they make use of the pattern and combination of the words or sentences.

He also helped students to understand the importance of analysing words and sentences.

In addition, he often related scientific knowledge to students' daily experience, so that students would not find science too remote. He never discouraged students even when they gave a wrong answer. In summary, he came across as a considerate and passionate science teacher.

Functions of L1 used by the teacher whose lessons were observed

1. Functions related to unpacking the field
The following example illustrates the functions of L1 in helping students access the content of the discipline. In these examples, the science teacher uses students' L1 to explain scientific terms, which he seems to believe are not easy for the students to comprehend. (English translations of the Cantonese utterances are placed in square brackets: [].)

Example 1

The teacher is explaining the process of condensation. He wants students to understand that the word ending '-tion' commonly appears in the names of scientific processes (e.g. condensation, filtration, evaporation, distillation and so on).

Teacher: Condensation 睇唔睇到個特點呀？個字尾係咩吖？
            [Can you see the characteristic of it? What is the suffix of the word?]
Student: 'tion'
Teacher: Condensation 都係 'tion', 識唔識點串呀？
            [is also] [Do you know how to spell it?]
Student: 'tion'
Teacher: 'tion' 係唔係呀? 睇吓個字表，我頭先無講錯呀，所有 D 辦法, 方法, 成套嘢就係 'tion', 所以將佢擺埋一齊，一次過記嚟, 乜嘢 filtration, 乜嘢 condensation, evaporation 吖, distillation 吖, 都係 'tion' 囉, 所以講緊呢個係 condensation.
            ['tion' Right? Look at the word list. What I said earlier is right. All about methods, ways, and all of these are presented as 'tion'. Therefore, try to put them together and remember them. No matter if it is filtration, condensation, evaporation or distillation, it ends with 'tion'; so this is condensation.]

In the above example, we can see that the teacher tries to explain the abstract concept of 'condensation' in students' L1, saying that it is the process of conversion of a gas into liquid (將氣體變翻做液體). If he had tried to do this in the students' L2, the students may not have been able to understand what it is, as they would need to have understood several other terms such as 'process', 'gas' and 'liquid' simultaneously.

2. Functions related to negotiating different role-relationships
There are, comparatively, more examples of the interpersonal functions. Apart from teaching science, the science teacher spent quite a large proportion of the lesson time dealing with students' attitudes towards English, their L2 and discipline issues. It is easy to understand why he places so much stress on the importance of discipline, because following instructions is crucial in science lessons, and especially so when conducting experiments in the science laboratory, in order to avoid accidents.

During the lesson observation, there were occasions when the teacher tried to negotiate a greater social distance with the students, especially when disciplining the class. Sometimes, however, he tried to negotiate a closer relationship with them in order to alleviate the tense atmosphere. In keeping with this notion of social distance, he alternately took up a stricter role, and then a more considerate one, helping students to overcome the barrier created by English. Below are some of these examples.

Example 2

The teacher asks the students to pay attention to him.

Teacher: 我講緊嘢就望我，聽咗我先，每樣嘢有佢適當嘅時候，你唔跟住群體活動，同一個既定嘅時間及流程呢，你只有阻礙我嘅時間啫。我講完都會做嗰個，掛住搞嗰個、睇嗰個，睇魚、睇其他，我要去講你嘅秩序呢，做正經嘢 D 時間又拖耐咗.
[When I am talking, listen to me first. Everything has to be done at the appropriate time. On the whole, we have to follow a certain schedule and flow. Talking only interrupts and wastes my time. After I have finished talking, we will do the experiment. If you go and look at something else like watching the fish and others, I will have to talk about discipline. Then the schedule for doing meaningful activities will be delayed and time will be wasted.]

In Example 2, the teacher is trying to play a stricter role. He asks the students to look at him when he is talking, telling them that they should pay attention to him and not be distracted by other objects in the laboratory. They should not disturb normal classroom proceedings in order that valuable class time isn't lost. Here, the teacher seems to be appealing to the students to cooperate by stressing an implicitly shared goal: not to waste time when they are performing lesson tasks. He uses L1 at length here (without code-switching to L2) to negotiate a closer relationship with his students, appearing almost like a concerned father, urging them not to waste precious learning time.

Example 3

The teacher is lighting up the Bunsen burner in preparation for an experiment. However, the match goes out, and in order to create a more relaxing atmosphere, he tells the students jokingly that the match has gone out because of his talkativeness.

Teacher:　Ai yayayaya too much nonsense 太多廢話，佢熄咗。

　　　　　[Ai yayayaya too much nonsense. Too much nonsense. It extinguished.]

太多廢話 is a Cantonese phrase meaning 'too much nonsense'. He means that talking too much nonsense has put out the match. Of course, the match does not go out because of his talking, but he is using this notion as a metaphor to indicate that nonsense talking should be avoided, especially when conducting an experiment.

Attention should also be paid to the nonsense syllables of 'Ai yayayaya'. He is very dramatic when uttering these syllables, and this creates a rather humorous atmosphere. This was not the only occasion when the teacher tried to create this kind of atmosphere. When drops of distilled water appeared, the teacher said 'Yeah!', making a victory sign with two fingers. This gesture is very common among young people in Hong Kong. Whenever they take photos, girls in particular like making that gesture.

In the three extracts included in Example 4 below, the science teacher comes across as a considerate teacher, and the use of L1 helps him to negotiate a closer relationship with his students, almost like a concerned parent urging his children to learn and not to waste time. He tries to encourage students and helps them to see that English is not as difficult as they think.

Example 4: Extract (1)

The teacher explains in English the preparations he has made before conducting an experiment, and he then switches to Cantonese to assure students that they will eventually understand what he is talking about if they think, listen and follow closely.

Teacher:　基本上 … 頭先聽得明吖，係嗎？所以慢慢嚟，想下你就會跟得
到，聽得明嘅啦.
[Basically … you understand what I have just mentioned,
right? Therefore, if you think, gradually you will understand.]

In Extract (1) the teacher suggests that students should ultimately
come to understand what he is explaining. It is a matter of time and of
processing the knowledge in the mind.

Example 4: Extract (2)

After revising and explaining the procedure several times, the teacher
once again assures students that they will understand if they pay attention to him.
Teacher:　但大家都留心，噤就係噤樣，其實聽得明嘅，你留心 D就聽得明
啦。
[All of you concentrate and that is it. You will understand.
When you pay attention, you will understand.]

In Extract (2), the teacher emphasizes the importance of concentration. If students pay attention to the teacher, they will understand
what the teacher says eventually.

Example 4: Extract (3)

The teacher tells the students that all the impurities will be left behind.
To help students to understand the phrase 'left behind', he explains
what it is in Cantonese. Then he tells the students to learn the phrase in
order that they can use it or understand it when the teacher mentions it.
Teacher:　left behind 係咩呀？即係留底係度囉！唔郁囉！係咪呀？噤跟
住就應該學咗呢個噤嘅詞語佢，以後唔係識用或者起碼老師講就
聽得明囉。噤樣每日學 D 每堂學 D 累積上去，你課堂就知講乜
喇，如果唔係十世都唔知人講緊乜。
[What is 'left behind'? That is 'remain here'. Don't move.
Right? Then the next is that you have to learn this phrase.
After that, you will be able to use it or at least you will understand when the teacher mentions it. As a result, you will learn
bit by bit every day and after accumulating those bits, you
will know what the teacher is saying; otherwise you will never
know what other people are saying.]

In Extract (3), the teacher stresses that once students have learned an
expression, they have to remember it. Then, lesson by lesson and day
by day, they will build up their knowledge and understand what the
teacher is talking about.

From these extracts, we can see how the teacher uses students' L1, the students' most familiar and comfortable language, to help them to overcome, psychologically, the barrier between them and English. It is difficult to imagine how the same effect could be achieved by using only the students' L2. L1 is used to negotiate a closer relationship with the students – with the teacher acting like an encouraging parent, who is also humorous.

3. Functions related to signalling topic shifts
In principle, both L1 and L2 can be used to give signposts or advance organizers (i.e. an overview or roadmap) during a lesson, but it is in the switching between two languages that topic shifts are highlighted, almost like changing the colour of a pen when marking a shift in topic or focus.

Example 5 demonstrates the use of L1 to signal a topic shift.

Example 5

The teacher explains what fluoride is and its use.
Teacher: The only one thing I want you to know of this chapter, I would like you to understand, in tap water, yes, in tap water, we add, we put something in. The name is fluoride. How to spell fluoride? F-L-U-O-R-I-D-E, fluoride. This is in the title 個標題唔係囉. F-L-U-O-R-I-D-E, fluoride. 好似 flower 噤樣，好似朵花，不過有個 u 係度，後面有個 R-I-D-E, ride 個字.
[The only thing I want you to know of this chapter, I would like you to understand, in tap water, yes, in tap water, we add something in. The name is fluoride. How to spell fluoride? F-L-U-O-R-I-D-E, fluoride. This is in the title, right? It is like 'flower' but there is a 'u' and at the end there is the word R-I-D-E, ride.]

In this example, the teacher first announces to students in L2 the major learning goal of this lesson and then explains in detail what he expects them to learn. It helps to provide students with an advance organizer in order to summarize their learning in this lesson. Then he switches to L1 to signal a change in topic – to focus on the word *fluoride*.

As seen from the above examples, the teacher seems to switch to students' L1 systematically to carry out different functions: for example, unpacking technical content (functions related to helping students to access the discipline), negotiating different social relationships with the students to encourage them or to discipline them, or to liven up the atmosphere by using everyday humorous L1 words, and signalling shifts in topic or focus. In the next section, we will examine how students view the flexible use of classroom language.

2.3.4 Interviews with students

In this section, we look at students' responses to some of the questions put to them when they were interviewed, especially those relating to bilingual practices.

The target students were invited to give their views on the practice of switching from their mother tongue to their second language, English. Students whose performance in the pre- and post-tests was not outstanding admitted that switching from their second language to their L1 did, to a certain extent, help them understand the concepts and ideas taught in the class. However, surprisingly, they pointed out that they would prefer the teacher to speak totally in English given that they will eventually have to learn science in English.

For instance, one of the students, Keung, said: 'Like Chinese students studying in America, they will eventually be able to speak in English.' Another student called Ming also said: 'As we are going to learn and answer questions totally in English in Form 3, it is better that Mr Chan speaks in English.'

However, Tom, who had quite a poor result, said, 'It is better that more Chinese is used.' This indicates that students who have poor results because of their weakness in English do want the teacher to speak more Cantonese, their mother tongue. This idea is supported by the group of students who performed better. They stated that flexible use of classroom language did help to enhance their study. Fai said: 'It helps those who are weak in English.'

Furthermore, when asked about the difficulties they encountered when studying science in English, all of them agreed that the scientific terms acted as an obstacle to their progress. The terms were long and difficult to read, and they needed the Chinese equivalents so that they could understand the terms and eventually understand the concepts. They also found it difficult to spell the scientific terms. However, one student supported the teacher's claim that knowing the pronunciation of the words would help them with the spelling, saying that this was useful.

The students' views are further verified by the results of the pre- and post-test mentioned earlier. The students' performance in both tests were compared. It was found that in Form 1D, the elite class, more students, 27 in total, did improve in the post-test. This correlates with the claims of those students with outstanding performance that the flexible use of classroom language did help to enhance their study.

The performance of Form 1A students was not the same. Twelve out of the 35 students did show some improvement, suggesting that bilingual practice helped some of them to boost their study. However, 16 of the 35 students had fewer marks in the post-test. This may be due to the fact that the students in this class were less motivated and less competent in English. The teacher's use of English thus created a certain degree of difficulty for these students and in consequence fewer students performed well. Despite the fact that some of these students wanted their teacher to speak totally in English, they seemed to lack the ability to cope with tests in English. This explains why the student who did poorly said that he'd prefer to have more Chinese in the lessons.

The above findings indicate that the flexible use of classroom language does help students who have some basic English proficiency to learn Integrated Science better. Even though some students think that it is better not to switch between the two languages, they do find that their L1 helps, especially in understanding difficult scientific terms. However, for students with limited English and who lack motivation, the use of L1 does not seem to help much.

2.3.5 Implications

Based on the above findings, we can come up with the following tentative implications. First, the use of L1 does seem to help in the teaching and learning of science, but this statement has to be qualified by the important proviso that students must be motivated to make the effort to bridge the gap between their existing L2 proficiencies and those required for L2 learning; furthermore, they must not be at a very limited level of L2 proficiency as this will make their learning in L2 far too frustrating for any amount of L1 use to sufficiently counter it.

Second, collaboration between the English teachers and the Integrated Science teachers is crucial. Cross-subject materials should be designed and adopted. For instance, science texts can be selected as extensive reading materials. However, how much help the English teachers should offer is still a matter for investigation.

Third, the team spirit of the science teachers is a decisive factor. If only one or two teachers are willing to take on the extra workload, or there is no consensus among the members, it will be difficult to achieve positive results or sustain the results achieved.

Last but not least, teachers play a significant role as models. They must be competent in both languages to be linguistically responsive subject teachers. The science teacher in this study provides a good example; his mother tongue is Cantonese and he has no problems giving L1 instructions. Importantly, however, he is also competent in English and seems to have language awareness (e.g. noticing the common word endings of a number of technical terms such as 'condensation' and 'evaporation'). Armed with this language awareness, he can draw students' attention to the linguistic aspects of the L2 that are important for academic content learning. In other words, his proficiency in both languages means that he is able to unpack science texts, which are more academic and contain more abstraction in English, and use students' L1 to make the discourse more accessible for them and thereby help students overcome the difficulties they encounter in learning science in the L2. Not only does he unpack the texts, but he also makes use of students' L1 to help them re-pack the texts so that they know how to answer questions in English. For example, students can look for key words common to both L1 and L2, such as *draw* (畫) and *use* (用途). He also demonstrates how to answer questions with the help of Cantonese. He even encourages students to answer the questions in Cantonese first and then translate the answers into English. He shows students the similarity between L1 and L2 word-formation processes, as shown, for example, in words such as *high*er 高咗, *low*er 低咗, *high*est 最高. He is a science teacher with cross-lingual awareness, and he helps his students to acquire this cross-lingual awareness too.

Finally, teachers who empathize with their students will come up with good teaching strategies that will enhance their students' learning. Having a sense of humour may also help teachers to develop a closer relationship with their students and create a more relaxing atmosphere, which benefits the process of teaching as well as learning.

2.4 Conclusion

The fine-tuning of Hong Kong's MOI policy since 2010 has led many secondary schools to switch from Chinese to English to teach Integrated Science, and this is mainly in response to the expectations of parents. There is a tendency for school authorities to believe that it is easier to start with Integrated Science because students are not required to read and write a large number of texts. However, research has shown that this belief may be unsound and that the opposite may in fact be the case: the language of science is highly abstract and condensed, and this may create problems for junior secondary students in particular. Careful planning and the support of all members of the school are necessary to enhance the teaching and learning of science in English.

Given the efforts of the team of science teachers, this school does seem to provide a model for flexible yet systematic bilingual language use as a pedagogical resource. Nevertheless, it should be stressed that this is just a preliminary study, involving only two classes, which were observed within a rather short period of time; more work is required in order to obtain a more comprehensive picture of the practices that may eventually lead to the discovery of a principled bilingual approach to classroom teaching and the conditions required for these practices to succeed. To this end, we suggest the following: increasing the number of informants participating in the study, conducting classroom observations over a longer period of time – preferably at least a full semester – and preparing a questionnaire to collect data on students' attitudes towards English and Chinese, as attitudes, to a great extent, influence how they view the MOI adopted for the subject and whether they are willing to work with the teachers to bridge the gaps between their existing proficiencies and those required of them by L2 learning.

Appendix: Interview questions

1. Do you like science?
2. Why?
3. How do you find what you have to learn in science?
4. Do you find this useful in your daily life?
5. Which topic do you find the most interesting?
6. Which topic do you find the least interesting?
7. Do you find the terms in science difficult?
8. In what way do you find the terms difficult? Can you give an example?
9. Are you happy with using English to study Integrated Science (IS)?
10. What are the easiest things in using English to study IS?
11. What are the most difficult things in using English to study IS?
12. Have you experienced any difficulties when you study IS in English?
13. How do you cope with it?
14. What kind of language support do you want to have?
15. In what ways do you think the teacher can help you? How can the teacher help you in this?
16. What do you think of the way that your teacher talks sometimes in English and sometimes in Cantonese in science lessons?
17. Are there any other things you want to tell me about learning science in your class?

References

Bray, M. and Koo, R. D. Y. (2004). Language and education. In M. Bray and R. D. Y. Koos (eds.), *Education and Society in Hong Kong and Macao: Comparative Perspectives on Continuity and Change* (2nd edn) (pp. 141–58). Hong Kong: Comparative Education Research Centre, the University of Hong Kong.

Cenoz, J. (2009). *Towards Multilingual Education: Basque Educational Research from an International Perspective.* Bristol: Multilingual Matters.

Cook, V. (1995). Multi-competence and learning of many languages. *Language, Culture and Curriculum,* 8(2), 93–8.

Cook, V. (2001). Using the first language in the classroom. *The Canadian Modern Language Review,* 57(3), 402–23.

Cook, V. (2002). Language teaching methodology and the L2 user perspective. In V. Cook (ed.), *Portraits of the L2 User* (pp. 325–44). Clevedon: Multilingual Matters.

Cummins, J. (2007). Rethinking monolingual instructional strategies in multilingual classrooms. *The Canadian Journal of Applied Linguistics,* 10(2), 221–40.

Duff, P. and Polio, C. (1990). How much foreign language is there in the foreign language classroom? *The Modern Language Journal,* 74, 154–66.

Fang, Z. (2005). Scientific literacy: a systemic functional linguistics perspective. *Science Education,* 89(2), 335–47.

Lin, A. M. Y. (2008). Code-switching in the classroom: research paradigms and approaches. In K. A. King and N. H. Hornberger (eds.), *Encyclopedia of Language and Education* (2nd edn), Vol. X: *Research Methods in Language and Education* (pp. 273–86). New York: Springer Science.

Lin, A. M. Y. (2013). Classroom code-switching: three decades of research. *Applied Linguistics Review,* 4(1), 195–218.

Polio, C. and Duff, P. (1994). Teachers' language use in university foreign language classrooms: a qualitative analysis of English and target language alternation. *Modern Language Journal,* 78, 313–26.

Swain, M., Kirkpatrick, A. and Cummins, J. (2011). *How to Have a Guilt-Free Life Using Cantonese in the English Class: A Handbook for the English Language Teacher in Hong Kong.* Hong Kong: Research Centre into Language Acquisition and Education in Multilingual Societies, Hong Kong Institute of Education.

Turnbull, M. (2001). There is a role for the L1 in second and foreign language teaching, but … *The Canadian Modern Language Review,* 57, 531–40.

Turnbull, M. and Dailey-O'Cain, J. (2009). *First Language Use in Second and Foreign Language Learning.* Bristol: Multilingual Matters.

3 Linking content, linking students: a cross-linguistic pedagogical intervention

Susan Ballinger

3.1 Towards cross-linguistic immersion pedagogy

It might sound odd to call French immersion a 'grassroots' bilingual programme today, but it originally represented a community's response to a local need. At a time when the French language was shifting from a position of disadvantage to a position of prestige in Quebec (d'Anglejan, 1984; Genesee & Gándara, 1999; Lamarre, 1997), parents in St Lambert, Quebec, mobilized to create a more intensive French L2 programme to help their children succeed in Quebec's changing linguistic environment. What emerged was a programme that was tailored to the L2 learning needs of this homogeneous group of anglophone students and that launched cutting-edge approaches to communicative language teaching.

Those cutting-edge approaches included combining content and language learning goals by instructing at least half of the curriculum through the medium of French. This approach is based on the same principle as the Direct Method of language teaching which posits that students are supposed to learn the L2 through the L2, not through the L1, and that the L1 and L2 should be kept separate in the classroom (Stern, 1992; Cook, 2001; Cummins, 2007). According to the Direct Method, we can learn a language best if we learn it in the same way that we learned our L1 – through exposure to that language. Further influencing this approach to language instruction within French immersion was Krashen's Input Hypothesis, which argues that passive exposure to comprehensible input is the only 'essential ingredient' (1985: vii) for acquiring either an L1 or an L2.

These ideas on second language education translated to a pedagogical practice in which immersion teachers did not explicitly teach language because learners were supposed to be able to absorb their L2 without focused effort (Dalton-Puffer, 2007). Furthermore, in order to prevent the L1 from interfering with acquisition of the L2, the French immersion model maintained strict separation of the two languages of instruction. The L1 was considered an obstacle, or at least irrelevant, to the learning of the L2 (Cook, 2001), and separation of languages in the classroom was intended to separate the languages in the students' minds (Jessner, 2006).

Much has changed in the years since French immersion began. Not only has the programme become commonly offered at schools throughout Quebec and Canada, but it has also been exported to other countries and has influenced the creation of various content-based L2 programmes such as two-way immersion in the United States and Content and Language Integrated Learning (CLIL) programmes in Europe (Day & Shapson, 1996; Dalton-Puffer, 2007). This model is widely considered to be a successful method of helping students achieve high levels of L2 proficiency, and French immersion students tend to reach high levels of receptive proficiency in their L2 (Genesee, 1987).

Nevertheless, the theoretical grounding of the model has come into question over the years because studies have shown that French immersion students' productive abilities lag behind their receptive abilities and that immersion students tend to focus on conveying meaning, not accuracy, in their interactions (Swain, 1985; Lyster, 1987; Harley, 1989; Genesee, 1994), resulting in a kind of classroom pidgin that does not resemble native-like language use (Lyster, 1987). Many researchers have viewed these results as confirmation that the cognitive processes guiding L2 learning are essentially different from those that guide L1 learning, and the addition of an L2 to one's repertoire is not equivalent to the addition of a second L1.

Meanwhile, other researchers have questioned the merits of maintaining complete separation of the L1 and L2 in bilingual programmes and have argued that it does not make good academic or pedagogic sense to do so. From an academic standpoint, Cummins (2007), who refers to the separation of French immersion languages as the 'two solitudes' approach to language teaching, has noted that building walls between bilingual students' languages is not in keeping with theories on students' development of a common underlying language proficiency (Cummins, 1991) that serves to strengthen skills in all of their languages. According to Jessner (2006: 122), a pedagogical attempt to prevent contact between a bi- or multilingual student's languages:

contradicts the results of research on multilingualism, which evidenced the links between the multilingual individual's languages in the brain. The emerging qualities and synergies which develop in the form of metalinguistic and metacognitive abilities due to the contact between the languages form a crucial part of multilingual proficiency which should be fostered in multilingual schooling.

Other researchers have referred to this practice as 'parallel monolingualism' (Heller, 1999), 'bilingualism through monolingualism' (Swain, 1983) and 'separate bilingualism' (Creese & Blackledge, 2010). Many such researchers take issue with the fact that bilingual and multilingual students are frequently instructed as if they were monolingual speakers of one language at a time, rather than bilingual or multilingual speakers at all times. They claim that this pedagogical practice suppresses, rather than supports, bilinguals' natural process of drawing on all of their linguistic resources to make sense of new information (García, 2009; Cenoz & Gorter, 2011; Hélot & Ó Laoire, 2011, and also García et al., this volume).

In recent years, these researchers have increasingly called for changes to be made to the pedagogy within bilingual programmes such as immersion. These changes include the development of a more dynamic model for bilingual pedagogy that builds bridges instead of walls between students' languages and that allows bilingual students to 'translanguage', or to cross freely between languages in accordance with their needs (Cummins, 2007; García, 2009; Creese & Blackledge, 2010; see also Creese et al., this volume). This dynamic model would include methods that purposefully make cross-curricular links between material taught in both languages to reinforce and deepen students' understanding of content as well as language.

Finally, because of the dramatic increase in Allophone populations in Canadian cities, bi- and multilingualism are now the norm, rather than the exception, in many French immersion classes. Thus, many researchers have argued that it is time for immersion programmes to make changes that support the L1s of students from non-English backgrounds (Swain & Lapkin, 2005; Cummins, 2007; Duff, 2007; Lyster & Lapkin, 2007). They have noted the necessity of bringing a language-as-resource approach to bilingual education in which 'linguistic diversity is seen as a societal resource that should be nurtured for the benefit of all groups' (Cummins et al., 2006: 299; see also Ruiz, 1988). Such an approach would view learners' other languages as a resource, rather than a burden, in the L2 classroom.

The following study responds to these calls for changes to bilingual pedagogy that include building cross-linguistic bridges between students' languages and introducing pedagogical approaches that recognize and build upon students' existing linguistic resources. This study can also be seen as an effort to have French immersion once again serve the needs of the community that it sprang from, as in the school board where French immersion began, 38% of the students now claim French, not English, as the language that they speak at home (Hobbs & Nasso-Maselli, 2005). In a number of individual schools within the school board, one can find equivalent numbers of English-dominant and French-dominant students learning in the same classroom or even more French-dominant than English-dominant students.

Nevertheless, previous research in this context has shown that teachers and administrators have not noticeably adjusted their pedagogical approach to address the students' changing needs for L1 and L2 learning support. Although in any given class, half of the students may be native speakers of the language of instruction, teachers only rarely reference their students' expertise to help non-native-speaking students. Moreover, the programme still maintains a strict separation between the languages of instruction (Lyster et al., 2009).

French immersion has come a long way since its inception, but changes in our knowledge of second language acquisition as well as changes in the composition of French immersion classes mean that the programme model must become more responsive to students' language learning needs, which have shifted and become more diverse over the years. Essentially, the programme must become flexible enough to adapt itself to new demographics. In the school board where French immersion began, this means accommodating the needs and taking advantage of the knowledge of both French- and English-dominant learners. Thus, in addition to making cross-linguistic links between content taught in French and English, the intervention described in this chapter also taught English- and French-dominant students strategies that would allow them to share their linguistic knowledge with each other during collaborative activities.

The focus on peer interaction in this study was influenced by several prominent immersion issues related to the quality of students' L2 production and student–student peer interaction. Student–student L2 interaction in the immersion classroom is problematic for two main reasons. First, in North American one-way and two-way immersion programmes, students tend to resist speaking the non-English language extensively with their peers. Second, immersion students tend to produce grammatically and semantically inaccurate language when speaking their L2 (Harley & Swain, 1984; Swain, 1985; Genesee, 1987; Lyster, 1987). Immersion teachers note that by Grade 3 or 4 (8–9 years old), students have discovered that they can sacrifice grammatical and semantic accuracy in their L2 and still be understood (Harley, 1989). Therefore, practising the L2 may be more likely to result in the fossilization of certain kinds of errors in the students' interlanguage and in the creation of a kind of classroom variety (Aston, 1986; Lyster, 1987) than in enhanced L2 acquisition. And yet, the opportunity to speak and practise the L2 with peers remains one of the potential core benefits of the immersion model. If students are truly going to be 'immersed' in a language and to use their L2 as authentically as possible, then speaking the L2 with their peers is crucial.

Based on the above issues, the research questions guiding the current investigation were:

1. What were teachers' and students' impressions of a cross-linguistic pedagogical intervention?
2. How much collaborative interaction did focal pairs of French L1 and English L1 students engage in during the intervention?
3. What other factors interacted with students' awareness and ability to take advantage of reciprocal learning opportunities?

3.1.1 Complementary language backgrounds

When two second language learners are simultaneously learning each other's first, or dominant, language, they can be described as having 'complementary language backgrounds'. Their language backgrounds 'complement' each other because they create a situation in which students can simultaneously learn language from and teach language to one another. This was the case for the English- and French-dominant student participants in this study. One might assume that this situation is unique to this particular research context, but it has been documented in content-based language programmes in a number of international contexts such as the Spanish Basque country (Cenoz, 1998), Cataluña (Artigal, 1991), Ireland (Hickey, 2001), Wales (Baker, 2003) and, finally, the United States, where two-way immersion programmes purposefully enrol students of complementary language backgrounds, in part so that they can better learn one another's language and culture (Lindholm-Leary, 2001).

While it is important to seek methods of promoting reciprocal learning through peer interaction in all L2 learning contexts, it is of even higher priority that researchers address this goal in contexts where students are naturally disposed to act as both novice and expert during peer interaction. Thus, one of the overarching goals of this research intervention was to seek methods of exploiting the reciprocal learning opportunities posed by participating students' complementary language backgrounds. Students were assigned a partner according to their language dominance so that English-dominant students were paired with French-dominant students. In keeping with research based on sociocultural theory that has emphasized the fluidity of expert/novice roles in student interactions (Lantolf, 2000; Storch, 2002; Angelova et al., 2006), the partner assignments remained the same for the intervention period. This allowed the role of expert and novice to be played by the same individual, depending on whether the language of instruction was their L1 or L2.

3.2 Teaching learners to collaborate for L2 learning

3.2.1 Pair interaction dynamics

Research indicates that learner pairs working on collaborative and communicative tasks naturally develop specific interaction styles. To determine how interaction style might tie in with L2 learning, Storch (2002) examined ten learner dyads in an Australian ESL class who were engaged in a language-focused writing task. Using two scales that measured the pairs' level of equality (equality of task control) and mutuality (level of engagement with their partners' contributions), she found that the pairs tended to follow one of four patterns of interaction: collaborative, expert–novice, dominant–dominant and dominant–passive. She found that learners with collaborative and expert–novice interaction styles showed the most L2 learning based on learner uptake of linguistic forms addressed during previous peer interactions. Subsequent studies have applied Storch's framework to analyse dyadic interactions for various purposes: to determine their effect on performance during paired oral examinations (Galaczi, 2008), to investigate the influence of a partner's proficiency on collaborative L2 learning in second and foreign language classrooms (Kim & McDonough, 2008; Watanabe & Swain, 2007) and to examine affordances for bilingual language learning in two-way immersion (Martin-Beltrán, 2010). As a whole, these studies have found that a more collaborative interaction style creates more opportunities for more effective L2 learning.

3.2.2 Training students to engage in metatalk

It is therefore only logical to seek the best methods of teaching students how to interact in a more collaborative manner. LaPierre (1994) and Swain and Lapkin (1998, 2002) investigated whether immersion students could be taught to use 'metatalk' – using language to talk objectively about language (Bouffard & Sarkar, 2008) – through teacher modelling. They found that metatalk training did result in students' engagement in more 'language-related episodes' (LREs), or parts of interaction in which the speakers 'talk about the language they are producing, question their language use, or correct themselves or others' (Swain & Lapkin, 1998: 326). Some researchers have used pre-task modelling to train pairs of learners to both engage in LREs and to interact in a manner reflective of Storch's (2002) definition of collaborative interaction (Kim & McDonough, 2008, 2011; Martin-Beltrán, 2010). The results of this modelling have been mixed. Martin-Beltrán (2010) modelled collaborative writing and metatalk to two-way immersion students and gave them self-evaluation rubrics that listed criteria for collaborative behaviour. Despite the modelling, she found that student pairs did not uniformly display high levels of collaboration. Kim and McDonough (2011), which employed a quasi-experimental research design, modelled examples of correctly resolved LREs and demonstrated collaborative pair dynamics in the form of feedback, asking and responding to questions, and sharing ideas. They found that not only did the group who had received modelling engage in more LREs, but their LREs were more often resolved correctly, and they engaged in more collaborative behaviours.

3.2.3 Interactive strategy training

Several studies working with adult language learners have focused on interactive strategy training to help learners communicate more extensively in their second language, to learn from oral interactions and to teach other students. Rost and Ross (1991) taught strategic questioning to Japanese university students. Bejarano et al. (1997) designed interaction strategies for Grade 11 (usually 16 years old) Israeli ESL students to facilitate their comprehension and support their participation and learning as they engaged in collaborative group work. Lam and Wong (2000) focused on training Form 6 (usually 17 years old) ESL learners in Hong Kong how to seek and give clarification and to seek confirmation of comprehension. Naughton (2006) trained adult Spanish EFL students in 'cooperative strategies' which consisted of follow-up questions, requesting and giving clarification, repair, and requesting and giving help. Finally, Sato and Lyster (2012) trained university-level Japanese learners of English to provide one another with corrective feedback during communicative peer interaction tasks.

All of the interactional strategy studies found that learners engaged in significantly more strategy use after receiving training, although Lam and Wong (2000) found that many clarification attempts ended in participants simply moving on in the conversation without resolving their lack of comprehension. Lam and Wong concluded that strategy training can be useful, but that it must also be accompanied by linguistic scaffolding as well as peer help and cooperation. Based on this last finding, Naughton (2006) argued that creating a cooperative learning environment is crucial for successful student interactions. Her research design therefore included getting students to engage in a series of structured cooperative games. The strategy that students used the least at the end of her study was the repair strategy. On the other hand, Sato and Lyster (2012), in which the only strategy taught was corrective feedback, demonstrates that learners can be trained to correct their partner's utterances and that engaging in corrective feedback may benefit their overall L2 proficiency.

We can summarize some of the findings and implications of the above metatalk, collaborative behaviour and interactional strategy studies as follows: (a) students can be trained to engage in modified interactional behaviours (b) it may be necessary to create a collaborative environment in the classroom for interactive strategy training to be effective for improved communication and language learning and (c) student–student repair is a cognitively demanding task that may require focused training.

3.3 L2 learning strategies

Language learning strategies (LLSs) have been defined as 'operations, steps, plans, and routines used by the learner to facilitate the obtaining, storage, retrieval, and use of information' (Rubin, 1987: 18). More generally stated, they are actions that help learners learn language. The strategies developed for this study were based on Oxford's (1990) scheme of language learning strategies; however, while her scheme takes an individualistic approach whose ultimate goals are to help learners help themselves, the strategies taught in the project were modified based on the idea of reciprocal learning. As such, participating students were instructed to focus on using strategies not only to help themselves learn but also to take advantage of their partner's expertise and to help their partner learn language. Thus, these peer strategies had the goals of raising their awareness of their L2 production and enhancing its accuracy, as well as increasing their awareness of themselves and their peers as language learning resources.

3.4 Methodology

3.4.1 Design

The study included a seven-week classroom intervention in one Grade 3 early partial French immersion (50/50) and one Grade 3/4 early total French immersion (90/10) classroom that enrolled both English- and French-dominant students. The teaching intervention aimed to bridge the students' L1 and L2 through (a) a 'biliteracy' project that linked English and French language arts content and (b) the instruction of collaborative language learning strategies designed to enhance students' ability to engage in reciprocal language learning.

In the first week of the intervention, students received two hour-long introductory strategy lessons, one in their English class and one in their French class. The following six weeks of the project consisted of a biliteracy project in which students' English and French teachers read to them from the English and French versions of three picture books. Following each reading, students engaged in collaborative literacy tasks that spanned their two language classes. During the intervention, students also received seven 20-minute strategy lessons. To the greatest extent possible, each student was assigned to a pair consisting of one French-dominant and one English-dominant partner, which gave all partners the potential to act as both expert and novice in their English and French language arts classes.

Data collection consisted of (a) participant observations, (b) student, teacher and parent interviews and (c) audiotaped interactions between eight focal student pairs as they worked on the collaborative tasks. Interaction data were collected before, during and two months after the teaching intervention and were analysed both qualitatively and quantitatively to examine how students displayed their language awareness, their awareness of opportunities for reciprocal language learning and their general collaborative behaviour under the conditions of the intervention.

3.4.2 Materials

BILITERACY PROJECT ACTIVITIES

The L2 activities created for the biliteracy project centred on themes and content drawn from the picture books. Larger tasks were broken down into smaller component activities that were completed in a consecutive fashion across language classes. For example, in conjunction with *The Montreal of My Childhood* (di Thomasis, 1994), a book about growing up in Montreal in the 1940s, the discussion and activities centred on comparing the differences and similarities between childhood in the 1940s and childhood today. Students were asked to interview someone who had grown up in the 1940s. In English class, they worked with their partners to generate interview questions. After conducting the interviews as homework, in the following French class they discussed their results, creating bulleted lists of what was the same and what was different between their findings. In the final English class, they wrote a more formal paragraph comparing and contrasting their findings.

STRATEGY INSTRUCTION LESSONS

Strategy instruction consisted of role plays, games and discussions. Students were shown role plays demonstrating both good and bad methods of interacting for language learning, and students were asked to name and discuss the strategies that they had observed. They were then asked to enact the strategies through their own role plays or by playing games in which they were required to use the strategies. This was again followed by class discussion (see Wenden, 1987; Oxford, 1990; Chamot, 1998; Cohen, 1998).

DATA ANALYSIS

Students' and teachers' perceptions of the intervention were based on a qualitative analysis of their interviews (pre- and post-intervention for teachers; post-intervention for students). The analysis of the participant interaction data, which totalled 22.5 hours of audiotaped interaction, adopted an 'embedded' mixed methods design. In other words, although the study was primarily qualitative in nature, the quantitative data set provided 'a supportive, secondary role' to the qualitative data set (Creswell & Plano Clark, 2007: 67). While quantitative analysis allows for a simplified overview of a classroom interaction phenomenon and for a clear portrait of or comparison between individuals or groups, it has been argued that the categorization of an utterance can be ambiguous since researchers are not privy to the speakers' intentions, the context of the utterance or the surrounding utterances of the interaction (Edwards & Westgate, 1994; Foster & Ohta, 2005; Sato & Ballinger, forthcoming). Nevertheless, since qualitative reports of interaction rely on excerpts, placing quantitative data in a supporting role to the qualitative data allows researchers to report on how representative that excerpt is of participants' behaviour (Edwards & Westgate, 1994).

The decision to use quantitative measures in this essentially qualitative study was made with two goals in mind. The first was to determine whether there were correlations between the frequency of 'collaborative' (partner-focused, on-task) turns and the frequency of LREs, corrective feedback (CF) and partner-directed questions (PDQs). These last three interactive behaviours were thought to be representative of quality collaboration for language learning. Therefore, the goal of these correlations was to explore the possibility of finding a formula that could be used to quantify the amount of quality collaboration taking place during peer interactions. The second goal of this analysis was to use patterns in the quantitative findings to guide the qualitative analysis by indicating which aspects of the interaction needed closer examination. Based on these quantitative findings, the qualitative analysis looked more closely at student interaction during LREs, and particularly during conversational episodes involving corrective feedback, to determine which additional interactional moves differentiated the quality of students' collaboration.

3.4.3 Measures

COLLABORATIVE TURNS

The first measurement of interaction data was the amount of individual and pair collaboration, operationalized as the percentage of individual and pair collaborative turns out of their total conversational turns. After the total number of conversational turns was calculated for each pair and for each partner, the data were pruned to include only 'collaborative' turns. This was done by eliminating all off-task interactions and all interactions that were not directed at an individual's assigned partner. In other words, all conversational turns directed at other students or at teachers or researchers that did not also involve partners were eliminated. All other measurements (LREs, CF and PDQs) were taken from this reduced set of collaborative interaction data.

LANGUAGE-RELATED EPISODES

Since one of the primary goals of the strategy instruction was to raise students' awareness of their and their partners' language production, their language awareness was operationalized as turns involving LREs, or turns in which the participants were engaged in metatalk.

CORRECTIVE FEEDBACK

Although all instances of CF are also by definition LREs, it was calculated separately as a combined measurement of students' strategy use (CF and asking questions were the two most emphasized strategies in this intervention), language awareness and awareness of reciprocal learning opportunities, another goal of the strategy instruction. In other words, the act of giving and receiving CF reflected all of the goals of the reciprocal strategy instruction.

PARTNER-DIRECTED QUESTIONS

Because one must ask questions in order to seek task- and language-related help from a partner, the act of asking one's partner these types of questions was one of the two most emphasized strategies during the instruction. The use of PDQs was therefore seen as a reflection of students' strategy use as well as a collaborative mindset.

3.5 Findings

3.5.1 Participants' impressions of the biliteracy project

Research question 1 addresses students' and teachers' responses to the biliteracy project, as measured through observations and student and teacher interviews.

TEACHERS' IMPRESSIONS

At the first school, the French teacher, Mme Madeleine (all names are pseudonyms), held nine years of immersion teaching experience, while the English language arts teacher was in her first year of service. The English teacher, Ms Thompson, did not have a classroom of her own and travelled from class to class throughout the day. She spent four hours per week with the Grade 3/4 students. The two teachers rarely spoke outside of class. Neither of them had ever collaborated with another teacher to plan or implement cross-linguistic lessons prior to the intervention. Mme Madeleine occasionally read to her students from science and other factual texts, while Ms Thompson read aloud from novels for approximately 10 to 15 minutes per week. Both teachers stated that they had not taught the students strategies prior to the project.

At the second school, the French teacher, Mme Éloise, had ten years of experience in immersion, and the English teacher, Ms Madison, had six years. Each teacher was with the Grade 3 students 50% of the time and their classrooms were adjoining. Students would travel back and forth between the classes, switching based on the day of the week. In addition, according to both teachers, they had good 'chemistry', and they had worked on projects together in the past. Both teachers read to their students often and had their students work in pairs and in groups quite often too. Although they both taught their students reading and writing strategies, they had never collaborated cross-linguistically, nor read aloud bilingually to the students.

Prior to the project, the teachers were generally optimistic, with only Ms Madison worrying that the students might become confused by the alternation between languages in the project. In their post-intervention interviews, the teachers were enthusiastic about and even surprised by the students' positive response to the readings and activities. Mme

Éloise remarked, 'Je dirais que ma classe a embarqué dans tous les livres. Même celui-là que je trouvais un peu plus difficile. Je trouve qu'ils sont laissés allés et c'était très agréable' (I would say that my class got into all of the books. Even the one that I found a little more difficult. I find that they let themselves go, and it was very enjoyable). Ms Thompson commented, 'They really surprised me because they got a lot more out of it than I expected', and Mme Madeleine stated that she discovered 'que les élèves ont une bonne capacité de travailler dans les deux langues simultanément avec le même materiel' (that the students have a strong capacity to simultaneously work in the two languages on the same content).

Although all of the teachers appreciated the biliteracy project and thought that it had engaged and benefited their students, they all stated that they did not think that they would have time to implement it. Their schedules did not afford them shared planning time, and it seemed too daunting for them to try to organize such an approach otherwise.

Their response to the strategy instruction and collaboration was more mixed. While several teachers commented that only the more mature students seemed to benefit from the strategy instruction, all teachers stated that they would teach these types of strategies in the future and that they seemed to be useful. However, they focused on teaching strategies to help students improve their 'teamwork' skills, and none of them mentioned the goal of teaching them to engage in reciprocal language learning.

STUDENTS' IMPRESSIONS

Based on observations of students' participation levels and their interview responses, they were highly engaged by both the bilingual readings and the collaborative tasks during the project. When asked whether they would change anything about the project, most of the students replied that they would not want to change anything because they had liked all of it. Additionally, several students stated that the bilingual readings were helpful because if they could not understand something in their L2, they could understand it in their L1. When asked whether they had learned anything from or taught anything to their partner, students almost always stated that they had both given and received language help as in the following example:

Example 1

Mitch: ... *Moi, je l'aidais en français et lui il m'aidait en anglais.* [... Me, I helped him in French and he helped me in English.]

Susan: Ok, *comment?* [OK, how?]
Jonah: Uh, I speaked in English and he speaked in French.
Susan: *Intéressant. Comment tu as aidé Jonah?* [Interesting. How did you help Jonah?]
Mitch: *A écrire les mots.* [To write the words.]

When asked which strategies they remembered learning about, students most often mentioned 'feedback' and 'asking questions', which were the two most emphasized strategies during the intervention. Most pairs stated that they did give each other corrective feedback, regardless of whether this was reflected in their interaction data.

3.5.2 Student interaction

Research question 2 investigated how much collaborative interaction focal pairs engaged in during their interactions.

QUANTITATIVE FINDINGS

A non-parametric correlational analysis (Spearman's rho) was run for the number of individual collaborative turns and the number of LRE turns for each individual; the number of individual collaborative turns and the number of PDQs asked by each individual; and the number of collaborative turns and the amount of CF initiated by each individual (see Table 3.1). The correlational analysis revealed significant positive correlations between collaborative turns and PDQs ($r = .000$) as well as between collaborative turns and LREs ($r = .002$). However, the correlation between collaborative turns and corrective feedback was found to be non-significant ($r = .080$).

Because corrective feedback is a type of LRE, and because it is an interactional behaviour that embodies the concept of peer language teaching, it was expected that individuals who focused more on completing a task with their partners would also engage in more corrective feedback. In fact, within each pair, the opposite tended to be true. In taking a closer look at the numbers, it was found that for six out of eight pairs, the partner who produced fewer collaborative turns also initiated more corrective feedback and vice versa. Why, for most of these pairs, was the partner who engaged with their partner less on the task seemingly more aware of their partner's language errors and more interested in providing corrective feedback? The question sparked by this seemingly contradictory behaviour helped guide the qualitative analysis of the interactions, which closely examined students' interactive behaviour within the LREs and CF episodes.

Table 3.1 Pair collaborative behaviours

	Collaborative turns	LRE turns	CF	PDQs
Pair 1	59.4 (190)	28.4 (54)	9.0 (17)	26.3 (50)
Pair 2	61.2 (363)	10.5 (38)	3.0 (11)	35.5 (129)
Pair 3	70.0 (222)	5.0 (11)	2.7 (6)	16.2 (36)
Pair 4	61.0 (427)	2.8 (12)	0.7 (3)	17.3 (74)
Pair 5	77.5 (966)	20.4 (197)	6.3 (61)	18.2 (176)
Pair 6	72.9 (806)	15.5 (125)	2.2 (18)	21.7 (175)
Pair 7	49.0 (735)	8.0 (113)	3.3 (24)	15.8 (116)
Pair 8	56.1 (786)	7.0 (55)	0.9 (7)	17.3 (136)

The qualitative analysis was further guided when contradictions were found between quantitative measurements of pair collaboration versus individuals' collaboration within pairs. Again, individual and pair collaboration were quantified by finding the percentage of collaborative turns out of overall conversational turns. These contradictions were most apparent when comparing Pair 5 and Pair 6, who were numerically the most collaborative pairs with 77.5% (Pair 5) and 72.9% (Pair 6) of their turns being on-task and partner-directed. Although Pair 5 had the highest rate of collaborative turns among all pairs, they also displayed the largest gap between the partners' individual collaborative turns as well as between the amount of CF that the partners initiated. Meanwhile, the partners in Pair 5 produced the exact same number of collaborative turns, and they were one of the two pairs in which the same partner who produced more collaborative turns also offered more CF. Thus, while these two pairs at first seemed to be at the same end of the collaborative spectrum, a look at individual partner contributions indicated that there might be something very different going on at the level of pair dynamics that the quantitative analysis was unable to reveal.

QUALITATIVE FINDINGS

In order to explore Research question 3, which asked what other factors might interact with students' awareness and ability to take advantage of reciprocal learning opportunities, the qualitative analysis used the contradictions from the quantitative findings as signposts to guide its more narrow examination of student interaction. This analysis began with a close contrastive analysis of Pair 5's and Pair 6's interaction during LREs and CF episodes. An initial reading of their transcribed interactions quickly revealed that although the partners in Pair 5 did indeed collaborate on task completion to a great extent, they also displayed frequent conflicts, breakdowns in collaboration and difficulties in resolving language-related problems, while Pair 6's interactions lacked conflict, were consistently polite and were productive in terms of both task completion and linguistic problem-solving.

A closer examination of the two pairs' interactions found that they were accompanied by two different sets of behaviours. Axelle and Chloe in Pair 5 frequently made emphatic assertions about content or language without confirming their partners' understanding or agreement, and although they did sometimes acknowledge their partner's contribution or offer of corrective feedback by repeating their words, explicit statements of approval were rare and monosyllabic (i.e. 'OK' or 'Oh'). During LREs, they did not elaborate on their partners' suggestions, and they displayed a lack of awareness of or respect for their partners' linguistic resources. Finally, their corrective feedback was often rejected, ignored or led to conflict. Meanwhile, the interaction between Cedric and Erica in Pair 6 was marked by acknowledgement and approval of the other's contributions, by elaborations on those contributions and by confirmations of the other's agreement or understanding. These behaviours seemed to show that the partners were aware and respectful of one another's linguistic knowledge.

Once these two sets of behaviour were established, the remaining pairs' LREs and CF episodes were analysed to verify whether these patterns held. Repeatedly, when these episodes were marked by the set of behaviours associated with Pair 5, they would end in conflict as in Example 2.

Example 2

Mohit: (Writing) Uh, *le poissonier.* Oh no. *Le* ... [Uh, the fishmonger. Oh no. The (masculine)...]
Stella: You wrote '*la*'. [You wrote 'the' (feminine).]
Mohit: *La* (mumbling). [The (feminine)]
Stella: You don't ... It, it's a boy, Mohit. *C'est un gar!* [It's a boy!]
Mohit: *La, le, la, le.*
Stella: *Je sais parce que si c'est une fille ou un gar, c'est un gar!* [I know because if it's a girl or a boy, it's a boy!]
Mohit: OK, you write it. I don't like it.

In this excerpt from Pair 2's interaction, Mohit is writing answers to reading response questions when he makes a mistake with French grammatical gender. Stella corrects him and, when he still seems confused, she insists in a critical and irritated tone of voice on the correct gender. Although this switch to focus on form represented an excellent opportunity for reinforcement of Mohit's knowledge of a grammar item that is notoriously difficult for French L2 learners to acquire, the intention behind Stella's correction is simply to get him to write the correct form on what is also her work; it is not meant to teach him how to use that form properly. Although she does give him a bit of an explanation for why he must use *le* instead of *la*, she makes no move to confirm whether he understands that explanation, which is another indication that she is not interested in teaching, but in correcting him. Furthermore, the manner in which Stella corrects Mohit pushes him to abandon the task. As others (Foster, 1998; Yoshida, 2008) have pointed out, giving corrective feedback is a face-threatening act, and Stella's tone of voice in delivering the feedback did little to 'save' Mohit's 'face'.

All pairs did sometimes acknowledge their partner's contribution or offer of corrective feedback by repeating their words. This behaviour happened most often during a read-aloud task when students would correct the way in which the other had read a word. Corrective feedback occurred at a much higher rate during this task, and it was accepted without question in most instances. Perhaps having the support from the text in front of them gave them more confidence to offer CF and more trust in the others' offer of CF.

Other than with Pair 6, using explicit statements of approval ('Yeah', 'Okay' or 'Good') were extremely rare. During LREs, the other pairs did not elaborate on their partners' suggestions. Instead, partner contributions were frequently ignored or rejected, or they served as the basis for an argument as in the following excerpt (Example 3).

The partners in Pair 6 were also the only ones to seek confirmation of the other's understanding or agreement:

Example 3

Erica: *Tu sais qu'il y a un trait ici, huh*? [You know that there is a hyphen here, huh?]
Cedric: I forgot.

It is notable that Erica's question is essentially an offer of corrective feedback. Cedric has left the hyphen out of '*grands-mamans*', and she wants him to rewrite it. However, she demonstrates her respect for his linguistic knowledge by framing the correction as a confirmation of this knowledge. Cedric responds with acknowledgement and acceptance of her CF.

Pair 5 repeatedly demonstrated their lack of awareness of or respect for their partner's linguistic knowledge. Although Chloe was strongly English dominant and Axelle was strongly French dominant, they both frequently refused to accept corrections of their L2 production from their native-speaking partner, as in Example 4.

Example 4

Chloe: *Ça ne se dit pas, en hiver.* [We don't say 'en hiver'.]
Axelle: *En hiver, oui.* ['En hiver,' yes.]
Chloe: *Mais je dis l'hiver.* [But I say 'l'hiver.']
Axelle: *Non, en hiver, Chloe. Chloe! C'est parce qu'il faut que tu écris qu'est-ce que je te dis. C'est* n'hiver (emphasizing pronunciation). *En hiver.* [No, 'en hiver', Chloe. Chloe! It's because you have to write what I say. It's 'n'hiver. En hiver'.]
Chloe: *Ça ne s'existe pas!* [That doesn't exist!]
Axelle: *Oui, ça l'existe!* [Yes, it exists!]
Chloe: *Mme Madeleine!* (asks teacher and returns). *C'est ça. Ça l'existe.* [That's right. It exists.]
Axelle: *C'est ça, en hiver. Ouais.* [That's right, 'en hiver'. Yeah.]

In this extract, the conflict can be resolved only when the teacher confirms Axelle's L1 knowledge that 'in winter' can be expressed as 'en hiver' but not as 'en l'hiver'. At other moments during their interactions, Axelle also demonstrated her lack of awareness of or respect for Chloe's knowledge. At one point, she even initiated an argument with Chloe about how Chloe's own name was spelled.

Pair 6 was also the only pair to both repeat and elaborate on their partners' statements during LREs. Example 5 demonstrates how their repetition and elaboration led to linguistic scaffolding and successful resolution of a language problem, in this case, French adjective placement.

Example 5

Cedric: *Notre beau gros vert gazon.* [Our beautiful big green grass.]
Erica: *Beau gros ...* [Beautiful big ...]
Cedric: *... notre gros, non ...* [... our big, no ...]
Erica: *Notre beau ... Non, notre beau vert, non. Long, beau vert.* [Our beautiful ... No, our beautiful green, no. Long, beautiful green.]
Cedric: *Long, vert gazon, non.* [Long, green grass, no.]
Erica: *Notre gazon vert.* [Our green grass.]
Cedric: *Notre gazon vert.* [Our green grass.]

Instead of focusing on whether the other partner was correct or incorrect, they focused on proposing solutions to a problem that they shared by showing their approval of their partners' contribution and building on it to try out new solutions. As soon as Erica found an appropriate solution, Cedric established that the problem was solved by repeating what she had said with descending intonation.

Additionally, in Example 6, below, Cedric code-switches, using the French word for 'breakfast' during a brainstorming task in English class.

Example 6

Cedric: Well, sometimes the people go at the morning. I remember. I already went, and they get a *déjeuner*.
Erica: Right, breakfast in the morning.
Cedric: Yeah, breakfast.

Before correcting his linguistic form, Erica first acknowledges the content of his contribution with an approving 'Right'. Then, she reformulates his *déjeuner* into the English 'breakfast', and finally she elaborates on this with 'in the morning'. Cedric follows her correction with another approving acknowledgement, 'Yeah', and then repeats her correction. Although they are engaging in a potentially face-threatening behaviour – peer correction – the fact that Erica's approval occurs before her correction, along with the polite manner in which she delivers this correction, prevents a minor language problem from derailing their communication as it often did with other pairs. It also allows them to successfully resolve language issues, to practise language forms in both English and French, and to learn through peer interaction in a variety of tasks.

3.6 Discussion and implications

3.6.1 Biliteracy in French immersion

This study's biliteracy approach to cross-linguistic pedagogy fits smoothly and naturally into both French immersion classes. Working on the various components of a larger task in both English and French did not confuse the students. Based on teacher and student reports, having the same themes and vocabulary presented in both languages increased their engagement with the lessons. This finding lends support to García's (2009) reflection that schools in the twenty-first century must shift their perspective on bilingual education to build programmes that support bilingual or multilingual students' natural proclivity to 'translanguage', or to cross back and forth between languages, rather than build imaginary boundaries between those languages.

Not only was cross-linguistic teaching a natural fit, but participating teachers and students believed that it benefited students' overall understanding of the language and content of the lessons. In keeping with Cummins's (1991) notion of the development of a common underlying language proficiency, teachers noticed and were impressed by students' ability to carry their knowledge across languages, and they believed that the bilingual readings served to reinforce students' overall understanding of the material. This likely functioned differently depending on which language the book was read in first. If the students heard the book in their non-dominant language first, the second reading probably helped them to fill in the holes in their understanding. If they heard the book in their dominant language first, the second reading may have allowed them to focus more attention on vocabulary and language structures in their L2 rather than being able to attend only to the global meaning in the story.

Finally, the repeated discussions of and exposure to the stories and their themes seemed to further engage the students rather than to bore them. This layering of information on the same topic across classes allowed them to have a more complete comprehension of complex themes such as identity and place. It gave them time to better personalize their understanding of concepts such as day-to-day life in the 1940s, which lay far out of their frame of reference. In sum, this cross-linguistic teaching approach was not only good second language pedagogy, but also simply good pedagogy.

3.6.2 Reciprocal strategies in French immersion

The student participants here were younger than in most other studies of interactional strategies. Although behaviour varied from pair to pair, all participating students engaged in extensive task collaboration. All student pairs engaged in PDQs, LREs and CF. Whether or not these behaviours were related to the intervention, they demonstrate that younger students are quite capable of autonomously using reciprocal strategies.

The positive correlations found between collaborative task interaction and PDQs as well as between collaborative interaction and LREs indicate that these behaviours may be more straightforwardly in line with an individual's overall collaborative mindset. Furthermore, these correlations offer clear support for raising students' awareness of language form during peer interactions as well as for training students to turn to their partner for help by asking questions. On the other hand, although CF was initially seen as an operationalized measure of students' engagement in collaborative reciprocal learning, this interactional move proved to be a less straightforward measure of collaborative interaction.

Primarily, pair dynamics seemed to play a critical role in students' initiation of CF as well as in their rejection or acceptance of the CF offered by their partner. Although Storch's (2002) scales of measurement were not employed in this study's analysis to categorize students' interactional patterns, it is very likely that examining pairs' interactional styles would have helped to explain why one partner tended to take a dominant role in offering CF while simultaneously taking a less active role in task collaboration. It may have also explained why Pair 6, whose partners produced the exact same number of collaborative turns, did not fit this dominant–passive pattern when it came to CF and why they were the only pair to engage in the additional collaborative behaviours uncovered in the qualitative analysis of conflictive and non-conflictive interactional behaviour.

The final issue that arises in examining reciprocal learning strategies is whether it is worthwhile to teach them, considering the power of pair interactional styles. While acknowledging that naturally occurring pair dynamics played a major role in students' reciprocal behaviour in this project, I would still argue that conflictive student pairs are not condemned to stay frozen in negative interactional patterns. Partners tend to reflect each other's behaviour. Thus, just as a rude rejection of one partner's contribution can lead that partner to reciprocate by rejecting future contributions, one acknowledgement of a contribution can lead to the reciprocation of collaborative behaviours, non-conflictive interaction and ideally to more learning during peer interaction.

3.6.3 Limitations

The primary weakness of this intervention was the lack of teachers' direct involvement in the planning of lessons and the delivery of strategy instruction. While the teachers worked very hard to cooperate with the demands of the research project, they themselves were not collaborative partners in its planning and implementation. Thus, despite all efforts to explain, discuss and promote the approach, they may not have been fully aware of, or in agreement with, the goals of the strategy instruction.

Furthermore, the intervention had no chance of becoming sustainable practice in the schools. The unfortunate fact is that no matter how feasible, relevant and potentially beneficial cross-linguistic teaching is for bilingual education, if teachers, such as those who participated in this study, do not have official time allocated to collaboratively plan with their colleagues, this approach may never be truly feasible.

3.7 Conclusions

As the pendulum of thought swings from a position in which languages should be separated in bilingual education to a position in which languages can and should be mixed in the bilingual classroom, bilingual educators need concrete ideas and guidelines to follow when attempting to implement these changes. This study was an attempt to do exactly that. While the two parts of the intervention – the biliteracy project and the reciprocal language learning strategy instruction – may seem like two separate studies at the outset, they were both part of a general movement towards a cross-linguistic pedagogy, which must help students make links between languages, whether it is through the content they are exposed to or through peer interaction. As researchers continue to work on the development of a cross-linguistic pedagogy for bilingual education, they must take into account the necessity of implementing this approach at these and other levels as well. Teachers must be trained in the approach, and changes must be made at the administrative and programmatic levels to seek logistical adjustments that facilitate the planning and sharing of the classroom curriculum across languages.

References

Angelova, M., Gunawardena, D. and Volk, D. (2006). Peer teaching and learning: co-constructing language in a dual language first grade. *Language and Education*, 20, 173–90.

Artigal, J. (1997). The Catalan immersion program. In K. Johnson and M. Swain (eds.), *Immersion Education: International Perspectives* (pp. 133–50). Cambridge: Cambridge University Press.

Aston, G. (1986). Trouble-shooting in interaction with learners: the more the merrier? *Applied Linguistics*, 7, 128–43.

Baker, C. (2003). Education as a site of language contact. *Annual Review of Applied Linguistics*, 23, 95–112.

Ballinger, S. and Lyster, R. (2011). Student and teacher language use in a two-way Spanish/English immersion school. *Language Teaching Research*, 15, 289–306.

Bejarano, Y., Levine, T., Olshtain, E. and Steiner, J. (1997). The skilled use of interaction strategies: creating a framework for improved small-group communicative interaction in the language classroom. *System*, 25, 203–14.

Bouffard, L.-A. and Sarkar, M. (2008). Training 8-year-old French immersion students in metalinguistic analysis: an innovation in form-focused pedagogy. *Language Awareness*, 17, 3–24.

Cenoz, J. (1998). Multilingual education in the Basque Country. In J. Cenoz and F. Genesee (eds.), *Beyond Bilingualism: Multilingualism and Multilingual Education* (pp. 175–91). Clevedon: Multilingual Matters.

Cenoz, J. and Gorter, D. (2011). A holistic approach to multilingual education: introduction. *The Modern Language Journal*, **95**, 339–43.

Chamot, A. (1998). *Teaching Learning Strategies to Language Learners.* Washington, DC: Center for Applied Linguistics.

Cohen, A. (1998). *Strategies in Learning and Using a Second Language.* London: Longman.

Cook, V. (2001). Using the first language in the classroom. *The Canadian Modern Language Review*, **57**, 402–23.

Creese, A. and Blackledge, A. (2010). Translanguaging in the bilingual classroom: a pedagogy for learning and teaching? *The Modern Language Journal*, **94**, 103–15.

Creswell, J. and Plano Clark, V. (2007). *Designing and Conducting Mixed Methods Research.* Thousand Oaks, CA: Sage.

Cummins, J. (1991). Interdependence of first- and second-language proficiency in bilingual children. In E. Bialystok (ed.), *Language Processing in Bilingual Children* (pp. 70–89). Cambridge: Cambridge University Press.

Cummins, J. (2007). Rethinking monolingual instructional strategies in multilingual classrooms. *Canadian Journal of Applied Linguistics*, **10**, 221–41.

Cummins, J., Chow, P. and Schecter, S. (2006). Community as curriculum. *Language Arts*, **83**, 297–307.

Dalton-Puffer, C. (2007). *Discourse in Content and Language Learning (CLIL) Classrooms.* Amsterdam: John Benjamins.

d'Anglejan, A. (1984). Language planning in Quebec: an historical overview. In R. Bourhis (ed.), *Conflict and Language Planning in Quebec* (pp. 29–52). Clevedon: Multilingual Matters.

Day, E. and Shapson, S. (1996). *Studies in Immersion Education.* Clevedon: Multilingual Matters.

Di Thomasis, A. (1994). *The Montreal of My Childhood.* Toronto, ONT: Tundra Books.

Duff, P. (2007). Multilingualism in Canadian schools: myths, realities and possibilities. *Canadian Journal of Applied Linguistics*, **10**, 149–64.

Edwards, A. and Westgate, D. (1994). *Investigating Classroom Talk* (2nd edn). London: Falmer Press.

Foster, P. (1998). A classroom perspective on the negotiation of meaning. *Applied Linguistics*, **19**, 1–23.

Foster, P. and Ohta, A. (2005). Negotiation for meaning and peer assistance in second language classrooms. *Applied Linguistics*, **26**, 402–30.

Galaczi, E. (2008). Peer-peer interaction in a speaking test: the case of the First Certificate in English Examination. *Language Assessment Quarterly*, **5**, 89–119.

García, O. (2009). *Bilingual Education in the 21st Century: A Global Perspective.* Malden, MA: Wiley-Blackwell.

Genesee, F. (1987). *Learning Through Two Languages.* Cambridge, MA: Newbury House Publishers.

Genesee, F. (1994). *Integrating Language and Content: Lessons from Immersion.* Santa Cruz, CA: National Center for Research on Cultural Diversity and Second Language Learning.

Genesee, F. and Gándara, P. (1999). Bilingual education programs: a cross-national perspective. *Journal of Social Issues*, 55, 665–85.

Harley, B. (1989). Functional grammar in French immersion: a classroom experiment. *Applied Linguistics*, 10, 331–59.

Harley, B. and Swain, M. (1984). The interlanguage of immersion students and its implication for second language teaching. In A. Davies, C. Cripers and A. Howatt (eds.), *Interlanguage* (pp. 291–311). Edinburgh: Edinburgh University Press.

Heller, M. (1999). *Linguistic Minorities and Modernity: A Sociolinguistic Ethnography.* London: Longman.

Hélot, C. and Ó Laoire, M. (2011). From language education policy to a pedagogy of the possible. In C. Hélot and M. Ó Laoire (eds.), *Language Policy for the Multilingual Classroom: Pedagogy of the Possible* (pp. xi–xxv). Bristol: Multilingual Matters.

Hickey, T. (2001). Mixing beginners and native speakers in minority language immersion: who is immersing whom? *The Canadian Modern Language Review*, 57, 443–74.

Hobbs, J. and Nasso-Maselli, M. (2005). *Elementary Programs Study.* St Lambert, Quebec: Riverside School Board.

Jessner, U. (2006). *Linguistic Awareness in Multilinguals: English as a Third Language.* Edinburgh: Edinburgh University Press.

Kim, Y. and McDonough, K. (2008). The effect of interlocutor proficiency on the collaborative dialogue between Korean as a second language learners. *Language Teaching Research*, 12, 211–34.

Kim, Y. and McDonough, K. (2011). Using pretask modelling to encourage collaborative learning opportunities. *Language Teaching Research*, 15, 183–99.

Krashen, S. (1985). *The Input Hypothesis: Issues and Implications.* London: Longman.

Lam, W. and Wong, J. (2000). The effects of strategy training on developing discussion skills in an ESL classroom. *ELT Journal*, 54, 245–55.

Lamarre, P. (1997). A comparative analysis of the development of immersion programs in British Columbia and Quebec: two divergent sociopolitical contexts. Unpublished doctoral dissertation, University of British Columbia.

Lantolf, J. (2000). Introducing sociocultural theory. In J. Lantolf (ed.), *Sociocultural Theory and Second Language Learning* (pp. 1–26). Oxford: Oxford University Press.

LaPierre, D. (1994). Language output in a cooperative learning setting: determining its effects on second language learning. Unpublished MA thesis, University of Toronto.

Lindholm-Leary, K. J. (2001). *Dual Language Education.* Clevedon: Multilingual Matters.

Lyster, R. (1987). Speaking immersion. *The Canadian Modern Language Review*, 43, 701–17.

Lyster, R. and Lapkin, S. (2007). Multilingualism in Canadian schools: an introduction. *Canadian Journal of Applied Linguistics*, 10, 145–82.

Lyster, R., Collins, L. and Ballinger, S. (2009). Linking languages through a bilingual read-aloud project. *Language Awareness*, 18, 366–83.

Martin-Beltrán, M. (2010). The two-way language bridge: co-constructing bilingual language learning opportunities. *The Modern Language Journal*, 94, 254–77.

Naughton, D. (2006). Cooperative strategy training and oral interaction: enhancing small group communication in the language classroom. *The Modern Language Journal*, 90, 169–84.

Oxford, R. (1990). *Language Learning Strategies: What Every Teacher Should Know*. New York: Newbury House Publishers.

Rost, M. and Ross, S. (1991). Learner use of strategies in interaction: typology and teachability. *Language learning*, 41, 235–73.

Rubin, J. (1987). Learner strategies: theoretical assumptions, research history and typology. In A. Wenden and J. Rubin (eds.), *Learner Strategies in Language Learning* (pp. 15–30). Englewood Cliffs, NJ: Prentice Hall International.

Ruíz, R. (1988). Orientations in language planning. In S. McKay and C. Wong (eds.), *Language Diversity: Problem or Resource?* (pp. 3–25). Cambridge, MA: Newbury House Publishers.

Sato, M. and Ballinger, S. (forthcoming). Raising language awareness in peer interaction: a cross-context, cross-method examination. *Language Awareness*, 21, 1–2.

Sato, M. and Lyster, R. (2012). Peer interaction and corrective feedback for accuracy and fluency development: monitoring, practice, and proceduralization. *Studies in Second Language Acquisition*, 34(4), 591–626.

Stern, H. (1992). *Issues and Options in Language Teaching*. Oxford: Oxford University Press.

Storch, N. (2002). Patterns of interaction in ESL pairwork. *Language Learning*, 52, 119–58.

Swain, M. (1983). Bilingualism without tears. In M. Clarke and J. Handscombe (eds.), *On TESOL '82: Pacific Perspectives on Language Learning and Teaching* (pp. 35–46). Washington, DC: TESOL.

Swain, M. (1985). Communicative competence: some roles of comprehensible input and comprehensible output in its development. In S. Gass and C. Madden (eds.), *Input in Second Language Acquisition* (pp. 235–56). Rowley, MA: Newbury House Publishers.

Swain, M. and Lapkin, S. (1998). Interaction and second language learning: two adolescent French immersion students working together. *The Modern Language Journal*, 82, 320–37.

Swain, M. and Lapkin, S. (2002). Talking it through: two French immersion learners' response to reformulation. *International Journal of Educational Research*, 37, 285–304.

Swain, M. and Lapkin, S. (2005). The evolving sociopolitical context of immersion education in Canada: some implications for program development. *International Journal of Applied Linguistics*, 15, 169–86.

Watanabe, Y. and Swain, M. (2007). Effects of proficiency differences and patterns of pair interaction on second language learning: collaborative dialogue between adult ESL learners. *Language Teaching Research*, **11**, 121–42.

Wenden, A. (1987). Conceptual background and utility. In A. Wenden and J. Rubin (eds.), *Learning Strategies in Language Learning* (pp. 3–13). Englewood Cliffs, NJ: Prentice Hall International.

Yoshida, R. (2008). Learners' perception of corrective feedback in pair work. *Foreign Language Annals*, **41**, 525–41.

4 The role of the native language in the literacy development of Latino students in the United States

Igone Arteagoitia and Elizabeth R. Howard

4.1 Introduction

English learners (ELs), particularly those from Hispanic backgrounds, represent one of the fastest-growing populations in the US public school system. The number of Latino students nearly doubled between 1990 and 2006, accounting for 60% of the total growth in public school enrolments over that period. Currently, 20% of the students attending US public schools are of Hispanic origin, and projections recently released by the US Census Bureau suggest that by 2050 there will be more Latino students in US public schools than those of European descent (Fry & Gonzales, 2008).

Despite the fact that the vast majority of the Latino K-12 students are US born, Spanish-speaking ELs lag behind native English speakers of the same age in text-level reading skills, and this puts them at risk of academic failure (August et al., 2005). As shown by results from the 2009 National Assessment of Educational Progress (NAEP), 39% of eighth-grade (ages 13–14) Latino students scored below the basic level in reading (Mather & Foxen, 2010). Raising the educational attainment of the fastest-growing segment of the population will be vital to the overall economic future and prosperity of the United States and as such should be a priority for education policy-makers.

While ELs exhibit word-level reading skills comparable to their English-only peers, their reading comprehension skills, which are necessary to master school work beyond third grade (ages 8–9) and have access to economic opportunity, are significantly lower (August & Shanahan, 2006). Differences in the reading performance of ELs and English native speakers begin to increase around Grade 4 or 5 (ages 10–11) when children transition from 'learning to read' to 'reading to learn', and these seem to be related to vocabulary and conceptual knowledge (Chall, 1983). Research on the acquisition of first language reading skills has demonstrated a strong relationship between knowledge of word meaning and ability to comprehend passages containing those words (Anderson & Freebody, 1981). In fact, the proportion of difficult words in a text has been found to be the single most powerful predictor of text difficulty, and a reader's general vocabulary knowledge the single best predictor of how well the reader can understand text (Anderson & Freebody, 1981).

While much less is known about how EL students become fluent readers at advanced levels, a review of experimental and quasi-experimental studies by the National Literacy Panel (August & Shanahan, 2006) emphasizes the importance of vocabulary knowledge for EL students' continued success in reading development beyond third grade. A number of studies (García, 1991; Jiménez et al., 1996; Carlisle et al., 1999; Laufer, 2003; Proctor et al., 2005; Proctor et al., 2006; Lesaux et al., 2010) have shown that English reading comprehension is an area of weakness for ELs in the United States and that this is in large part due to their low oral language skills (vocabulary knowledge, in particular) in both their first and second languages (L1 and L2). Thus, for example, in a longitudinal study with Spanish-speaking children from low socioeconomic backgrounds, Reese and colleagues found that English language proficiency, including oral language skills, and Spanish early literacy skills were predictive of English reading comprehension in middle school (Reese et al., 2000).

Further support for the relationship between L2 vocabulary and reading comprehension comes from a series of studies conducted with Turkish children in the Netherlands by Verhoeven (1990, 2000), in which he found that the word-reading and oral language skills of children in first grade predicted their reading comprehension in Dutch. Additionally, findings from his 1990 study show that by the end of second grade the role of oral language proficiency (vocabulary and syntax) had increased, while the role of word-reading skills had decreased. Similarly, Proctor et al. (2005) tested a structural equation model of L2 reading comprehension on a sample of fourth-grade Spanish-speaking ELs and found that while decoding skills (alphabetic knowledge and fluency) played an important role in predicting these students' English reading comprehension outcomes, they were less predictive than vocabulary and listening comprehension. Listening comprehension made an independent, proximal contribution to reading comprehension, while vocabulary knowledge contributed to reading comprehension directly and also indirectly through its strong relationship with listening comprehension. Similar findings were obtained in a more recent study conducted by Lesaux et al. (2010). These researchers followed a group of fourth-grade Spanish-speaking students into fifth grade and found that while students' word-level reading skills (L1 or L2) were not significantly related to English reading comprehension, students' L2 oral language skills were a strong and significant predictor of English reading comprehension.

4.2 The relationship between L1 vocabulary and L2 reading comprehension

When compared with monolingual English-speaking students, EL students possess an additional set of resources and abilities that are linked to their native language. There are only a handful of studies that have examined the relationship between native language and literacy skills and second language reading comprehension. In a follow-up to their 2005 publication, Proctor et al. (2006) studied the effects of Spanish language and literacy skills in Spanish on English reading comprehension for the same fourth-grade students. Results reveal that, after controlling for the effects of language of instruction and English decoding and oral language proficiency, Spanish vocabulary knowledge made a significant contribution to English reading comprehension, thus lending support for the transfer of vocabulary from the L1 to the L2. Different results were obtained by Lesaux et al. (2010) in a study conducted with fourth- and fifth-grade students instructed in Spanish from Kindergarten to Grade 3, in which the relationships between Spanish vocabulary skills and English reading comprehension were found to be very weak. The authors do not offer a conclusive explanation for the divergence between their outcomes and those of Proctor and colleagues but stress the need for more research on the role of L1 language and literacy skills in L2 reading comprehension.

One component of Spanish vocabulary that may be useful for Spanish-speaking EL students is cognate knowledge. Spanish–English cognates are words that are etymologically related and thus have similar form and meaning. The importance of Spanish–English cognate words is not limited to its quantity (estimates ranging from between 10,000 to 15,000), but to the fact that they tend to be low-frequency sophisticated words in English and account for from a third to as much as half of the active vocabulary of an average educated English speaker (Nash, 1997). Many words that are rare in oral language in English have cognates that are relatively common words in Spanish, and this may provide an advantage to Spanish-speaking EL students. So, if Spanish-speaking students know the meaning of the word *encontrar* in Spanish, equivalent to *find* in English, and are able to recognize the relationship between *encontrar* and *encounter* when they come across the word *encounter* in a text, their Spanish knowledge should provide them with substantial help unlocking its meaning.

There is some research evidence that (Spanish/English) biliterate students are able to recognize cognates in an English text (Nagy et al., 1993; Hancin-Bhatt & Nagy, 1994; Jiménez et al., 1996). For example, Jiménez et al. (1996), using think-aloud protocols, found that successful Spanish-speaking English middle-school (ages 12–14) readers were able to use their Spanish knowledge in English reading comprehension. However, the same was not true of less successful English readers, suggesting that the ability to use cognates may be subject to L2 language and literacy level.

Similarly, in a study conducted with upper-elementary Spanish-speaking biliterate students (Grades 4–6), Nagy et al. (1993) found that the ability to recognize cognates in text predicted performance on an English reading comprehension test containing cognates, but only if the meaning of the word in Spanish was known. The fact that students only selected half of the cognates that they encountered on a test of cognate identification was interpreted as evidence that explicit instruction may be needed for most students to make connections between the two languages (for similar findings see García, 1991). Word meaning in Spanish was measured using a 'yes/no vocabulary test', in which students were asked to report whether they knew the meaning of a series of cognate words in Spanish. These tests have some limitations in that students are not tested on the knowledge of the words but rather on their familiarity with them. So, students 'are likely to say that they know the meaning of a word even if they have only a limited or vague grasp of its meaning', as the authors themselves acknowledge (Nagy et al., 1993: 244). An assessment in which students are presented with the target words in context and asked to select a synonym among a number of options would provide a more direct way of assessing reading vocabulary knowledge.

Nagy and colleagues also tested the potential moderating effects of grade level (4–6) on cognate recognition and found that grade was not a significant predictor of cognate recognition in their sample. However, grade level made a difference in a different study conducted by some of the same researchers (Hancin-Bhatt & Nagy, 1994). Spanish-speaking students in Grades 4–8 (ages 10–14) showed higher recognition of cognate roots in derived words than in non-cognate roots, with older students exhibiting more cognate awareness than younger ones. These authors interpreted these findings as evidence that the ability to recognize cognates may be developmental. Nevertheless, as Proctor and Mo (2009) have indicated, it is possible that 'age may have been confounded with English language proficiency, opening a different, though clearly related, window on the developmental parameters of Spanish–English cognate recognition' (p. 127).

In their recent study Proctor and Mo (2009) investigated the relationship between knowledge of cognate reading vocabulary and English reading comprehension in Spanish-speaking biliterate fourth-grade students. Findings from their study revealed that higher reading comprehension was associated with higher cognate recognition for the Spanish-speaking students but not for a group of native English-speaking peers used as comparison. These findings must be viewed with some caution as the sample was rather small (n=30). Moreover, the fact that only fourth-grade students were included in the study does not permit exploration of the potential confusion between age and proficiency that they raised. Finally, the absence of Spanish literacy measures in the study is a drawback, as the authors themselves admit, as the interaction between the two languages would provide insights into the intricacies of biliteracy development and a more complete picture of such development.

In sum, there is some evidence that Spanish–English bilingual adolescent students are able to recognize cognates in English text, even though this ability seems to be developmental and possibly subject to L2 proficiency level and enhanced by explicit instruction. Furthermore, most of these studies collected only English language literacy data and determined the influence of the native language by comparing the performance of Spanish-speaking bilingual students and English monolingual students on English cognate and non-cognate items. Given that the ability to transfer the meaning of a cognate word from Spanish to English entails knowing the meaning of the word in Spanish, it would seem important to assess word meaning in Spanish.

Following this line of research and expanding upon it, the current study seeks to investigate the role that knowledge of Spanish cognates plays in the development of English vocabulary and reading comprehension skills in Spanish-speaking middle-school students. By studying students in different grade levels (6–8) and looking at different indicators of English proficiency (i.e. classification as EL and performance on an English vocabulary measure), we were able to discriminate between grade and English language proficiency differences in cognate recognition. Moreover, a measure of Spanish cognate knowledge allowed us to use L1 vocabulary knowledge as the developmental benchmark for a group of middle-school Spanish-speaking students to answer the following questions:

1. Does Spanish cognate knowledge predict concurrent English vocabulary when controlling for background characteristics for Spanish-speaking adolescent students?

2. Does Spanish cognate knowledge predict concurrent English reading comprehension when controlling for background characteristics and the effects of English vocabulary skills for these students?

4.3 Method

4.3.1 Participants

Participants were 230 Spanish-speaking students in Grades 6 through 8 in 21 different classrooms in a large urban middle school in Connecticut with a large percentage of native Spanish speakers. The data were collected as part of a larger study of 350 middle-school students that included a small percentage of speakers of other L1s as well as native English speakers. The study, a cognate-based curricular intervention focused on general English academic vocabulary called EVoCA (Enhancing Vocabulary through Cognate Awareness – www.cal.org/vias/subproject4/index.html), was developed with middle-school students in mind, with a specific interest in supporting the English academic vocabulary development and reading comprehension of adolescent ELs, and in particular native Spanish speakers.

The native Spanish-speaking focal students were predominantly of Puerto Rican or Dominican origin, and most of them had been born in the United States. Because the intervention was not designed for emergent ELs, participants were at least at an intermediate ESL level. At the time of the study, 30% of the native Spanish speakers were designated as ELs, with the remaining 70% either having been reclassified as fully proficient or never having been identified as EL because of sufficient English proficiency at the time of entry into the district. The sample of 230 students was fairly balanced with regard to gender, with 48% female students. Most (90%) were from low socioeconomic status backgrounds, as measured by their eligibility for free or reduced lunch at school (characteristics that have been associated with low academic achievement: Suárez-Orozco & Suárez-Orozco, 2001). Finally, a small percentage of students (14%) were receiving some type of special education service.

4.3.2 Measures

A variety of instruments including both standardized assessments and researcher-developed tests were used to assess language and literacy skills in both languages. Of those, the three measures that are relevant to the current study (the English Vocabulary Test, the Spanish Cognates Test and the Gates–MacGinite (reading) comprehension subtest) will be briefly described in this section.

READING COMPREHENSION

The comprehension subtest from the fourth edition of the *Gates–MacGinitie Reading Tests* for Levels 6 (Form S) and 7/9 (Form T) (MacGinitie et al., 2000) is a whole-group administered multiple-choice test, in which students have 35 minutes to read 14 grade-level short passages from expository and narrative texts and complete 48 multiple-choice questions. This norm-referenced measure is a widely used assessment of students' global reading comprehension. The developers provide Kuder-Richardson Formula 20 (KR-20) reliability coefficients for raw total and subtest scores across grade levels and forms for two time points, as well as extensive validity evidence. For Levels 3 through 10/12, reliability coefficients for the total scores ranged from .93 to .96 and, for subtest scores, from .90 to .93.

VOCABULARY

The English Vocabulary Test is a researcher-developed assessment aligned with the EVoCA intervention. It is a group-administered multiple-choice assessment designed to measure students' baseline knowledge and growth on cognate words taught as part of the intervention as well as other words not taught (both cognates and non-cognates). Students are presented with a sentence in which the target word is underlined, and they are asked to choose the answer option (out of four) that has the same or almost the same meaning as the underlined word.

The Spanish Cognates Test follows the same format as the English Vocabulary Test, but the instructions and the four choices are presented bilingually (in Spanish with English translations in parentheses) to make sure that students are given as many opportunities as possible to show their knowledge of Spanish. The Spanish Cognates Test measures prior knowledge of the Spanish equivalents of the English cognate words in the English Vocabulary Test. The purpose of this assessment is to determine the extent to which the Spanish-speaking participants in the study are in fact already familiar with the Spanish equivalents of the English words targeted in the intervention, in order to help predict the extent to which they may be able to capitalize on their knowledge of Spanish to unlock the meanings of the English target words. (Sample items for the Spanish Cognates Test and the English Vocabulary Test are provided in the Appendix.)

Earlier versions of the English Vocabulary Test and the Spanish Cognates Test were field-tested, and the information obtained from the item analyses (Rasch) was used to revise the assessments and develop the versions of the tests used in the current study. An investigation of the psychometric properties of the two measures revealed their reliability and construct validity. The estimated internal consistency reliability in the study sample for the English Vocabulary Test was high (Cronbach's alpha = .90) and moderate for the Spanish Cognates Test (Cronbach's alpha = .81). Principal Axis Factor (PAF) analysis conducted on the English and Spanish measures separately revealed the existence of one dominant factor in each, thus providing evidence for the construct validity of each of the measures. Furthermore, the strong significant correlation between the English Vocabulary Test and the vocabulary subtest of the *Gates–MacGinitie Reading Tests* ($r = .71$) provides additional support for the validity of the former. Unfortunately, it was not possible to obtain criterion validity for the Spanish Cognates Test, as data on standardized assessments of Spanish language and literacy were not available at the time the study was conducted.

4.3.3 Procedure

The English assessments were group-administered to classrooms of students by trained research assistants on two different testing sessions. Students were gathered in the library in groups of 20 or fewer to take the Spanish assessment, as the classrooms had mixed groups of L1 speakers. All three assessments were administered over the course of one week.

4.3.4 Analyses

Multiple regression analyses were conducted using performance on the Spanish Cognates Test as a predictor of performance on (1) the English Vocabulary Test and (2) the Gates–MacGinitie comprehension subtest controlling for English vocabulary scores and student background characteristics (grade, gender, ethnicity, eligibility for free/reduced lunch and classification as EL). Prior to running the regression analyses, we calculated the sample means, standard deviations and simple correlations on each observed measure.

4.4 Results

4.4.1 Descriptive statistics

Table 4.1 displays the means, medians, standard deviations, and minimum and maximum scores on the three measures (raw scores for

Table 4.1 Means, medians, standard deviations, minimum and maximum scores for outcome variables

	Mean	Median	SD	Minimum	Maximum
Spanish cognate knowledge (52 items)	23.77	23	7.53	8	42
English vocabulary knowledge (74 items)	30.64	29	11.93	2	65
English reading comprehension (48 items)	504.05	501	30.16	431	619

the two researcher-developed instruments and Extended Scale Scores, ESSs, for the Gates–MacGinitie comprehension subtest). ESSs, like normal curve equivalents (NCEs), measure reading achievement in equal units, and thus, for example, a difference of 25 units represents the same difference all along the scale. However, gains in ESSs are not the same from year to year to account for the differences in reading growth that take place during the school years, with gains being greatest in the primary grades.

As shown in Table 4.1, both the English Vocabulary Test and the Spanish Cognates Test were rather challenging, with very few participants scoring at the high end. The percentage of correct responses across items in the Spanish test was 46% and 42.5% in the English test. These findings are in line with those obtained for English reading comprehension as measured by the Gates–MacGinitie comprehension subtest. As a group, participants' reading comprehension scores were well below average, as shown by the mean ESS score of 504, which is equivalent to a National Percentile Rand (NPR) of 50 in the winter of Grade 5.

PREDICTING ENGLISH VOCABULARY FROM SPANISH COGNATE KNOWLEDGE

Multiple regression analyses were conducted to evaluate the contribution of Spanish cognate knowledge to English vocabulary knowledge, controlling for the effects of student background characteristics (grade, gender, ethnicity, eligibility for free/reduced lunch and classification as EL). The correlations among these variables are presented in Table 4.2.

As shown in Table 4.2, the English vocabulary measure was significantly correlated with three other variables, the correlation between

Table 4.2 Correlations between study variables (reading comprehension not included)

Indicators	1	2	3	4	5	6	7
1. English vocabulary raw score (n=74)	—						
2. Gender	−.001	—					
3. Grade	.309**	−.055	—				
4. EL classification	−.277**	.043	.044	—			
5. Meal status	−.005	.092	.034	.147*	—		
6. Ethnicity	−.058	.068	.086	.158**	.127	—	
7. Spanish cognates raw score (n=52)	.546**	−.158*	.342**	.009	.012	.102	—
Means	31.04	—	—	—	—	—	24.07
(Standard deviations)	(11.981)						(7.490)

* $p < .05$.
** $p < .01$.

the two vocabulary measures being the strongest ($r = 0.55$). The positive moderate correlation between these two variables indicates that participants with strong Spanish (cognate) vocabulary skills also have strong English academic vocabulary skills. This finding is promising given that the purpose of the larger project (the EVoCA intervention) was to enable Spanish-speaking students to capitalize on their knowledge of Spanish to unlock the meanings of English academic words via a cognate-based English vocabulary intervention. English vocabulary scores are also positively and significantly correlated with grade level, showing that students in Grade 8 had higher English vocabulary scores than those in Grade 7, who likewise had higher scores than those in Grade 6. Finally, the negative significant correlation between English vocabulary and classification as EL denotes that students classified as EL performed more poorly on the English vocabulary test than those who were not. This is not surprising, as EL classification is an indication of English proficiency, and it makes sense that students with less developed English proficiency would not perform as well on a measure of English vocabulary as students with better developed English proficiency.

Table 4.3 Regression models investigating the role of L1 cognate knowledge on L2 vocabulary, controlling for student background characteristics

Model	R	R^2	R^2_{adj}	SEE	Change statistics				
					ΔR^2	ΔF	df_1	df_2	Sig. ΔF
1	.429[a]	.184	.165	10.920	.184	9.674	5	215	.000
2	.645[b]	.416	.399	9.259	.232	85.056	1	214	.000

[a] Predictors: (Constant), Ethnicity, Gender, Grade, Meal status, EL classification
[b] Predictors: (Constant), Ethnicity, Gender, Grade, Meal status, EL classification, Spanish cognate

Table 4.3 displays the regression analysis output with English vocabulary as the dependent variable. All background variables were entered simultaneously into Model 1. In Model 2 an additional variable, performance on the Spanish Cognates Test, was added to Model 1 in order to obtain the unique contribution of Spanish cognate knowledge.

As shown in Table 4.3, Spanish cognate knowledge is a significant predictor of English (academic) vocabulary knowledge, accounting for 23.2% of the variance ($\Delta R^2 = .232$, $\Delta F_{(1, 214)} = 85.056$, $p < .001$). Once the effects of students' background characteristics are controlled for, each one point increase on the Spanish Cognates Test is associated with a 0.83 point increase on the English Vocabulary Test (see Table 4.4).

Hancin-Bhatt and Nagy (1994) suggested that cognate awareness seems to be developmental, with older students being more able to use cognate knowledge than younger ones. In order to evaluate this phenomenon, we conducted an interaction effect test to investigate whether grade level moderates the contribution of Spanish cognate knowledge on English vocabulary skills (see Table 4.5).

As shown in Table 4.5, the interaction effect between grade and the Spanish Cognates Test scores is positive and statistically significant ($\hat{\beta} = .276$, $t = 2.418$, $p = .016$). In other words, after controlling for student background characteristics, the influence of Spanish cognate knowledge on English vocabulary knowledge increases as students move through the middle-grade levels. This indicates that the role of cognate knowledge on English academic vocabulary skills is affected by students' age and developmental level.

Table 4.4 Unique contribution of L1 cognate knowledge on L2 vocabulary, controlling for student background characteristics

Model	Unstandardized coefficients		Standardized coefficients		
	B	SE	Beta	t	Sig.
1 (Constant)	−.534	7.273		−.073	.942
Gender	.719	1.483	.030	.485	.628
Grade	4.900	.930	.327	5.269	.000
EL classification	−7.502	1.633	−.289	−4.593	.000
Meal status	1.185	2.556	.029	.464	.643
Ethnicity	−2.453	3.317	−.047	−.740	.460
2 (Constant)	−1.118	6.167		−.181	.856
Gender	2.531	1.273	.106	1.989	.048
Grade	2.346	.836	.156	2.808	.005
EL classification	−7.315	1.385	−.282	−5.282	.000
Meal status	1.080	2.167	.027	.498	.619
Ethnicity	−4.799	2.824	−.091	−1.700	.091
Spanish cognate	.833	.090	.521	9.223	.000

Note: Dependent variable: English vocabulary

Table 4.5 Testing interaction between L1 cognate knowledge and grade level

Model	Unstandardized coefficients		Standardized coefficients		
	B	SE	Beta	t	Sig.
1 (Constant)	46.236	20.515		2.254	.025
Gender	2.466	1.259	.103	1.959	.051
Grade	−4.319	2.878	−.288	−1.501	.135
EL classification	−7.730	1.380	−.298	−5.600	.000
Meal status	1.145	2.143	.028	.534	.594
Ethnicity	−4.869	2.793	−.093	−1.744	.083
Spanish cognate	−1.141	.822	−.713	−1.389	.166
Grade X Spanish	.276	.114	1.453	2.418	.016

Note: Dependent variable: English vocabulary

PREDICTING ENGLISH READING COMPREHENSION FROM SPANISH
COGNATE KNOWLEDGE

A second set of regression analyses were conducted to determine the role of Spanish cognate knowledge in English reading comprehension. Table 4.6 presents the correlations for all of the measured variables including the Gates–MacGinitie comprehension subtest.

Consistent with previous findings on the role of vocabulary in reading comprehension, English vocabulary knowledge was found to be positively and significantly related to English reading comprehension. Perhaps more interesting is the fact that there is also a positive significant correlation between Spanish cognate knowledge and English reading comprehension, lending support for a relationship between English reading ability and Spanish (cognate) word knowledge. As we saw with English vocabulary, the correlation between English reading comprehension and grade level is also positive and significant, but not as strong. Finally, English reading comprehension and EL classification are significantly and negatively associated, denoting that EL students performed more poorly on the reading comprehension test than non-EL students, a finding consistent with the literature.

Given the interrelationships between English reading comprehension and vocabulary, it is essential to examine the predictive power of Spanish cognate knowledge above and beyond that provided by this known predictor of reading performance. The results of the multiple regression analysis are displayed in Tables 4.7 and 4.8. The same procedure used with English vocabulary as the dependent variable was used, this time with the performance on the Gates–MacGinitie comprehension subtest as the dependent variable. All background variables and English vocabulary were entered into Model 1. In Model 2 an additional variable, performance on the Spanish Cognates Test, was added to Model 1 in order to obtain the unique contribution of Spanish cognate knowledge.

As shown in Tables 4.7 and 4.8, regression analysis confirmed the importance of well-developed English vocabulary skills to English reading ability. However, a truly interesting finding is the fact that knowledge of Spanish cognates had a significant and positive effect on English reading comprehension above and beyond English vocabulary knowledge and the background characteristics included in the model. The contribution of Spanish cognate knowledge to English reading comprehension, which accounts for 2.5% of unique variance ($\Delta R^2 = .025$, $\Delta F_{(1, 206)} = 8.541$, $p = .004$), is smaller than its contribution to English vocabulary, but in line with Proctor et al.'s (2006) findings.

Table 4.6 Correlations between Gates–MacGinitie Reading Tests (comprehension subtest) and other study variables

Indicators	1	2	3	4	5	6	7	8
1. Gates comprehension ESS (n=48)	—							
2. Gender	-.064	—						
3. Grade	.258**	-.050	—					
4. EL classification	-.245**	.026	.062	—				
5. Meal status	.008	.098	.062	.166**	—			
6. Ethnicity	-.039	.068	.093	.157*	.138*	—		
7. English vocabulary raw score (74 items)	.598**	.001	.294**	-.284**	-.002	-.054	—	
8. Spanish cognates raw score (52 items)	.460**	-.162**	.339**	.034	.003	.108	.553**	—
Means	504.64						31.04	24.07
(Standard deviation)	(30.285)						(11.981)	(7.490)

$*p < .05.$
$**p < .01.$

Table 4.7 Regression models investigating the role of L1 cognate knowledge on L2 reading comprehension, controlling for L2 English vocabulary and student background characteristics

Model	R	R^2	R^2_{adj}	SEE	Change statistics				
					ΔR^2	ΔF	df_1	df_2	Sig. ΔF
1	.614[a]	.377	.359	24.245	.377	20.891	6	207	.000
2	.634[b]	.402	.382	23.815	.025	8.541	1	206	.004

[a] Predictors: (Constant), English vocabulary, Gender, Ethnicity, Meal status, Grade, EL classification
[b] Predictors: (Constant), English vocabulary, Gender, Ethnicity, Meal status, Grade, EL classification, Spanish cognate

Table 4.8 Unique contribution of L1 cognate knowledge on L2 reading comprehension, controlling for L2 English vocabulary and student background characteristics

Model	Unstandardized coefficients		Standardized coefficients		
	B	SE	Beta	t	Sig.
1 (Constant)	436.521	16.362		26.678	.000
Female	−3.556	3.348	−.059	−1.062	.289
Grade	3.875	2.231	.102	1.737	.084
EL classification	−6.648	3.920	−.100	−1.696	.091
Meal status	2.721	5.982	.026	.455	.650
Hispanic	−.375	7.386	−.003	−.051	.960
English vocabulary	1.363	.153	.539	8.894	.000
2 (Constant)	435.630	16.075		27.100	.000
Female	−1.516	3.362	−.025	−.451	.653
Grade	2.743	2.226	.072	1.233	.219
EL classification	−9.073	3.939	−.137	−2.303	.022
Meal status	3.467	5.881	.033	.590	.556
Hispanic	−3.409	7.329	−.026	−.465	.642
English vocabulary	1.069	.181	.423	5.908	.000
Spanish cognate	.828	.283	.205	2.923	.004

Note: Dependent variable: *Gates–MacGinitie Reading Tests* (comprehension subtest)

In order to investigate whether grade level moderates the contribution of Spanish cognate knowledge on English reading comprehension skills, we conducted an interaction effect test between grade and the Spanish Cognates Test scores (see Table 4.9).

The interaction was not statistically significant ($\hat{\beta} = -.372$, $t = -1.211$, $p = .227$), indicating that, after controlling for English vocabulary knowledge and student background characteristics, the effects of Spanish cognate knowledge on English reading comprehension did not vary by grade level.

Some have proposed that rather than being a developmental phenomenon, cognate awareness may be influenced by English language proficiency, such that only those students with enough proficiency

Table 4.9 Interaction testing between L1 cognate knowledge and grade level

| Model | Unstandardized coefficients | | Standardized coefficients | | |
	B	SE	Beta	t	Sig.
1 (Constant)	371.433	55.394		6.705	.000
Gender	–1.447	3.359	–.024	–.431	.667
Grade	11.715	7.735	.307	1.514	.131
EL classification	–8.331	3.982	–.126	–2.092	.038
Meal status	3.142	5.881	.030	.534	.594
Ethnicity	–3.164	7.324	–.024	–.432	.666
English vocabulary	1.101	.183	.436	6.028	.000
Spanish cognate	3.471	2.201	.858	1.577	.116
Grade*Spanish	–.372	.307	–.777	–1.211	.227

Note: Dependent variable: *Gates–MacGinitie Reading Tests* (comprehension subtest)

level in English can make use of their L1 vocabulary knowledge (Proctor & Mo, 2009). Findings from the regression analyses revealed that both performance on the English Vocabulary Test and EL status were significantly associated with English reading comprehension. Thus, we decided to examine whether performance on these two variables may have a moderating effect on the contribution of Spanish cognate knowledge on English reading comprehension. Findings revealed that the interaction effects were not statistically significant, indicating that the effects of Spanish cognate knowledge on English reading comprehension did not vary depending on the students' English vocabulary knowledge ($\hat{\beta} = .013, t = .744, p = .458$) or on their classification as EL ($= -.486, t = -.946, p = .345$).

4.5 Discussion

The purpose of the study was to investigate the role that knowledge of Spanish cognates may play in the development of English vocabulary and reading comprehension skills in Spanish-speaking middle-school students. The issue is important because Latino students in the United States lag behind their native-English-speaker peers in text-level reading skills as measured by national assessments (Mather & Foxen,

2010). Given the prominence of Spanish/English cognate words in academic English and the fact that many of them are higher frequency in Spanish than in English, Spanish-speaking students could potentially use their L1 vocabulary knowledge to unlock the meaning of complex words while reading in English (Lubliner & Hiebert, 2011). The L1 would thus become a useful tool in the development of L2 reading skills. Yet, to date, very few studies have examined the potential role of L1 vocabulary on L2 reading achievement, and the few that have done so used small samples and rarely included direct tests of knowledge of word meaning in Spanish.

Findings from the present study are consistent with those found in the literature regarding the role of English vocabulary on reading comprehension, and also add to the scarce cross-linguistic literature on the role of L1 vocabulary on L2 reading comprehension. Moreover, they show that despite students' low vocabulary scores in both languages and their underachievement as a group in English reading comprehension, a significant portion of the variance in their reading comprehension was explained by their Spanish (cognate) vocabulary knowledge, after the effects of English vocabulary were accounted for. This finding is consistent with that of Proctor et al. (2006).

The high correlation found between English and Spanish vocabulary, while not surprising given the focus on cognate vocabulary and the fact that the same cognate words were tested in both languages, is encouraging for the development of interventions that focus on cognate vocabulary. Our results show that Spanish cognate knowledge is predictive of English reading comprehension skills. Since the data used for the present study were collected before the onset of the intervention, these results represent the contribution of Spanish cognate knowledge before explicit instruction on cross-language relationships had been delivered. Preliminary findings from a cognate-based intervention carried out with a larger sample of middle-school students, which included the students in the present study, suggest that the intervention had a positive effect on the English vocabulary skills of students who participated in the treatment.

In order to shed light on whether cognate knowledge might be developmental or influenced by L2 proficiency, we examined the moderating effects of grade and English proficiency on the contribution of Spanish vocabulary to English reading comprehension. Two different variables were used as measures of English proficiency: whether or not a student was identified as EL and performance on a vocabulary assessment. The interaction effects between these two variables and Spanish vocabulary were not statistically significant, showing that the effects of Spanish cognate knowledge on English reading comprehension were not affected by students' English language proficiency. So, it seems that, at least when it comes to students at an intermediate ESL level or beyond, English proficiency level does not have a moderating effect on the contribution of Spanish cognate knowledge to English reading comprehension. It is possible that the L2 proficiency level of participants in the study was beyond the proficiency threshold needed for cognate recognition, since while they had varying levels of English language proficiency, there were no beginning ESL students in the sample. Students at different ESL levels, including beginning-level students, must be assessed in order to be able to test this hypothesis.

Our results likewise indicate that the effects of Spanish vocabulary on English reading comprehension were not moderated by grade. Nagy et al. (1993), investigating the contribution of cognate knowledge in students in Grades 4–6, obtained similar results in that they did not find any significant interactions between grade and any other measured variables. However, in their study on cognate roots recognition in derived words, Hancin-Bhatt and Nagy (1994), working with students in Grades 4–8, did find a grade effect, such that eighth-graders exhibited more cognate awareness than fourth-graders, even after controlling for other measured variables. It is possible that a larger grade span, five grade levels as opposed to three, which is what Nagy et al. (1993) and the present study worked with, is needed to find grade differences. Another possibility is that older students may be more able to apply their Spanish cognate knowledge at the word level than at the text level. Findings from our study provide support for this possibility in that they show that grade had a moderating effect on the contribution of cognate knowledge to English word knowledge but not to English reading comprehension. Given all the possible explanations laid out, it is clear that more research on the role of the L1 is needed to be able to better understand its effects on English reading ability.

4.6 Limitations and future research

This study represents a first attempt at examining the cross-linguistic data collected for the larger study, and as such it has some limitations that warrant further research. First, it was not possible to conduct analyses at the item level that would allow us to examine the structural characteristics of cognate pairs and study to what degree they play a role in cognate knowledge. There is some evidence that cognate pairs that share phonological and orthographic features are more easily recognized than those that do not. Thus, it would be important to look at the different cognate pairs and investigate the extent to which they share semantic and orthographic overlap and how this affects cognate knowledge. Second, while an attempt was made to select cognate pairs that were high frequency in Spanish and low frequency in English, which would facilitate transfer, not all cognate pairs followed this pattern to the same extent. Hence, it would be interesting to study to what extent the frequency of the word in Spanish might influence cognate knowledge.

Third, as this was the pilot phase of the larger study, we were limited to administering only the most essential assessments and were unable to administer additional assessments that might shed light on the relationships under investigation. As a result, it was not possible to use individually administered assessments of English and Spanish vocabulary and other predictors of reading comprehension, such as reading fluency, as has been done in studies with smaller samples (Proctor et al., 2006; Lesaux et al., 2010). Moreover, while we were able to develop a Spanish cognate knowledge measure and include it in the study, we were limited to single measures of reading vocabulary in both languages and a single measure of reading comprehension in English, and we were unable to administer a more global assessment of English proficiency. Finally, it was not possible to collect information on students' Spanish language and literacy practices at home to examine how these may influence students' L2 reading ability. The full study conducted the subsequent year did include such measures and will therefore allow for a better developed and more nuanced analysis.

Fourth, more research is needed into cognate relationships in languages that are semantically and orthographically linked, such as other Romance languages (e.g. French or Portuguese) and English. Studies that investigate cognate relationships in other languages will shed light on whether a degree of universality relative to cognate knowledge exists and contribute to the body of knowledge on how to best capitalize on the use of cognates for instructional and academic achievement.

4.7 Conclusion

This study provides supporting evidence for a small body of research that has found that the development of English academic vocabulary and reading comprehension skills can be enhanced by L1 knowledge, particularly in the case of relatively closely related languages like Spanish and English (August & Shanahan, 2006; Genesee et al., 2006). While the facilitative role of the native language in the development of second language literacy skills was put forward by Cummins (1979, 1984) more than three decades ago, the amount of empirical research on this topic is scant. Research with adolescent and adult L2 learners has for the most part ignored the L1 and focused on the development of L2 literacy skills.

Our findings suggest that Spanish cognate knowledge contributes to English vocabulary and reading comprehension ability for Spanish-speaking adolescent students. However, the variation in L2 reading comprehension explained by the Spanish cognate knowledge in the study was very small and should be viewed in relationship with other variables that influence English reading comprehension for Spanish-speaking adolescent learners. Because the full study included measures of English fluency and global English proficiency, as well as measures of more discrete language components, such as morphology and spelling, it will be possible to examine relationships among a number of different variables related to reading comprehension.

Findings from this study have instructional implications. Specifically, since our findings indicate that Spanish word knowledge contributes to both English word knowledge and English reading comprehension, there is support for instructional approaches that develop academic language skills in the native language, or that at least capitalize on them, such as cognate instruction. The curriculum developed for this study accomplishes that through a 40-day instructional sequence comprising six units and 50 general academic vocabulary words, all of which are cognates. Students are taught the words in the context of topics that are of interest to adolescents, such as bullying, and are provided [with] instruction in word-learning strategies such as contexting, word study (i.e. segmenting words into prefixes, roots and suffixes), dictionary skills and cognate awareness. Future analyses will investigate the effects of this intervention on students' vocabulary, morphology and comprehension skills.

Appendix

Sample items from vocabulary assessments

English Vocabulary Test

Directions: Read the sentence and choose the word that means the same or almost the same as the underlined word.

1. He encountered a difficult situation.
    a.   found
    b.   feared
    c.   imagined
    d.   expected

2. Try to <u>convey</u> your ideas in a simple way.
   a. develop
   b. draft
   c. connect
   d. express

3. I am <u>profoundly</u> aware of the situation.
   a. extremely
   b. fortunately
   c. probably
   d. hardly

Spanish Cognates Test

Directions: Lea la frase y escoja la palabra que tenga el significado más parecido a la <u>palabra subrayada</u>. Read the sentence and choose the word that means the same or almost the same as the <u>underlined word</u>.

1. Lo pensó <u>profundamente</u>.
   a. tranquilamente (*calmly*)
   b. instintivamente (*instinctively*)
   c. temporalmente (*temporarily*)
   d. intensamente (*intensely*)

2. Cuatro botellas de agua es <u>suficiente</u>.
   a. razonable (*reasonable*)
   b. demasiado (*too much*)
   c. necesario (*necessary*)
   d. bastante (*enough*)

3. Van a <u>castigar</u> a tres estudiantes.
   a. acusar (*accuse*)
   b. dar un susto (*scare*)
   c. reformar (*reform*)
   d. dar una lección (*punish*)

References

Anderson, R. C. and Freebody, P. (1981). Vocabulary knowledge. In J. T. Guthrie (ed.), *Comprehension and Teaching: Research Reviews* (pp. 77–117). Newark, DE: International Reading Association.

August, D. and Shanahan, T. (eds.) (2006). *Developing Literacy in Second-Language Learners: Report of the National Literacy Panel on Language-Minority Children and Youth*. Mahwah, NJ: Lawrence Erlbaum Associates.

August, S., Carlo, M., Dressler, C. and Snow, C. (2005). The critical role of vocabulary development for English language learners. *Learning Disabilities Research & Practice*, 20, 50–7.

Carlisle, J. F., Beeman, M., Davis, L. D. and Spharim, G. (1999). Relationship of metalinguistic capabilities and reading achievement for children who are becoming bilingual. *Applied Psycholinguistics*, 20, 459–78.

Chall, J. S. (1983). *Stages of Reading Development*. New York: Harcourt Brace.

Cummins, J. (1979). Linguistic interdependence and the educational development of bilingual children. *Review of Educational Research*, 49, 222–51.

Cummins, J. (1984). Wanted: a theoretical framework for relating language proficiency to academic achievement among bilingual students. In C. Rivera (ed.), *Language Proficiency and Academic Achievement* (pp. 2–19). Clevedon: Multilingual Matters.

Fry, R. and Gonzales, F. (2008). *One-in-Five and Growing Fast: A Profile of Hispanic Public School Students*. Washington, DC: Pew Hispanic Center.

García, G. E. (1991). Factors influencing the English reading test performance of Spanish-speaking Hispanic students. *Reading Research Quarterly*, 26, 371–92.

Genesee, F., Lindholm-Leary, K., Saunders, W. M. and Christian, D. (eds.) (2006). *Educating English Language Learners: A Synthesis of Research Evidence*. New York: Cambridge University Press.

Hancin-Bhatt, B. and Nagy, W. (1994). Lexical transfer and second language morphological development. *Applied Psycholinguistics*, 15, 289–310.

Jiménez, R. T., García, G. E. and Pearson, P. D. (1996). The reading strategies of bilingual Latina/o students who are successful English readers: opportunities and obstacles. *Reading Research Quarterly*, 31, 90–112.

Laufer, B. (2003). Vocabulary acquisition in a second language: do learners really acquire most vocabulary by reading? Some empirical evidence. *The Canadian Modern Language Review*, 59, 565–85.

Lesaux, N., Crosson, A. C., Kieffer, M. J. and Pierce, M. (2010). Uneven profiles: language minority learners' word reading, vocabulary, and reading comprehension skills. *Journal of Applied Developmental Psychology*, 31, 475–83.

Lubliner, S. and Hiebert, E. H. (2011). An analysis of English-Spanish cognates as a source of general academic language. *Bilingual Research Journal*, 34, 76–93.

MacGinitie, W. H., MacGinitie, R. K., Maria, K., Dreyer, L. G. and Hughes, K. E. (2000). *Gates–MacGinitie Reading Tests* (4th edn). Itasca, IL: Riverside.

Mather, M. and Foxen, P. (2010). *America's Future: Latino Child Well-Being in Numbers and Trends*. Washington, DC: National Council of La Raza.

Nagy, W., García, G. E., Durgunoglu, A. Y. and Hancin-Bhatt, B. (1993). Spanish–English bilingual students' use of cognates in English reading. *Journal of Reading Behavior*, 25, 241–59.

Nash, R. (1997). *NTC's Dictionary of Spanish Cognates*. Chicago, IL: NTC Publishing Group.

Proctor, C. P. and Mo, E. (2009) The relationship between cognate awareness and English comprehension among Spanish–English bilingual fourth grade students. *TESOL Quarterly*, 43(1), 126–36.

Proctor, C. P., August, D., Carlo, M. S. and Snow, C. E. (2006). The intriguing role of Spanish vocabulary knowledge in predicting English reading comprehension. *Journal of Educational Psychology*, 98, 159–69.

Proctor, C. P., Carlo, M., August, D. and Snow, C. (2005). Native Spanish-speaking children reading in English: toward a model of comprehension. *Journal of Educational Psychology*, **97**, 246–56.

Reese, L., Garnier, H., Gallimore, R. and Goldenberg, C. (2000). Longitudinal analysis of the antecedents of emergent Spanish literacy and middle-school English reading achievement of Spanish-speaking students. *American Educational Research Journal*, **37**, 633–62.

Suárez-Orozco, C. and Suárez-Orozco, M. (2001). *Children of Immigration*. Cambridge, MA: Harvard University Press.

Verhoeven, L. T. (1990). Acquisition of reading in a second language. *Reading Research Quarterly*, **25**, 90–114.

Verhoeven, L. T. (2000). Components in early second language reading and spelling. *Scientific Studies of Reading*, **4**, 313–30.

5 A nexus analysis of code choice during study abroad and implications for language pedagogy

Glenn S. Levine

5.1 Ideal worlds and real worlds

The purpose of this chapter is to analyse the code-choice practices of a group of US university students studying abroad in Germany, in part in order to gain insights into how those practices might inform our thinking about foreign language pedagogy and teaching practice.[1] The approach taken is an adaptation of Scollon and Scollon's (2004) nexus analysis, which allows us to examine code choice at the nexus of multiple, intersecting discourses, as one element in the complex system that is the student living, studying and using languages abroad. I will show here that in order to orient pedagogy towards meaningful training in *being multilingual*, it is useful and productive to consider aspects of second language (L2) learners' assessments and experiences of using their first and second languages while abroad.

At the start I own up to a certain bias: As a language teacher and a former study-abroad student myself, I envision each student's experience of living abroad in a new language and culture as a series of challenging and meaningful connections with the Other, as the development of intercultural competence comprising new skills, perspectives and forms of critical knowledge (Byram, 1997), as 'immersion' in the L2 and the multiple worldviews and cultural frames of its speakers in ways that bring the student to critically examine her or his own worldviews and cultural frames. My approach to the design of a language curriculum in German often imagines the students' study-abroad experience in this way.

The reality of it is, of course, quite different, and immensely variable from individual to individual, which always makes thinking about curriculum and teaching difficult. Some students may not 'immerse' themselves in the L2, may not engage extensively with people in the L2 society and perhaps are not as transformed as language teachers or they themselves would imagine or hope for (Kinginger, 2010). As participants in the L2 society, they may remain on the periphery, looking in from the outside, not entirely unlike the way they studied the L2 and its culture remotely in the language classroom back home, but now with the unmitigated experience of *being there*, of seeing, hearing, feeling, tasting and smelling it first-hand rather than having it mediated through books, recordings and websites. Now, this is not to diminish students' curiosity about or motivation or desire to be a part of the L2 society; most students who undertake to study abroad in an L2 environment for a semester or a year certainly do so because they have a desire to learn about and connect with the new language and culture, and to put themselves outside of their home-life 'comfort zone'. However, there is a gap between being there with the senses and the mind, and accessing the social worlds at work in the new culture, as numerous studies have shown us (Pellegrino-Aveni, 2005; Papatsiba, 2006; Jackson, 2008; Kinginger, 2008; Levine, 2008). What I aim to do here is examine what a group of students' language-use choices, which I refer to as code choices, suggest about that gap and look for ways to think about language pedagogy in relation to it. To accomplish this, I will adapt a method of analysis that Scollon and Scollon (2004) call 'nexus analysis' to examine learners' self-reports about code-choice practices during study abroad. Nexus analysis is a type of discourse analysis, one that allows the analyst to consider both linguistic and non-linguistic factors, but without viewing non-linguistic factors as merely 'language external'. It allows us to consider the immediate, situated aspects of context as well as the historical trajectory of that situated context. In addition, the analysis is geared not only towards the description of a given set of social actions or practices but also towards their *transformation*; this is where pedagogy comes into consideration, for ultimately my aim is to propose ways of thinking about teaching and learning that accord to the greatest extent possible with what we know of how students live and act while abroad (see also Kinginger, 2010).

Why nexus analysis? Because the phenomenon in which we are interested – the code choices of the US university student studying abroad – is inherently complex and, as mentioned, highly variable from individual to individual, and the quality and learning outcomes of each person's sojourn is so different as to appear to prevent any sort of larger-scale conclusions, let alone generalizations. What is needed is a method of analysis that will allow us to consider both the complexities of the context in which we are interested and the interests of the analyst her- or himself. In this case I am interested in how the code choices of a particular group of students might inform pedagogical thinking and decision-making, or at least help us begin to do so.[2]

The central focus of a nexus analysis is exploration of the 'nexus of practice', which Scollon and Scollon offer as a means of unifying the micro-analysis of unfolding moments of social interaction and a 'much broader socio-political-cultural analysis of the relationships among social groups and power interests in the society' (2004: 8). They argue that 'the most mundane of micro-interactions are nexus through which the largest cycles of social organization and activity circulate' (p. 8). Elsewhere, Scollon points out that the nexus of practice is the (admittedly imperfect) meeting point of a network of social practices, where that 'network itself is the basis of the identities we produce and claim through our social actions' (2001: 142). This means that the analyst's questions themselves help determine the nexus of practice, as well as what factors or elements might be of relevance to those questions. The nexus of practice of interest here is primarily code choice during the study-abroad sojourn, which I suggest represents a dimension of micro-level interactions of L2 learners/users that relates to the larger cycles of social organization and activity of both the 'study-abroad experience' and the 'L2 learning experience'. Further, I will relate this outward, or backward in time if you will, to the larger cycle of social organization and activity that is US foreign language education. *Code choice* is defined as the day-to-day uses of the language user's languages, which include in this case first language (L1) English and L2 German. In earlier work I have shown that in the instructed L2 setting, the students' L1, and other languages, should and does play a part in learning and communication and thus should be part of our consideration in designing instruction and teaching (Levine, 2011). I also argued that in order for the L1 to contribute to what Macaro (2009) calls 'optimal use' of both the L1 and the L2 in the language classroom, the management of code choices should be principled and part of critical reflection about language use and learning overall. The present chapter aims to add further nuance to the principles for code choice.

5.2 The components of nexus analysis

A nexus analysis consists of three parts: identifying, navigating and transforming the nexus of practice. *Identifying the nexus of practice* means identifying the meeting point of the historical body, the interaction order and discourses in place (these terms will be explained shortly) that are to be analysed, relative to the questions or issues in which the analyst is interested.

Navigating the nexus of practice is the main work of the nexus analysis, according to Scollon and Scollon, which involves examining what is happening at that nexus and describing it in terms of the historical body, interaction order and discourses in place, the insights of which would then lead to a transformation of that nexus of practice.

Transforming the nexus of practice means quite specifically bringing about positive social change; for them this is the entire purpose of the previous steps. For us, considering the pedagogical context of instructed L2 learning, as well as fairly truncated adaptation of the method (a nexus analysis can be conducted over many years), social change is imagined on a smaller scale, and perhaps in a less direct fashion than intended by Scollon and Scollon. But, as proponents of critical pedagogy in language education would point out (e.g. Reagan & Osborn, 2002), the classroom holds great potential for the microgenesis of change by building a questioning or transformation of the social or political status quo through teaching and learning practice. To do this, it would be necessary first to understand the implications of unquestioned pedagogical practices, which includes the teacher's and the learners' ways of making code choices.

The three main tasks in a nexus analysis are identifying and navigating the historical body, the interaction order and the discourses in place of the nexus of practice. The *historical body* is adapted from Nishida's (1958) term, defined as 'a lifetime of person habits [that] come to feel so natural that one's body carries out actions seemingly without being told' (Scollon & Scollon, 2004: 13). Related to Bourdieu's (1977) concept of the *habitus*, Scollon and Scollon opt for Nishida's concept because 'it situates bodily memories more precisely in the individual human body' (2004: 13).

The *interaction order* is based on Goffman's (1983) concept, and 'any of the many possible social arrangements by which we form relationships in social interactions' (Scollon & Scollon, 2004: 13). Goffman's concept is intended to provide the units of analysis of people's face-to-face interactions, with allowances, for he says the 'telephone and the mails provide reduced versions of the primordial real thing' (1983: 2). In today's world we could reasonably add the full range of digital communication, though with a critical questioning of whether these constitute 'reduced versions' of face-to-face communication (Thorne, 2003). The micro-level nature of the interaction order allows the analyst to move beyond limiting and reductionist concepts such as 'social roles', and it is contingent upon the situated contexts of interaction in space and time, even if these are indexed by social arrangements with their own historical trajectories (historical bodies; Goffman, 1983: 3). The interaction order is all of the features of that interaction itself, which presumably can be observed and listed.[3]

With regard to *discourses in place*, Scollon and Scollon (2004: 14) state:

All places in the world are complex aggregates (nexus) of the many discourses which circulate through them on different timescales ... Some of these discourses are very distant and of little direct relevance to particular social actions occurring in that place, such as the design specifications of the table at which two friends are having coffee. Some of the discourses are directly relevant such as the menu from which the snack selection is made.

In our discussion later on, I will consider the ways in which the whole issue of 'place' is complicated by simultaneous participation in face-to-face, digital and hybrid discourses.

5.3 The students and the study

There has been a robust amount of research in recent years on many aspects of the study-abroad experience, and in a range of theoretical frameworks and with diverse research questions and goals. Studies of students in L2 environments have often focused on the development of language features and language skills (e.g. Brecht et al., 1995; Lapkin, Hart & Swain, 1995; Milton & Meara, 1995; Dewey, 2004; Kinginger, 2008). Numerous studies have also explored a range of aspects of sociocultural or pragmatic competence (Isabelli-García, 2006; Magnan & Back, 2007; Jackson, 2008; Kinginger, 2008; Regan, Howard & Lemée, 2009). Those studies that delve into the subjective experiences of learners have shown us that the experience often is not the 'ideal' one that classroom teachers and students may imagine it to be before departure (Pellegrino-Aveni, 2005; Kinginger, 2010). It is an experience fraught with risks and danger to the student's sense of self, and self-worth, one which – even if in the end it is a growth experience – may move them out of their 'comfort zone' in ways that feel neither productive nor transformative in the moment.

One of the ways that students from many different language groups appear to head off those threats to self – or exert control in a situation inherently characterized by lack of control – is to spend time, and of course use language, with fellow L1 speakers (Papatsiba, 2006; Kinginger, 2008). Yet to date there has been little study explicitly considering L2 learners' code-choice practices abroad (see, however, Levine, 2008). The present study aims to add to that body of work. As a more or less exploratory study, the following two research questions related to code choice were quite open-ended and mostly descriptive:

1. When and how are the participants using German, English or other languages?

2. How are they using digital media, how often, with whom, in what contexts; and what language are they choosing when they use digital media?[4]

The study was conducted through a study-abroad programme at a large university in southern Germany, a long-standing programme based at a small liberal-arts college in the US Midwest. After appealing for participation through the director of the programme and emails to the students ahead of my arrival in Germany, thirteen students volunteered to participate: six women and seven men. The students came from different institutions, both small and large, around the United States. Though participation was voluntary, each participant did receive one unit of 'experiential' credit from the study-abroad programme.[5]

Data on code choice came from three sources. First, participants completed an initial survey in which they provided biographical information and details about their language background and their experiences with German. There they also self-reported their skill level with speaking, writing, reading in German, and on their uses of German and of digital media prior to and during their study-abroad sojourn. The form also asked them to provide information about their feelings of homesickness and difficulties adjusting to life abroad (which will not be addressed in the current analysis).

The second and main data source on code choice is what I called the 'Study-Abroad Communication and Digital Media Use Log' (henceforth 'Log'). Students were asked to go online and complete this survey as often as they could or wished. The students completed the form ranging from five to fifteen times total. It asked them to report about the preceding 24 hours only: on their various uses of language – German, English or other languages; their uses of digital media of all sorts; the social interactions they had, both face-to-face and online; and any experiences or feelings of homesickness or difficulties communicating. The goal was not necessarily to see how the experiences changed over the semester (though if clear trends were to emerge from the data it would be interesting), for it was assumed from the outset that students' uses of language and digital media would vary considerably over the course of the semester, and not in any sort of linear progression, for instance from less to more use of digital media. In this sense this is not a longitudinal study. Rather, these are a series of synchronic pictures of a day in the life of the student, based on self-reports, which hopefully all together give a picture of the overall experience. Further, I was interested in the ways that students' own assessments of the importance of acculturating or 'immersing' in German society might relate to their day-to-day choices to use more or less German or English.

The third data source includes the students' Facebook postings. While I did expect to see students posting primarily in English to Facebook, in terms of code choices and social networks I also was interested to see whether or how students might be connecting to people in Germany while abroad (see also Levine, 2014). Five of the thirteen students chose to share their Facebook postings.

All thirteen students completed the initial survey and at least five of the Logs. All thirteen reported growing up as monolingual speakers of US English and learning German as adolescents or adults. Twelve of them reported learning German in an instructed setting in high school and/or college; one reported learning German autodidactically.

In terms of self-reported speaking proficiency in German, on a four-point scale from *Anfänger* 'beginner' to *fließend* 'fluent', seven students marked *sehr gut* 'very good' and five marked *gut* 'good'. Only one, whom I call Amelia, marked *Anfänger*.

In the following I will draw from the data to first identify the nexus of practice, followed by a detailed description of navigating the nexus of practice, which includes consideration of the historical body, interaction orders, students' uses of digital media and discourses in place. Finally, I address transforming the nexus of practice pedagogically, considering ways that we might orient language instruction towards affecting learners' code-choice practices in ways that might foster optimal L2 use (Macaro, 2009) both in the classroom and during a study-abroad sojourn.

5.4 Identifying the nexus of practice

Earlier I stated that the nexus of practice of interest in this chapter is the students' code-choice practices while studying abroad. But this particular nexus of practice should be considered critically before accepting it out of hand. Why code choice? What might understanding it better bring us in our larger consideration of L2 learning and teaching? Let us begin at home, in the classroom, and thereafter consider dimensions of the same practices abroad, where the student can no longer be considered a student in a foreign language classroom, but rather a multilingual user of at least two languages in an L2 environment.

Beginning in the middle part of the twentieth century, as language teaching, particularly in the United States, began approaching language learning primarily for the purpose of communicating with real people in the real world, as opposed to learning a language for reading literature or for translating texts, a bias developed among teachers, curriculum planners and textbook producers for what many have called an 'exclusive target language' approach to managing communication in the classroom (Cook, 2001; Macaro, 2001, 2009). The ideal has been to exclude the learners' L1, if not entirely, then to the greatest extent possible. Language programme directors and other administrators who make policy for language programmes at all levels of education often have forbidden teachers from using anything but the L2 from day one of instruction. Language textbooks going back to the Audio-lingual Method (ALM) series (e.g. Winkler, 1969) and through variations of communicative approaches (e.g. Krashen & Terrell, 1983; Savignon, 2002) were all designed around the assumption that teacher and students would use the L2 exclusively in the classroom, and this even for textbooks with extensive passages in English (such as activity instructions or 'culture capsules'). In classrooms in which the L1 was not expressly forbidden, its use was then, and still is, viewed as 'resorting to' the L1. In other words, as Blyth (1995), Cook (2001, 2002), Macaro (2001) and I (Levine, 2011) have asserted, almost all pedagogical approaches have at worst stigmatized the use of the learner's L1 as part of the L2 teaching and learning, and at best attempted to limit the uses of the L1 in the classroom.

The exclusive use or stigmatizing of the L1 is admittedly understandable, for at some level it is an intuitive way of thinking about the instructional setting: *of course* one would want to use the L2 as much as possible and have the learners do the same. This assumption went unquestioned for a long time, both in language pedagogy and in applied linguistics research (Auer, 2007; Macaro, 2009; Ortega, 2010). However, a good deal of empirical research has taught us not only that the L1 plays a role in both teaching and learning, whether the textbook or the teacher wishes it (Cook, 2001; Macaro, 2001; Levine, 2011), but also that it should play a role, for it can facilitate learning and communication in myriad ways (Antón & DiCamilla, 1999; Cook, 1999; Swain & Lapkin, 2000; Liebscher & Dailey-O'Cain, 2004; Dailey-O'Cain & Liebscher, 2009; Evans, 2009). Just as learners' own strategies for learning and communicating contribute to learning and language use, and just as factors such as the quality and nature of the students' exposure to the L2 are crucial, so too are the ways the learners make use of their L1 for learning and communication, as one tool among many for developing multilingual capacities in a new language (Scott, 2010). For this reason, code choice, as defined earlier, is as valid a nexus of practice towards understanding aspects of L2 development and approaching pedagogical practice as any other aspect of L2 learning and use, such as turn-taking or the use of particular grammatical forms.

In this vein, another way of thinking about code choice makes it an excellent nexus of practice for our analysis, and that is as a point of intersection with societal bilingualism or multilingualism. There is likely no multilingual setting in the world in which the users of multiple languages do not routinely and creatively make use of their languages, and for a wide range of interactional, social and even political purposes (see Myers-Scotton, 1993; Zentella, 1997; Li Wei, 1998; Myers-Scotton & Bolonyai, 2001; Garafanga, 2009; Roberts, 2009). Thus, it would be reasonable to consider code choices being made by L2 learners as study-abroad students, perhaps in part to look for areas of similarity and difference within multilingual speech communities, but more importantly, to bring the 'real world' of these L2 learners and users into consideration in approaching language pedagogy. For this reason as well, then, our study-abroad students' code choices make for a useful and viable nexus of practice.

The nexus of practice we identify consists of the ways that a group of study participants report using the L2 and the L1, in what contexts and with whom. This includes the amount and types of L2 and L1 use in digital as well as face-to-face contexts.

5.5 Navigating the nexus of practice

For Scollon and Scollon (2004: 9), this is the 'main body of work of a nexus analysis' as the analyst 'works his or her way through the trajectories of participants, places, and situations both back in time historically and forward through actions and anticipations to see if crucial discourse cycles or semiotic cycles can be identified'. Admittedly, the analysis presented here is not a full nexus analysis as proposed and described by the Scollons; it might better be labelled a sort of preliminary, or even exploratory, nexus analysis, because, as Scollon and Scollon note, a proper nexus analysis can take months or years, depending on the 'circumfencing' of the analysis; that is, the circles of people, places and things under consideration (p. 9). For our purposes we have the discursive history of US students' instructed language learning to which we can make reference, and we have enough information about the basic code-choice practices, attitudes and beliefs of this group of students to be able to navigate our way through our nexus of practice.

5.5.1 Historical body

With regard to code choice, what is the 'lifetime of personal habits [that] come to feel so natural that one's body carries out actions seemingly without being told' (Scollon & Scollon, 2004: 13)? In this context we have the lifetime of monolingual English usage of these particular students and the much shorter period of time in which they have developed as bilingual users of German and English. There are two features of the students' background that should be highlighted here, though arguably there would be many additional features of relevance. The first is the above-mentioned monolingual bias, not only in language teaching and applied linguistics but also in US society overall that privileges English over any number of 'foreign' languages (Simon, 1980; Blyth, 1995; Cook, 1997, 2002; Kramsch, 1997, 1998, 2009; Horner & Trimbur, 2002; Auer, 2007; Ortega, 2010). The second is the pedagogical paradigm in which all but one of these students was instructed in German, namely some variation of communicative language teaching (CLT). While CLT is based on an ideal of extensive or even exclusive use of the L2, used in simulations of ostensibly authentic situations, and designed to get students talking and using the language appropriately in a range of communicative contexts (see Savignon, 2002), in fact the CLT setting contributes to maintaining the tension between the dominant L1 (English) and the L2. CLT as an approach no doubt succeeds at getting students talking in a range of contexts, but it also serves to essentialize L2 language and culture, to keep the L2 'exotic' and 'foreign' (Horner & Trimbur, 2002; Reagan & Osborn, 2002). An alternative pedagogy would be oriented not towards keeping the L2 strange and exotic and foreign, but rather towards creating affordances for the *students* to feel strange and foreign, but in a way that acknowledges their legitimate place in the L2 society as multilingual language users. In other words, it would simulate aspects of being the foreigner that students experience in the host country when they study abroad.

A third feature of the historical body, also to be traced back to the CLT instructional setting, is what could be called the 'performative' dimension of L2 use. Based on Lyotard's (1984) notion of the performative (see also Phipps & Gonzalez, 2004), this means that the system in which students have learned L2 German is aimed primarily at creating learners who can successfully produce and manipulate language, that is, acquire and demonstrate language 'skills'. For some students, the larger purpose of the endeavour appears limited to the acquisition of these skills and the achievement of good marks based on demonstrating skills mastery, rather than (primarily) oriented towards the development of the learner as a multilingual person interacting with people in the L2 society (Phipps & Gonzalez, 2004; Kramsch, 2009). To be sure, students' motivations for learning and using L2s will always remain complex and dynamic, even in the context of a particular introductory or intermediate language class, and certainly when the student moves to the more advanced levels of instruction.[6] The point here relates to students' code choices, and what feels 'so natural that one's body carries out actions seemingly without being told'. Essential in this feature of the historical body is that up until their arrival in Germany, students' uses of German in instructional contexts were primarily set up as language-use-for-performance, and likely almost always tied to the assessment of that performance and the assignment of a grade for it.

A fourth feature of the historical body is also tied to this performative perspective and derives from the students' own reports. In surveys administered at the start of the study, the students were asked how important it was to be able to function as a normal participant in German society. Eleven of the thirteen reported that it was somewhat important or very important to them, while two reported that it was not important. Yet statements such as the following were typical of the prose comments students offered:

Michael: It was important to connect with Germans in order to speak German and have them correct me if I said something wrong. I helped one girl in my dorm apply for a semester abroad in England and we practiced my German and her English in conversation where I would speak German and she would correct it and she would speak English and I would correct it.

All of them also reported that it was important to them to use German every day, and to speak and use as much German as possible. To the question of how important it was to use German every day, the following was also typical of the responses:

Alex: I sort of forced myself to use a bit of German every day. One of the major goals while in Germany was to improve my German ability.

Note that in both instances the focus is on the performative, on the improvement of language skills. This suggests that an aspect of the students' historical body is a conviction that using a lot of German while abroad, and connecting to the people there, is important, a given, though connecting with people may also be about exploiting means of 'mastering' German. Even if they reported this because they perceived that such a response was expected of them, many of their responses to questions about the importance of connecting with Germans and using German appear to index a largely pedagogical discourse about the nature and purpose of study abroad. Without wishing to diminish the value of each student's experience, we can call this an aspect of the historical body.

5.5.2 Interaction order

In this section I present some of the findings of the study of students' code-choice practices while in Germany, based on students' self-reports. Here I will also unpack some of the observed relationships between reported code-choice patterns and the digital vs. non-digital settings of language use. I will orient the discussion in this and the next sections around the two research questions presented earlier. The first of these is as follows: When and how did the students use German and English?

The initial survey, completed after the students had been in Germany for one to three months, asked them to estimate the amounts of German and English they used on a day-to-day basis. The Log entries they subsequently completed added detail to this estimation, as they reported on their uses of German and English, as well as of digital media, in the preceding 24 hours. When asked what their most regularly used languages were while in Germany, and to rank them from most to least frequently used, eight of the thirteen students reported using English most frequently, and German second. Of note, however, is that all of them reported using English during the preceding day, and in different modes: speaking, reading, writing, watching TV or videos. In addition, all of them had multiple English-speaking acquaintances or friends, including other (non-US) international students. Six of them reported using English primarily with their non-US international student friends.

In the Logs the students marked how many hours they had used German and English in the previous 24 hours. Not surprisingly, there is no generalizable pattern across the group, or even within a single individual, except for the crucial point that *all* of the students used German for at least an hour most days, and that they used English without exception every day for at least two hours, in some way(s). Combining the responses of all 13 students for all 109 Log entries (see Table 5.1), the mean amount of time they reported speaking German in the previous 24 hours was 3.1 hours, with a standard deviation of 2.05. The mean amount of time students reported speaking English in the previous 24 hours was 4.1 hours, with a somewhat smaller standard deviation of 1.78.

For this adaptation of a nexus analysis of students' code-choice practices, the question of *how* the students were using the two languages

Table 5.1 Aggregated reported time speaking English and German in the previous 24 hours for all 109 responses (N =13 students)

	Time spent speaking German in the previous 24 hours	Time spent speaking English in the previous 24 hours
Minimum	0.7	2
Maximum	7.4	9.4
Mean	3.1	4.1
Standard deviation	1.78	2.05

day to day is in fact more important than the number of reported hours, which varied depending on what the students' schedules included (e.g. on days they had instruction, the amount of German would be higher than on days they stayed in their room and did not socialize with others). Figure 5.1 presents selected students' prose comments about the ways they had been using German and English in the previous 24 hours. The selection is representative of the range of types of comments students made. Each row represents one day's comments and so reflects their use of both German and English on that day. Also, though most students provided many comments over the weeks of the study, here I reproduce just a few per student, to give the reader a sense of the topics and purposes for English and German use. Their selection was based on whether they represented repeating comments observed across all of the surveys. (Note that the orthography here is as students provided it in their surveys.)

Name	GERMAN USE PREVIOUS 24 HOURS	ENGLISH USE PREVIOUS 24 HOURS
James	Spoke and listened to german at the library, in the meeting, at my internship, and in class read german in class	watched a james bond movie, talked to my friend in english, and wrote some things on facebook also skyped a friend back home in English
	The church I go to has services in both english and german so I go to the german one and I watched tv for a while in german and spoke german with my american friends for a while	I spoke english while cooking dinner and on skype with my family

(continued)

Name	GERMAN USE PREVIOUS 24 HOURS	ENGLISH USE PREVIOUS 24 HOURS
Amelia	Mostly only used in my German class about society and literature around the turn of the century.	I talked a little bit with some of my classmates before and after class in English, and spoke to my boyfriend later on at night in English, and watch TV/movies in the evening in English.
Evan	Listening to, speaking German in church, watching a german cartoon on tv, reading for class, writing for class	internet, movies
	I had two German classes, corrected an essay in German, spoke as much as possible to all friends, including my American friends here	I spent 3 hours at the internship, which is run in English; I spent some time on the internet; and I spoke mostly English at my friends apartment and the club because there are so many different cultures together there that English works best and because the club was too loud for me to understand German
	The meeting was entirely in German, and I wrote about 3 pages of essays in German.	Speaking with friends, reading websites, watched about two hours of a movie and a tv show.
	I read from my powerpoint on Kulturwissenschaft, proofread an essay, and read out loud in class for a grade	Anything online, particularly in the morning and before bed. Talking to friends throughout the day in person.
Liz	I had 3 hours of class, as well as a meeting for my program and speaking with friends while we were in our student center.	Whenever I am with my American friends, we speak English, and I've also spent some time catching up with friends from home.
	I've been working on all of the German assignments that I must hand in within the next week.	I spent a lot of time with my American friends, and I'm hooked on a book in English, so I've read a lot in the past day.
Miles	spoke german at lunch and in class	talking casually with friends here is the biggest culprit

(continued)

Name	GERMAN USE PREVIOUS 24 HOURS	ENGLISH USE PREVIOUS 24 HOURS
	Reading "Ein fliehendes Pferd" for class, and writing a paper on it. Also spoke some german last night going out	Spoke mostly english last night, also watched a few youtube videos in English
	I spoke german the entire day yesterday at my internship. I work from 8:00 to 16:00 and my co-workers only speak german. At dinner we only spoke english. Today in class we read and listened to German folksongs. Right now I am currently writing a paper in German	dinner with friends last night
Mia	All evening when we were out with German students, I only used my German	Aside from my praktikum, I used English at lunch
	I had a lot of German homework so I spent most of my day reading and writing, however, no speaking.	only at lunch did I really speak at all today, and it was in English
	I spoke German the entire time with my exchange student/ friend from high school. I am very comfortable using my German with her and she is very easy to talk to.	I spoke English for the three hours in my practicum teaching English to 11th and 13th graders.
	I used German while studying for my test and doing homework.	I only used english on FB today!!
Nancy	Spoke German in the kitchen. Read and wrote German homework.	Spoke English with my American friend while cooking/eating dinner. Also spoke English with a couple friends on Facebook. Watched an couple episodes of an English TV show before I went to bed.
	Studied and took 2 German exams today. Also spoke some German with friends and while ordering food.	Spoken some English with my German friends. Wrote in English on Facebook.

(*continued*)

Name	GERMAN USE PREVIOUS 24 HOURS	ENGLISH USE PREVIOUS 24 HOURS
	Spoke, read and wrote German in class. I have also been working on writing to papers in German today. I also practiced reading German out loud.	Spoke English with English speaking friends. Read and wrote in English online.
Susan	Did hw and practiced reading in my room for a couple of hours	Watched some Sex and the City before bed. Had minimal contact with people in the center. Spent most of my day going on walks or in my room.
	Spoke a mix of german and english with my friend at the bar.	spoke some english with my friend at the bar, read for a bit before bed. Worked on a personal essay for a few hours. Watched Sex and the City.
	Spoke German with the program director, had class, read and translated a story for class, wrote two essays, and practiced reading for a while.	Spoke some English with friends on cigarette breaks and read for a bit before bed.
Sam	used it obviously in class and for the afternoon to work on referat and papers	primarily for research and talking with friends
	internship…and met with tandem partner and went shopping	spoke with home about coming trip, read news articles, studied and watched a little show
	had class for 3 hrs, read and worked on my paper, also was at internship	personal use including reading news, writing emails and watched a show
Mark	I used German frequently today, I had 2 meetings all in German and a class which was in German. Then I ate dinner with friends and spoke German.	We only speak German in our classes, so my time speaking English was while I was with friends after dinner and while meeting with my language partner
	used german in class and during rugby practice	talking with friends here and from back home.

Figure 5. Sample comments by individual students on their day-to-day uses of German and English

What is striking is that if one categorizes in particular the recurring uses of German and English, many of the categories appear to be complementary. With a few exceptions, such as Mia's use of German to socialize with her German friend from high school, the students tended to use German for certain purposes or in certain contexts, and English for different purposes and in different contexts. The students' uses of German appear to fall into the following categories:

- Course-related reading and writing (including preparing presentations)
- Class presentations
- Speaking with professors and others in educational settings
- While working at their assigned internship (though for some this involved only English)
- Watching television shows
- Conversing with friends in cafés and the study centre
- Listening to sermons in church

Of these, only the last three are arguably unrelated to performative uses of language as discussed earlier.

As for English usage, the purposes and contexts fall into these categories:

- Conversing with friends (often fellow programme participants or flatmates)
- Communicating with family and friends back home through digital media (Skype, Facebook, email)
- Arranging meetings or planning excursions with fellow programme participants through Facebook
- Watching videos on YouTube, television shows and movies
- Reading books
- Writing journal entries

Of note here is that students do not appear to use English primarily or often to work on German-language course assignments, as has been found to happen in instructed L2 settings (Swain & Lapkin, 2000). Instead, English appears to serve as the primary language of social activity, both with people in Germany and of course people back home. What these comments suggest, in combination with the reported amounts of time, is what we might call a *diglossic interaction order*. The students indeed appear to tend towards complementary sets of contexts in which German or English are used or preferred.

A key observation for our consideration of language pedagogy is that no matter how important the learning or 'mastering' of German may be for the students, in fact English plays an important part in each person's day-to-day life, and not in ways that can be dismissed as simply disruptive of the students' largely performative language learning goals. Put another way, the discourses which intersect or circulate through code choices are all part of the larger constellation of discourses of US language education and contemporary manifestations of study abroad (Kinginger, 2010); however, these results prompt the question of whether these discourses are sufficient for students to move beyond performative functions of the L2 and social-networking functions of the L1 towards greater access to L2 social networks and their own critical awareness of the many discourses at work in the L2 environment. This transformation of the nexus of practice will be considered shortly, after a brief look at the students' use of digital media.

5.5.3 Uses of digital media

In their Logs the students reported a significant amount of digital media usage every day for which they completed logs, as also indicated in the prose comments presented earlier. This was often in the form of time on the Internet (e.g. watching YouTube and using Facebook), but also using Skype, email and instant messaging programmes. According to their initial surveys, these uses did not differ markedly from those prior to the study-abroad programme, except in a few key ways. The first is in terms of the communication, synchronous or asynchronous, with family and friends at home; they communicated with family and friends often about their activities in Germany, and they often (more often than previously, it appears) checked in on what was going on with people back home.

Second, internet access was somewhat more restricted than at home. This meant several used the Internet primarily when they were in the programme's study centre, rather than at home in their shared apartments or dorm rooms, where they reported no or very slow connections. And this, of course, meant that most spent overall less time on the Internet in Germany than they had at home prior to the programme.

A third way that digital media usage differed from uses prior to the start of the programme was the nature of the digital social networks in which the students engaged. We already noted the networks of friends and family, but all of the students engaged in frequent communications with fellow study-abroad programme participants. The purposes were usually logistical, that is, planning events, outings or trips. However, often they were to share photos and comments about outings or trips they had taken together.

In terms of the language choice of digital media usage, the main finding was that English was by far the most frequent language used in those media. In fact in all of the postings of the five students who shared their Facebook pages, there were just a few instances of German usage, and all but one was a simple insertion of German in an otherwise English-language posting, and not for communicating with German speakers.

5.5.4 Discourses in place

In their book-length treatment of discourses in place, Scollon and Scollon (2003) observed that even in books on intercultural communication, 'scant attention is focused on the question of how the physical/ material characteristics of language in the world give meaning to communications and how those meanings may be radically different from place to place in the world' (pp. x–xi). They demonstrate how meanings of particular uses of language are influenced by, and influence, the physical location of that language use. What does being in Germany mean for these students? What does using German in Germany mean to them? Put another way, does German *mean* differently when used in Germany rather than in the language classroom? What are the discourses in place at work in this context? In pre-digital generations, studying and living abroad meant minimal contact with social networks or communities of practice outside of those in the study-abroad site. To be sure, like this group of students, even pre-digital-era students engaged with social networks that served as a facsimile of their at-home social networks, socializing with fellow participants or other compatriots and, of course, using their L1 for those interactions. What is new about these students' situation? New in this system is the very multiplicity of social networks, both digital and non-digital, as well as those that I would call a *hybrid social space*, where the students interact digitally with local compatriots with whom they also interact face-to-face. Social networks in which the students participate digitally can be anywhere, and the students' comments suggest that they themselves don't seem to draw distinctions between the 'here' and the 'over there' with regard to communications as located in a particular place. Thus, the whole idea of 'place' is both complex and somewhat problematic, because for the students, 'being' in Germany is just one part of their experience. They are in essence *being* back home, in Germany and online-as-place arguably all at the same time. Because of this fluidity of discourses in place – discourses which are dominated by English usage for these students – concerns can be raised about whether students' hybrid social spaces contribute to optimizing L2 use, let alone engaging with German social networks, whether face-to-face or digital. It is these hybrid social spaces that point towards transforming the nexus of practice, for we might exploit pedagogically the students' own unconcern with whether discourse is physically located in the room or mediated through various digital media. The aim would be to create greater affordances for rich hybrid social spaces right in the L2 classroom which make use of both L1 and L2 in training students themselves to make avid use of the L2, join L2 social networks and use language as developing multilinguals; all of this in advance of studying abroad.

5.6 Transforming the nexus of practice

It appears that for these students, living and studying in a new country and exploring a new culture and language means operating in that new language for a range of purposes. But for many of the students in my study, the L2 serves instrumental or performative purposes of mastering German successfully in the course of study, that is, using German in class, for assignments and for a range of service encounters. These students entered into and maintained social networks primarily in English, both in person with fellow programme participants and digitally through email, Facebook and other media (cf. Kinginger, 2008, 2010; Levine, 2014). These uses of English appeared to elicit regret or even guilt feelings in some, but nonetheless appeared to be an integrated and important part of their everyday lives. What comes to the fore in the students' responses, in particular in the Logs, is that English appears to remain important for students' sense of control and security, as proposed by Pellegrino Aveni (2005). English is thus both a tool for navigating their developing bilingual identity as English/German speakers (Turnbull & Dailey-O'Cain, 2009) and a sort of parallel linguistic track that remains active much of the time. In terms of transforming the educational nexus of practice, perhaps what may be needed is what Kinginger (2010: 225) calls an 'activist stance' to language education, whereby we, as language educators, need to 'upgrade our ability to argue in favor of meaningful study-abroad experiences explicitly including an emphasis on language learning as negotiation of difference'. Arguably, these students' inclination to build and maintain their own English-based social networks is an indication of their coping with difference, rather than eschewing it, on their own terms. A transformed nexus of practice would thus allow a principled, viable role for the study-abroad students' L1, but would, crucially, shift the emphasis to the optimization of L2 use (see Macaro, 2009) and engagement in L2 social networks, both non-digital and digital.

The reader may object to any sort of generalizations from this small group of learners to L2 study-abroad settings at large. There is, admittedly, a paucity of data on just what learners are using their different languages for while abroad (see, however, Kinginger, 2008; Levine, 2009). Yet, just as we know that learners' L1 plays a part in L2 learning and for getting through their days and accomplishing a range of tasks and objectives, we can safely assert that even the most dedicated of 'immersion' students uses her or his L1, if only for non-study-related activities like reading a novel, watching a video in English or communicating with people back home.

A second point that emerges from this exploratory examination of the students' reported code-choice practices, and what they reported in writing about their beliefs and attitudes, is that for several of them, 'immersion' in the L2 may not be that important, and 'being there' in Germany and 'being at home' digitally don't come across as completely separate things. In other words, for some there does not appear to be a notable distinction between connecting digitally with fellow programme participants or family members thousands of miles away and connecting directly with others, such as Germans, in Germany. Whether this means these students are genuine 'digital natives', as proposed by Prensky (2001a, 2001b), or whether engaging with English through digital media provided just one more layer of security and control in the face of the uncertainty of living abroad, the indication is that perhaps there is no such thing as a pure state of 'being there' in the L2 environment. Let us turn now to the pedagogical implications of this, which includes consideration of how we might transform how educators employ digital media with and for students.

5.7 Implications and proposals for teaching

There are four key implications for pedagogy that present themselves, which I formulate as proposals for approaching curriculum design and teaching. The first is the role of English in developing a 'multilingual self', as described by Kramsch (2009), rather than a poor imitator of a native speaker (Belz, 2002, 2003). Indeed, the whole idea of 'immersion' may not be any more important to many of our classroom learners than it is to many of the students who study abroad. Perhaps it is time for teachers and curriculum planners to think in larger terms about who the student is or could be when they are abroad, grappling with complex issues of identity, which themselves are constantly changing, but which undeniably involve the learner's full range of linguistic, cultural and social competences (Cook, 2002). Our pedagogy should also include consideration of these competences. This would translate into tasks and activities in language classes that ask learners to reflect upon and analyse aspects not of the L2 culture and language alone, but of their own sense of identity both in their L1 and in the nascent L2. To this end I would make use of (excerpts from) any number of what Kramsch (2009) presents as 'linguistic memoirs'; in the activities she describes, students are also asked to write and discuss their linguistic autobiographies (see also Kramsch & Huffmaster, this volume). The point here is that the learners move beyond being the 'talking heads' (Kramsch, 2009: 28) that just receive and produce language and investigate interesting declarative knowledge about the L2 culture (which is important but not sufficient) and instead come to see themselves as 'owning' their knowledge of and dynamic capacities in the L2 on their own terms, mediated unavoidably through the symbolic system of the languages they already know (these increasingly involve not just English but any number of other languages our students have learned and regularly use).

The study described here points towards a second proposal for teaching that would expand the range of conventional CLT instruction, namely including principled use of the L1 in the design of classroom tasks that would more realistically reflect not the life of the monolingual L2 speaker but rather the 'on-the-ground' reality of the student studying abroad. While this can and should include learning about and critically studying the ways that people in the L2 society use multiple languages (e.g. immigrant or migrant communities; prominent multilingual individuals; language policy issues in the target country), it should also include explicit consideration of how the learners themselves would need and use the L2 in their daily lives in the L2 society, as visitors, sojourners or study-abroad students. Consideration of this 'on-the-ground' reality would necessarily include reflection on the ways students would use their L1 (and/or other languages) while abroad. Towards this end, I would suggest making use of some excerpts from applied linguistics scholarship as material for activity design, even quotes from the students, such as those provided in this chapter. This does not mean we are trying to turn our language students into applied linguists, but in my experience students often appreciate having access to authentic voices not only of members of L2 communities but of fellow learners or other multilingual users of the L2 (see also Blyth, 2009). The critical awareness of nuanced language-use issues that many will gain from this sort of activity in class may enrich the students' learning of L2, at the very least by making it more real because they can better imagine themselves in those situations.

The third implication relates to the fuzzy boundaries between the digital and the non-digital. Admittedly, today the range of uses of digital media of all sorts for classroom teaching has expanded dramatically, so that arguably there is little distinction to be made between the uses of digital media in society and those for pedagogy. Teachers today are aware of and accustomed to employing digital media as pedagogical tools. But as Prensky observed in his seminal essays regarding the 'digital native' (2001a, 2001b), one of the key advantages of digital media for learning is that it allows for inherent 'random access' to tasks and activities, guided by learners. While our uses for digital media in language classes may support all sorts of learning, they tend to follow conventional models of instructional design; the digital media are embedded into linear sequences of lessons, and the learners then employ the digital media as the teacher intended. This is understandable and intuitive, but like Prensky I suggest that we could learn from the students in this study that the choice of and means of employing digital media take a secondary role to the desired language learning outcomes. This would mean setting up tasks and activities and allowing learners to engage in digital communication as they see fit and to use various digital media of their choosing, depending on their preferences and needs. This could range from closed-ended tasks that involve the learning of language forms, vocabulary or declarative or critical cultural knowledge, to tasks involving communicating with speakers of the L2 elsewhere. Ultimately, I propose that language curriculum designers and classroom teachers move away from viewing digital media as something distinct from face-to-face communication and learning, let alone as an 'ancillary', and from the implicit assumption that student-guided uses of digital media would always lead to more L1 use at the expense of the L2. In the design of activities, students should be given as much choice about the means, timing and speed of task completion. This will put the onus on materials creators and teachers to effectively communicate L2 learning goals in terms that students understand and can 'own'. And this in turn could necessitate reevaluating aspects of our typically linear curricula based on sequences of form and lexical learning.

A fourth implication also goes to the very nature of conventional CLT methodologies, and to the best ways of preparing students to succeed and thrive while studying abroad (and arguably providing a valuable experience to the many students who do not end up going abroad). At the start of this chapter, I confessed that in my ideal conceptualization the student's study-abroad experience would mean a complete 'immersion' experience in which the student engaged in multiple L2 social networks, as people in the L2 society would experience them. One of the findings of the study described here is that despite their participation in programme-arranged internships, for the most part these students did not connect up with the sorts of social networks of which Germans themselves are a part. Instead, they created their own sorts of social networks, ones that were perhaps transpositions of those they had back home, but which represented something quite different from those in which Germans would participate (see Kinginger, 2010). While we may have to accept this as a normal part of the study-abroad experience for many students around the world, at least for the time being (see Papatsiba, 2006; Kinginger, 2008, 2010), we must ask what we could do in the classroom, well before students go abroad, to give them the capacities and tools to connect with L2 social networks if they wish to. To this end we could adapt an approach developed by Roberts et al. (2001) for helping students to be 'ethnographers' of the L2 culture, which details case studies of several students' experiences abroad. In the light of the ubiquitous availability of digital media and communications at home, I believe we can design instruction that would facilitate students not only to imagine themselves as part of L2 social networks but also, in fact, to conduct research towards actually doing so in advance of a study-abroad sojourn. This could be as simple as researching social networks based on their interests (e.g. a student interested in soccer could delve into the activities of a local soccer club in Germany) or as involved as joining Facebook or other online groups in which people are communicating asynchronously or synchronously, or both. An even more committed approach could include cross-cultural, telecollaborative projects.

5.8 Conclusion

This examination of code choice during study abroad had three purposes. First, I sought to gain a picture according to self-reports of how a group of US students studying abroad in Germany were using German and English in their day-to-day lives. Second, I sought to determine how and with whom the students were using digital media, and which languages they were choosing for digital communications of all sorts. And finally, I was interested in linking insights from the students' code-choice practices to a critical examination of curriculum design and teaching practice, in particular, CLT curriculum and teaching. Specifically, I aimed at rethinking aspects of language teaching to be more in line with what students actually experience when they go abroad, but also to foster learners' inclination and preparedness for using the L2 during study abroad in optimal ways, both for learning and for engaging with L2 social networks, digital and non-digital.

Nexus analysis was employed here as a method of structuring the pursuit of these three goals, in order to delve into the discursive aspects of students' code choices while abroad. Students' choices to use German and English appear to obtain along fairly diglossic lines, and the nexus analysis showed, I hope, that these can be traced not only to the day-to-day interactions in which the students engaged but also to the social networks in which they participated, and further, to the pedagogical model in which these students learned German as an L2. Examination of this last point meant interrogating some of the underlying assumptions of CLT, in particular the Lyotardian performative basis of university CLT instruction, to suggest that these students' code choices may in fact be well in line with a continuation of that model. In addition, the analysis suggested that students created and were involved in social networks in Germany that were not so much continuations of those from back home as a sort of transposition of familiar social networks to their new environment, which included primarily English use and the blending of the digital and non-digital.

Further research into students' code choices would need to examine in particular two things. First, it would need to capture aspects of their actual usage of different languages from day to day, in order to establish whether these students' self-reports reflected the reality of their situations. Second, it would need to capture some of the changes in code-choice patterns over time, such as a semester or an academic year. Of particular interest would be to learn whether study-abroad students use more or less of the L2 the longer they are in the study-abroad country, with whom and in what contexts. In this regard, a study involving a pedagogical intervention based on some of the observations and findings of the present study, whereby students' primary uses of the L2 appeared to be guided by a performative orientation, would be welcome. This would allow the researcher not only to be the 'fly on the wall' tracking what students do with their languages but also actually to influence critical awareness of language use towards the optimization of L2 use and learning, which is still the idealistic goal many language educators have for their students.

Notes

1. I would like to thank the editors, Jasone Cenoz and Durk Gorter, for their excellent editing of this manuscript. I express my deepest gratitude to the staff and students at the study-abroad programme in Germany. It was a transformative and delightful experience to meet and work with them. I am also grateful for support and helpful feedback from Hanne Heckmann, Celeste Kinginger, Claire Kramsch and Jaime Roots at key stages of the project.
2. There is significant overlap between the underlying assumptions and tenets of nexus analysis and those of complexity theory and dynamic systems theory, as

these have been adapted or repurposed for applied linguistics in recent years (de Bot, Lowie & Verspoor, 2007; Ellis, 2008; Larsen-Freeman & Cameron, 2008). Indeed, though never directly linked with the scholarship in these areas, Scollon and Scollon's model lends itself well as a methodology for moving beyond the metaphors of language, language learning and language use as interconnected and interdependent complex systems; it is thus a useful framework for linking theory, empirical observations and pedagogical practice.

3. In his landmark presidential address (1983), Goffman details 11 interaction units that can be observed and analysed. These are summarized in Scollon and Scollon (2003: 61).

4. The reader should note that the discussion of students' code choices here represents just part of the overall study, and as such this chapter is not a conventional research report. There is a broader set of research questions that were used for the data collection, including those related to socialization experiences in Germany, students' feelings of homesickness and overall difficulties communicating with people in German, but as these are not directly germane to the issue of code choice, they will not be addressed in the present analysis.

5. All human subjects (IRB) protocols were reviewed and approved, and students gave full informed consent for all components of the project, with assurances that they could withdraw from the study at any time.

6. See Dörnyei (2009), Pavlenko (2002), Schmidt and Watanabe (2001) and Ushioda and Dörnyei (2009) on the complexities of L2 learner motivation.

References

Antón, M. and DiCamilla, F. J. (1999). Socio-cognitive functions of L1 collaborative interaction in the L2 classroom, *The Modern Language Journal*, 83(2), 233–47.

Auer, P. (2007). The monolingual bias in bilingualism research, or: why bilingual talk is (still) a challenge for linguistics. In M. Heller (ed.), *Bilingualism: A Social Approach* (pp. 319–39). London: Palgrave Macmillan.

Belz, J. A. (2002). The myth of the deficient communicator. *Language Teaching Research*, 6(1), 59–82.

Belz, J. A. (2003). Identity, deficiency, and first language use in foreign language education. In C. Blyth (ed.), *The Sociolinguistics of Foreign-Language Classrooms: Contributions of the Native, the Near-Native, and the Non-Native Speaker* (pp. 209–48). Boston: Heinle.

Blyth, C. (1995). Redefining the boundaries of language use: the foreign language classroom as a multilingual speech community. In C. Kramsch (ed.), *Redefining the Boundaries of Language Study* (pp. 145–83). Boston: Heinle.

Blyth, C. (2009). The impact of pedagogical materials on critical language awareness: assessing student attention to patterns of language use. In M. Turnbull and J. Dailey-O'Cain (eds.), *First Language Use in Second and Foreign Language Learning* (pp. 156–78). Bristol: Multilingual Matters.

Bourdieu, P. (1977). *Outline of a Theory of Practice* (trans. R. Nice). Cambridge: Cambridge University Press.

Brecht, R., Davidson, D. and Ginsberg, R. (1995). Predicting and measuring language gains in study abroad settings. In B. F. Freed (ed.), *Second Language Acquisition in a Study Abroad Context* (pp. 37–66). Amsterdam: John Benjamins.

Byram, M. (1997). *Teaching and Assessing Intercultural Communicative Competence*, Clevedon: Multilingual Matters.

Cook, V. J. (1997). Monolingual bias in second language acquisition research. *Revista Canaria de Estudios Ingleses*, 34, 35–49.

Cook, V. J. (1999). Going beyond the native speaker in language teaching. *TESOL Quarterly*, 33(2), 185–209.

Cook, V. J. (2001). Using the first language in the classroom. *Canadian Modern Language Review / La revue canadienne des langues vivantes*, 57(3), 402–23.

Cook, V. (2002). Language teaching methodology and the L2 user perspective. In V. Cook (ed.), *Portraits of the L2 User* (pp. 327–44). Clevedon: Multilingual Matters.

Dailey-O'Cain, J. and Liebscher, G. (2009). Teacher and student use of the first language in foreign language classroom interaction: functions and applications. In M. Turnbull and J. Dailey-O'Cain (eds.), *First Language Use in Second and Foreign Language Learning* (pp. 131–44). Bristol: Multilingual Matters.

de Bot, K., Lowie, W. and Verspoor, M. (2007). A dynamic systems theory approach to second language acquisition. *Bilingualism: Language and Cognition*, 10(1), 7–21.

Dewey, D. P. (2004). A comparison of reading development by learners of Japanese in intensive domestic immersion and study abroad contexts. *Studies in Second Language Acquisition*, 26(2), 303–27.

Dörnyei, Z. (2009). The L2 motivational self system. In Z. Dörnyei and E. Ushioda (eds.), *Motivation, Language Identity, and the L2 Self* (pp. 9–42). Bristol: Multilingual Matters.

Ellis, N. C. (2008). The dynamics of second language emergence: cycles of language use, language change, and language acquisition. *The Modern Language Journal*, 92(2), 232–49.

Evans, M. (2009). Codeswitching in computer-mediated communication: linguistic and interpersonal dimensions of cross-national discourse between school learners of French and English. In M. Turnbull and J. Dailey-O'Cain (eds.), *First Language Use in Second and Foreign Language Learning* (pp. 50–86). Bristol: Multilingual Matters.

Garafanga, J. (2009). Code-switching as a conversational strategy. In P. Auer and Li Wei (eds.), *Handbook of Multilingualism and Multilingual Communication* (pp. 279–313). Berlin: Mouton de Gruyter.

Goffman, E. (1983). The interaction ritual. *American Psychological Review*, 48(1), 1–17.

Horner, B. and Trimbur, J. (2002). English only and U.S. college composition. *College Composition and Communication*, 53(4), 594–630.

Isabelli-García, C. L. (2006). Study abroad social networks, motivation, and attitudes: implications for SLA. In M. DuFon and E. Churchill (eds.), *Language Learners in Study Abroad Contexts* (pp. 231–58). Clevedon: Multilingual Matters.

Jackson, J. (2008). *Language, Identity, and Study Abroad: Sociocultural Perspectives*. London: Equinox.

Kinginger, C. (2008). *Language Learning in Study Abroad: Case Studies of Americans in France*. Special Monograph issue of *Modern Language Journal* 92 (Supplement s1), 1–124.

Kinginger, C. (2010). American students abroad: negotiation of difference? *Language Teaching*, 43(2), 216–27.

Kramsch, C. (1997). The privilege of the nonnative speaker. *Publications of the Modern Language Association*, 112(3), 359–69.

Kramsch, C. (1998). The privilege of the intercultural speaker. In M. Byram and M. Fleming (eds.), *Language Learning in Intercultural Perspective: Approaches Through Drama and Ethnography* (pp. 16–31). Cambridge: Cambridge University Press.

Kramsch, C. (2009). *The Multilingual Subject: What Foreign Language Learners Say about Their Experience and Why It Matters*. Oxford: Oxford University Press.

Krashen, S. and Terrell, T. (1983). *The Natural Approach: Language Acquisition in the Classroom*. Hayward, CA: Alemany Press.

Lapkin, S., Hart, D. and Swain, M. (1995). A Canadian interprovincial exchange: evaluating the linguistic impact of a three-month stay in Quebec. In B. F. Freed (ed.), *Second Language Acquisition in a Study Abroad Context* (pp. 67–94). Amsterdam: John Benjamins.

Larsen-Freeman, D. and Cameron, L. (2008). *Complex Systems and Applied Linguistics*. Oxford: Oxford University Press.

Levine, G. S. (2008). Language learners as discourse analysts: exploring intercultural communicative competence through L2 learners' intercultural moments. In R. Schulz and E. Tschirner (eds.), *Zur Entwicklung interkultureller Kompetenz in Deutsch als Fremdsprache: Lernziele, didaktische Ansätze, Evaluierung* (pp. 191–216). Munich: Iudicium.

Levine, G. S. (2009). Building meaning through code choice in L2 learner interaction: a D/discourse analysis and proposals for curriculum design and teaching. In M. Turnbull and J. Dailey-O'Cain (eds.), *First Language Use in Second and Foreign Language Learning* (pp. 145–62). Bristol: Multilingual Matters.

Levine, G. S. (2011). *Code Choice in the Language Classroom*. Bristol: Multilingual Matters.

Levine, G. S. (2014). From performance to multilingual being in foreign language pedagogy: lessons from L2 students abroad. *Critical Multilingualism Studies*, 2(1), 74–105.

Liebscher, G. and Dailey-O'Cain, J. (2004). Learner code-switching in the content-based foreign language classroom. *Canadian Modern Language Review / La revue canadienne des langues vivantes*, 60(4), 501–25 (repr. in *The Modern Language Journal*, 89(2) (2005), 234–47).

Li Wei (1998). The 'why' and 'how' questions in the analysis of conversational code-switching. In P. Auer (ed.), *Code-Switching in Conversation: Language, Interaction, and Identity* (pp. 156–76). London: Routledge.

Lyotard, J.-F. (1984). *The Postmodern Condition: A Report on Knowledge* (trans. G. Bennington, B. Massumi and F. Jameson). Minneapolis, MN: University of Minnesota Press.

Macaro, E. (2001). Analyzing student teachers' code-switching in foreign language classrooms: theories and decision making. *The Modern Language Journal*, 85(4), 531–48.

Macaro, E. (2009). Teacher use of code-switching in the L2 classroom: exploring 'optimal' use. In M. Turnbull and J. Dailey-O'Cain (eds.), *First Language Use in Second and Foreign Language Learning* (pp. 35–49). Bristol: Multilingual Matters.

Magnan, S. S. and Back, M. (2007). Social interaction and linguistic gain during study abroad. *Foreign Language Annals*, 40(1), 43–61.

Milton, J. and Meara, P. (1995). How periods abroad affect vocabulary growth in a foreign language. *Annual Review of Applied Linguistics*, 107/108, 17–34.

Myers-Scotton, C. (1993). *Social Motivations for Codeswitching: Evidence from Africa*. Oxford: Clarendon Press.

Myers-Scotton, C. and Bolonyai, A. (2001). Calculating speakers: codeswitching in a rational choice model', *Language in Society*, 30(1), 1–28.

Nishida, K. (1958). *Intelligibility and the Philosophy of Nothingness*. Tokyo: Maruzen Co. Ltd.

Ortega, L. (2010). The bilingual turn in SLA. Plenary address at the American Association for Applied Linguistics conference, Atlanta, Georgia.

Papatsiba, V. (2006). Making higher education more European through student mobility? Revisiting EU initiatives in the context of the Bologna Process. *Comparative Education*, 42(1), 93–111.

Pavlenko, A. (2002). Poststructuralist approaches to the study of social factors in second language learning and use. In V. Cook (ed.), *Portraits of the L2 User* (pp. 277–302). Clevedon: Multilingual Matters.

Pellegrino Aveni, V. (2005). *Study Abroad and Second Language Use: Constructing the Self*. Cambridge: Cambridge University Press.

Phipps, A. and Gonzalez, M. (2004). *Modern Languages: Learning and Teaching in an Intercultural Field*, London: Sage.

Prenksy, M. (2001a). Digital natives, digital immigrants. *On the Horizon*, 9(5), 1–6.

Prenksy, M. (2001b). Digital natives, digital immigrants, part II: Do they really think differently? *On the Horizon*, 9(6), 1–6.

Reagan, T. G. and Osborn, T. A. (2002). *The Foreign Language Educator in Society: Toward a Critical Pedagogy*, Mahwah, NJ: Lawrence Erlbaum Associates.

Regan, V., Howard, M. and Lemée, I. (2009). *The Acquisition of Sociolinguistic Competence in a Study Abroad Context*. Bristol: Multilingual Matters.

Roberts, C. (2009). Multilingualism in the workplace. In P. Auer and Li Wei (eds.), *Handbook of Multilingualism and Multilingual Communication* (pp. 405–22). Berlin: Mouton de Gruyter.

Roberts, C., Byram, M., Barro, A., Jordan, S. and Street, B. (2001). *Language Learners as Ethnographers*. Clevedon: Multilingual Matters.

Savignon, S. (2002). Communicative language teaching: linguistic theory and classroom practice. In S. Savignon (ed.), *Interpreting Communicative Language Teaching: Contexts and Concerns in Teacher Education* (pp. 1–27). New Haven, CT: Yale University Press.

Schmidt, R. and Watanabe, Y. (2001). Motivation, strategy use, and pedagogical preferences in foreign language learning. In Z. Dörnyei and R. Schmidt (eds.), *Motivation and Second Language Acquisition* (pp. 313–59). Technical Report #23. Honolulu: University of Hawai'i, Second Language Teaching and Curriculum Center.

Scollon, R. (2001). *Mediated Discourse: The Nexus of Practice*. London: Routledge.

Scollon, R. and Scollon, S. W. (2003). *Discourses in Place: Language in the Material World*. London: Routledge.

Scollon, R. and Scollon, S. W. (2004). *Nexus Analysis: Discourse and the Emerging Internet*. London: Routledge.

Scott, V. M. (2010). *Double Talk: Deconstructing Monolingualism in Classroom Second Language Learning*. Upper Saddle River, NJ: Pearson Education.

Simon, P. (1980). *The Tongue-Tied American: Confronting the Foreign Language Crisis*. New York: Continuum.

Swain, M. and Lapkin, S. (2000). Task-based second language learning: the uses of the first language. *Language Teaching Research*, 4(3), 251–74.

Thorne, S. L. (2003). Artifacts and cultures-of-use in intercultural communication. *Language Learning & Technology*, 7(2), 38–67. Retrieved from http://llt.msu.edu/vol7num2/pdf/thorne.pdf, 1 October 2013.

Turnbull, M. and Dailey-O'Cain, J. (2009). Concluding reflections: moving forward. In M. Turnbull and J. Dailey-O'Cain (eds.), *First Language Use in Second and Foreign Language Learning* (pp. 189–92). Bristol: Multilingual Matters.

Ushioda, E. and Dörnyei, Z. (2009). Motivation, language identities and the L2 self. In Z. Dörnyei and E. Ushioda (eds.), *Motivation, Language, Identity and the L2 Self* (pp. 1–8). Bristol: Multilingual Matters.

Winkler, G. (1969). *A-LM German: Level One*. New York: Harcourt.

Zentella, A. C. (1997). *Growing up Bilingual: Puerto Rican Children in New York*. Oxford: Blackwell.

6 Multilingual practices in foreign language study

Claire Kramsch and Michael Huffmaster

6.1 Introduction: the paradox of the foreign language classroom in an age of globalization

The teaching and learning of foreign languages at secondary and post-secondary institutions around the world is confronted with a major paradox. On the one hand, mindful of their mission to teach the national language, literature and culture of a given national speech community, teachers strive to impart a mastery of the standard language that will enable learners to become educated users of the language, to communicate with native speakers and to read the literature written by and for native speakers. On the other hand, as global communications have become more and more multimodal and multilingual, and potential interlocutors are not necessarily monolingual native nationals but other multilingual non-native speakers, foreign language learners have to learn, as the 2007 Report of the Modern Language Association advocates, how to 'operate between languages' (MLA, 2007: 237), that is, how to develop a linguistic and cultural competence across multilingual contexts. While this multilingual imperative has been theorized recently by applied linguists such as Makoni and Pennycook (2007), Peter Auer and Li Wei (2007) and Canagarajah (2007) and has been the theme of a special issue of the *Modern Language Journal* on multilingualism (Cenoz and Gorter, 2011), it has not yet been taken seriously by foreign language teachers in departments of foreign languages and literatures at educational institutions. The exclusive use of monolingual/national points of reference deprives the learners of the transnational, translingual and transcultural competencies they will need to use the language in today's multilingual environments.

The teaching of foreign languages still bears the traces of its historical antecedents in the teaching of classical Greek and Latin – prestige languages that in the nineteenth century contributed to the well-rounded education of national elites. The inclusion of living foreign languages into the academic curriculum in the early twentieth century coincided with a surge in nationalism among industrialized nations and with increased contacts, both touristic and commercial, across national borders. Following Benedict Anderson's notion of 'imagined communities' (1983), foreign languages, like nations, were imagined as belonging to clearly defined national communities of native speakers, as limited by clearly defined grammatical borders and as strictly policed by the standard rules of usage found in a nation's grammars and dictionaries. Such a view was supported by Saussure's structuralist and synchronic concept of *langue* as the common patrimony of a speech community (1916/1959) and by Herder (1772/1960) and von Humboldt (1836/1988), who gave this community a decidedly nationalistic meaning. It has been implicitly supported by linguists and psycholinguists in early research in second language acquisition, where notions of 'native speaker', 'competence/performance' and 'acceptability' were predicated on the existence of a native-speaker consensus on matters of grammaticality, the native speaker being usually seen as a foreign or formerly foreign national. Unlike teachers of English as a lingua franca, foreign language teachers therefore see their mission as acquainting their students with the language and cultural heritage of national communities, thereby reinforcing their appreciation of their own language and cultural heritage as citizens of their nation-state. As the MLA report indicates, foreign language majors should 'comprehend speakers of the target language as members of foreign societies and grasp themselves as Americans – that is, as members of a society that is foreign to others' (2007: 237).

However, the overwhelming spread of English as a lingua franca, the globalization of communication through the Internet and the sheer volume of international contacts through social networks have changed the expectations of foreign language students regarding translingual and transcultural communication and the demands that will be placed on them once they want to use the language in real-life contexts. Globalization presents an enormous challenge to the foreign language teacher, trained to teach according to principles of monolingual immersion in one target language and a communicative pedagogy based on the idealized grammar and pragmatics of the native-speaking national. We first review some recent research in linguistics and in literary studies that define the nature of the challenge and what we mean by multilingualism. We then discuss various possible multilingual practices within the monolingual context of the foreign language classroom. We finally consider some implications for the foreign language curriculum as a whole.

6.2 The nature of the challenge

While the initial attacks against the monolingual native-speaker norm came mostly from psycholinguists and foreign language educators (Davies, 1991; Firth and Wagner, 1997; Kramsch, 1997; Cook, 1999) anxious to set reasonable goals for language instruction, the current push towards multilingualism in language education comes from sociolinguists and critical applied linguists, who insist on taking into consideration the language variation and change typical of everyday global realities.

Already in 1990, the sociolinguist Ben Rampton had proposed some alternatives to the concept of native speaker that he called 'expertise, affiliation, and inheritance'. More recently Jan Blommaert (2010) has argued that the phenomenon of globalization forces sociolinguistics to unthink its focus on 'static variation, on local distribution of varieties, on stratified language contact' and to 'rethink itself as a sociolinguistics of mobile resources, framed in terms of trans-contextual networks, flows and movements' (p. 1). In this view people don't learn and use whole linguistic systems like French, German or English: 'We never know "all" of a language, we always know specific bits and pieces of it,' he argues. 'This counts for our "mother tongue" as well as for the languages we pick up in the course of a lifetime' (p. 23). Those bits and pieces he calls 'truncated repertoires'. Sociolinguists have to study *truncated multilingualism* or 'repertoires composed of specialized but partially and unevenly developed resources' (p. 23).

Other applied linguists call for taking into account the plurilingual needs of second language students. Auer and Li Wei (2007) and García et al. (2007) forcefully insist on broadening the notion of communicative context. The *Handbook of Multilingualism and Multiculturalism* (2007), edited by Peter Auer and Li Wei, destabilizes assumptions about the essential unity of language, nation and identity (see also Makoni & Pennycook, 2007). In this handbook, García, Bartlett and Kleifgen focus on *pluriliteracies*, what New Literacy Studies (Cope & Kalantzis, 2000) call *multiliteracies*, that is, 'literacy practices in sociocultural contexts, the hybridity of literacy practices afforded by new technologies, and the increasing interrelationship of semiotic systems' (García et al., 2007: 215). Following up on the idea that languages nowadays are not compartmentalized in neatly separated diglossic situations but rather overlap, intersect and interconnect, their pluriliteracies approach 'highlights the continuous interplay of multiple languages, scripts, discourses, dialects and registers' and 'calls attention to the ways in which multilingual literacies are enmeshed and rely upon multiple modes, channels of communication, and semiotic systems' (p. 217).

In his 2007 response to Firth and Wagner (1997) and in his contribution to the special issue of the *Modern Language Journal* on multilingualism, Canagarajah exhorts teachers of English to devise a multilingual pedagogy better adapted to the fluid communicative contexts of the large global urban centres in which various languages are used for various functions. He writes:

Research on lingua franca English (LFE) ... reveals what multilingual communities have known all along: Language learning and use succeed through performance strategies, situational resources, and social negotiations in fluid communicative contexts. Proficiency is therefore practice-based, adaptive, and emergent. These findings compel us to theorize language acquisition as multimodal, multisensory, multilateral, and, therefore, multidimensional. The previously dominant constructs such as form, cognition, and the individual are not ignored; they get redefined as hybrid, fluid, and situated in a more socially embedded, ecologically sensitive, and interactionally open model. (Canagarajah, 2007: 921)

In the face of such research, much of it conducted by scholars of English as a second or international language, foreign language educators will rightly point out that their role is quite different from that of English language teachers. They do not teach a lingua franca but a national language anchored in a national culture and tradition. Their goal, they would argue, is to acquaint their students with culturally authentic texts of various genres, written in standard national languages and addressed to educated native readers with full mastery of the national code. And yet, the growing diversification of languages, dialects, genres and registers within immigration countries, and the increased mobility and online accessibility of speakers and readers documented by the research mentioned above, cannot but raise questions regarding the traditionally monolingual speaker/reader that a monolingual immersion pedagogy strives to produce. How can foreign language teachers take into account the changing contexts of language use for which they are preparing their students without losing the historical and cultural awareness that comes from studying one national language, literature and culture?

One way out of this apparent paradox is to conceive of a multilingual foreign language education not merely as the juxtaposition of several linguistic codes but also, as Canagarajah (2011) suggests, as a 'multimodal, multisensory, multilateral, and, therefore, multidimensional' process of meaning-making through a variety of linguistic codes, modes of perception, modalities of expression, social genres and situational registers deliberately used not for their normativity but for their semiotic function. The 'language awareness' called for by the MLA report (2007) would then be less the traditional awareness of the rules of syntax and vocabulary but, rather, an awareness of the semiotic potential of switching linguistic codes, discourse structures and discourse modes, the symbolic potential of various media and modalities, and the way they position speakers and hearers, readers and writers. 'Operating between languages' as a multilingual practice would mean not only operating between multiple codes but also playing with various intertextualities (re-keyings, transpositions, transcriptions, transmodalities), engaging in translingual and transcultural practices (Kramsch, 2013) and deliberately experimenting with multivoiced discourse (heteroglossia) and multiple channels of perception (synaesthesia). In the next section, we explore what such multilingual practices might look like, based on our experiences teaching intermediate and advanced foreign language classes.

6.3 Multilingual practices in action

6.3.1 Translating translations

Translation represents one fairly obvious multilingual practice well suited to foreign language study. In order to avoid reinforcing outdated monolingualist notions of a standard national language, however, translation activities can be recast in such a way as to highlight the heteroglossic features of ostensibly monoglossic texts. The task of translating translations, for example, which are already by definition hybrid, can liberate learners from nationalist, monolingualist expectations of strict and unreflective fidelity to an idealized 'original' and allow for creative agency in the act of meaning-making. In a course on translation theory and practice at a small liberal-arts college in the United States, two intermediate-level German learners decided for their final course projects to translate German translations into English with the intention of foregrounding the language and culture of the original source texts.

One student chose a German translation of a Japanese fairytale, *Jukionna*, about two lumberjacks. The student noted in his commentary on his work that the German translator, in his introduction to his translation, explicitly expresses his goal of writing for an audience of German youth and admits that he accordingly changed, left out or replaced many passages (Heiser, 1912). Influenced by nineteenth- and early twentieth-century translation norms and nationalist attitudes towards language, the translator sought to Germanize the text and eliminate its foreignness. He was quite successful in this regard, for his translation reads not as a translation at all, but rather as though it were originally written in German, with only the names of the characters providing any indication of his text's provenance. The student who chose this text for his translation project, however, desired to emphasize the Japanese origin of the tale and thereby to restore the hybrid, heteroglossic dimensions of translation intentionally effaced by the German translator. His evolving drafts of one passage in particular illustrate well his attempts to achieve this effect. Initially, he rendered the phrase *ging jeden Tag zusammen in den Wald um Holz zu schlagen* as 'went every day together to the woods to chop wood', a strict, literal translation. Next he tried a lineated version of the text that had 'Each day together they went / To chop wood in the forest.' Finally, he settled on 'would go off to the forest together every day to fell cherry and oak'. His first two drafts show that he clearly understood the literal meaning of the German expression *Holz zu schlagen*, but his commentary explains his final choice of a freer translation: 'I like the image that the names of real trees give. I was trying to think of common trees that the Japanese have and I thought oak and cherry were good choices. I did some research to try to identify some common Japanese trees and it seems like those two are reasonable choices.' Significantly, by choosing to translate the generic term 'wood' into more specific expressions, the student is able to evoke richer imagery, which he feels is more aesthetically effective, as well as culturally specific detail. Though he does not explain his rationale for rendering *schlagen* (chop) as 'fell', the German word for lumberjack, *Holzfäller* (literally, 'wood-feller'), likely influenced his decision. The student notes further: 'I was thinking about using pine and maple, too, but the way cherry and oak sound together is so full in the mouth. Especially oak, it is such a rich sound and so familiar that it gives a feeling of comfort and familiarity.' We notice here that in addition to highlighting aspects of the original source culture, the student attends to multisensory aspects of language – an awareness perhaps encouraged by the process of translation – observing the way the sounds of the English words 'oak' and 'cherry' feel 'in the mouth'.

The other student chose to translate a passage from the German translation of J. K. Rowling's novel *Harry Potter and the Sorcerer's Stone*.[1] In discussing his translation of this German translation back into English, the student remarked that he 'heard a British voice' while translating, knowing that the original text was written by an English author and that the story's setting is in England. Though the German translation he was working from may have downplayed the Britishness of the original, except for titles and surnames, this student chose to emphasize it, following the 'British voice' he imagined. For an American, this decision translates into less colloquial and instead more formal, one might say, stilted syntax and diction. The result was effective and striking.

Formulations in the student's translation with stilted or elaborate syntax and diction were intended, in his words, to 'amp up the British feel' of the text. Due to copyright restrictions, we unfortunately cannot reproduce any part of the student's translation of the passage from the German translation of Rowling's text. But the following expressions and turns of phrase, invented by the authors, are offered as analogous examples to provide a sense of the effect the student strove to achieve in his translation: 'never in all of history had such a wondrous thing come to pass'; 'that it might conceivably occur remained their long-held hope'; 'would be truly remarkable': 'as could ever possibly happen'; 'as had yet, despite all concerted efforts, to occur'; 'we simply cannot see how we could possibly endure the inconvenience'. We iterate: these expressions are not taken from our data; they are not citations from the student's translation of the German translation of Rowling's text, nor are they reformulations or transpositions of the student's work, nor are they new translations of the German text or reformulations of Rowling's original. They are the authors' inventions, intended to convey the effect the student sought to impart with his translation. To an American ear, at least, the student's translation sounds even more 'British' than Rowling's original, which in comparison sounds more colloquial and informal, which is to say, more 'American'.[2] But despite the student's own perhaps simplistic formulation of his intention to 'amp up the British feel' in his translation, and despite any charges of stereotyping that the result may elicit, his work reveals an awareness of different registers and sociolects – aspects of heteroglossia within the supposedly uniform 'English' language – activated through the process of translating a translation that would otherwise go unnoticed in reading the original or in translating the original into another national language.

6.3.2 Translating across registers

The most successful examples of children's literature are those that manage effectively to capture the registers of both adults and children, the paragon case being Antoine de Saint-Exupéry's novella *The Little Prince*. The story speaks directly to children through its themes and imaginative fancy, while it also contains a rich subtext that makes it appealing to adults: commentary on politics and history, on the ways adults communicate with children and on how the process of maturation can lead to a sense of self-alienation. A major factor in this accomplishment, however, is the narrator's language, which displays a heteroglossic commingling of child and adult registers or 'voices'.

An advanced learner of French in the same course who chose to translate passages from *The Little Prince* remarked that although she knew the story intimately, it was the process of translation that first allowed her to discover this important feature of the text. Her commentary reveals the challenge of negotiating heteroglossia when translating children's literature:

It's difficult to find the appropriate vocabulary to make this story engaging for adults and children. The language also has to function as a go-between, so that no matter who reads it, the same sense and message is conveyed. If it's too childish, adults will dismiss the story. If it's too mature, children will get bored. So the language itself has to appeal to the inner child of adult readers and the individual children who might read it. It's tricky, particularly when I feel myself starting to slip into 'too childish' mode, which I feel is almost unfair to children. To use overly simplified language would be to condescend to children who might read the story.

Translating this piece just makes me realize more and more how brilliant it is, and why virtually any literate person can enjoy it – Saint-Exupéry maintains this go-between language perfectly. Despite this, it's still difficult to translate fluidly; part of me understands the French on an inherent level, I get the sense of it very well, and I think that's the childish part of the writing. On the other hand, my more intellectual understanding of the words is the adult part of my brain and personality grasping it on a different level, so it's almost as though I've got two translations ready to go when I read.

Some specific examples will illustrate the challenge that the text's heteroglossia posed for the student in her translation and that served to bring that very feature into relief. One salient case was the French expression *les grandes personnes*. The student considered various possible renderings of the expression in English, such as 'adults' or 'big people', but felt that the former was too adult, whereas the latter was too childish. She settled on 'grown-ups', a felicitous choice that captures both adult and child language as an expression that children use among themselves and that adults use in conversation with children. Another instance involved translating the expression *chef-d'œuvre*, which the student rendered as 'masterpiece'. Though this word might be considered more characteristic of adult language, the student notes the value of such choices 'because they underline the utmost importance of what the narrator's talking about. Most of the words [in the passage] are childish, or at least not adult, but these words indicate that the child is learning to assign value to a thing as an adult would do.'

The student employed the term 'go-between' to characterize this feature of the narrator's voice in *The Little Prince*, echoing the MLA report's call for an approach to language study that teaches translingual competence and the ability to 'operate between languages'. She also remarked how the multiple voices inherent in this example of children's literature first became conceptually salient for her during the process of translation: 'I find the concept of language as a go-between force really interesting; in this case [i.e. her translation], the language is going between a variety of places: between French and English, between children and adults, between French child culture and American child culture.' The multilingual practice of translating a text of children's literature evidently served to heighten her awareness of the heteroglossic nature of language in general.

6.3.3 Transposing across modalities: musical to verbal

In the same course, an advanced student of Spanish chose to translate into English the lyrics, or more precisely, the different musical styles, of two different versions of a popular Mexican song, 'La Jaula de Oro' ('The Cage of Gold'). The original was recorded in 1984 by the popular norteño group Los Tigres del Norte, which was composed of Mexican immigrants to the United States based in San Jose, California, and the second version is a cover by the internationally renowned American-born singer of Mexican heritage Julieta Venegas, released in 2009. Due to copyright restrictions, we cannot reproduce the lyrics of the song, but readers will find them readily available on the Internet. For the purposes of our argument, we hope a content summary will suffice to convey the important points we wish to make. As the song title and the information provided above concerning the artists' provenance and immigrant status indicate, the text deals with the conflicted feelings that long-term, first-generation Mexican immigrants to the United States experience. The lyric persona sings of how he has lived in the United States for a decade illegally, without documentation. He then relates that his wife and children came to join him when the children were still young and that they have consequently forgotten their origins in Mexico. He stresses that he himself has not forgotten his origins, however, and longs for his homeland, but he laments the realization that, as an illegal immigrant, he can never return. He acknowledges that he has been able to make a decent living in the United States, but he questions the value of material well-being when it comes at the cost of restriction of mobility, the inability ever to return to his homeland: hence the paradoxical song title, 'The Cage of Gold'.

The lyrics of the original Los Tigres del Norte and the Julieta Venegas cover versions of the song are identical, except for one seemingly minor difference. The original version includes a brief exchange of spoken dialogue between a father and son, immediately following the chorus the first time it is sung. The father's line, spoken in Spanish, asks if his son would like the family to return to Mexico, and the son's response, in English, emphatically rejects any such suggestion: 'No way!' Venegas's cover version, significantly, leaves this exchange out. In her translations of the two different versions of the song, the student sought to convey in the verbal mode the different musical styles of each version.[3]

For her rendition of the original Los Tigres del Norte version, she composed a translation with a discernible, palpable rhythm (though not a strict, regular metre) and with subtle but salient rhymes, such as 'established'/'U.S.' and 'had'/'wetback'. But beyond these rhymes in English that the student created in her translation, she also preserved two rhyme pairs from the original lyrics unchanged: *papeles/ilegales* and *nacion/prision*. By retaining these few select terms from Spanish in her English translation, the student not only managed to include more instances of rhyme, she also emphasized the source culture of the text she was translating as well as her own text's hybrid status as a translation. Such a strategy is designated in translation theory as **borrowing**.[4] The lexical items she chose for this strategy are by and large Latinate cognates in English, so they pose no difficulty for readers who do not know Spanish. In addition, one particular translation choice the student made may also be considered a unique instance of borrowing, solely on account of her decision to use italics. Though the English spelling of the name of the country Mexico is identical to its spelling in Spanish, by italicizing the word as *Mexico*, the student indicated that it is to be pronounced in her translation in Spanish rather than in English. Collectively, all of the student's choices for her translation of the original Los Tigres del Norte version of the song – the palpable rhythm, the rhymes, and the selective use of borrowing – were intended to convey in verbal form the traditional *rancheros* musical style of the song. Moreover, her targeted use of borrowing allowed her to evoke the bilingual culture of Mexican immigrants to the United States for whom the song resonated so strongly at the time, echoing the tensions embodied in the bilingual spoken dialogue between father and son in the original version, which she reproduced unchanged.

In contrast, the student's translation of Venegas's twenty-first century cover version of the song avoided borrowing entirely and rendered the lyrics systematically into contemporary colloquial American English, without rhyme or any recognizable regular rhythm. The result displayed characteristics more typical of spoken language than song. As with her translation of the original Los Tigres del Norte version, the student sought not only to translate the Spanish lyrics into English but also to transpose the musical style of Venegas's cover version into the verbal medium. Her translation of the song title as 'The Golden

Cage' for her rendition of Venegas's cover version, as opposed to 'The Cage of Gold' for her rendition of the original version, exemplifies well the effect she achieved in her second translation.

In her commentary on this translation, the student explained her stylistic choices as intended to reflect the musical style of Venegas's cover version as more contemporary 'indie-pop', with a corresponding appeal to a larger global audience. Significantly, her decision to translate Venegas's version into contemporary colloquial American English therefore simultaneously reflects the status of (American) English as a global *lingua franca*. As the student noted in her commentary on this translation, the audience of the original 1980s version by Los Tigres del Norte consisted mainly of Mexican immigrants to the United States at the time. Venegas's 2009 cover version, however, resonated with a global audience, including second- and third-generation Latino descendants of immigrants to the United States from the 1980s as well as contemporary listeners throughout Latin America, in addition to learners of Spanish as a foreign language across the globe, such as the student herself. Its language and lyrics aside, Venegas's cover version has a musical style that is less recognizable as belonging to any one particular traditional culture and instead aspires to (and indeed achieved) international pop status. Her version's omission of the exchange of bilingual dialogue between father and son that features so prominently in the original, combined with its international 'indie-pop' style, signals a transition from a world where supposedly monolithic national languages once stood opposed to one another to one in which different languages and various modalities of expression intermesh to spawn innovation. The student's two different translations of the song's lyrics, different transpositions from the musical to the verbal, encapsulate that transition.

6.3.4 Transposing across modalities: verbal to pictorial

In an undergraduate course for future secondary school teachers of English at a large university in the United States, students read the short story 'New Year's Sacrifice' written in 1924 by the Chinese writer Lu Xun (1990). The class read the text in its English translation.[5] In the story, the narrator comes back to his home town after having been gone a number of years. The small town is busy preparing for the celebrations of the Lunar New Year. The narrator meets a woman, Xiang-Lin, whom he has not seen in many years and who has become ostracized by the townspeople. He tells the story of that woman and how her little boy was eaten up by a wolf, a story that in her despair she cannot help but tell again and again. The townspeople turn against her. She becomes the 'sacrificial meal' offered to the gods on New Year's Day to secure good luck and prosperity. The narrator's phrase 'can't say for sure' – a recurring refrain in his narrative – becomes, as he says, 'a useful phrase' that helps deflect any responsibility for the sad fate of this woman.

The students had been asked to transpose the narrative into a visual design that would capture their interpretation of the story. They drew the five visuals on the following pages in chalk on the blackboard. As each drawing captured and foregrounded a different aspect of the story, the students were asked to offer verbal interpretations of their drawings. Together with the teacher, they fleshed out the following interpretations.

In Figure 6.1, the symbolic representation of a large question mark combined with different font letters renders the narrator's uncertainty even more graspable than in the text. It makes uncertainty and indeterminacy almost a metaphysical principle of life itself – a meaning the students had not been aware of to that extent while reading the story. The circular representation of hell, life, death and heaven with a question mark in the middle feels like a vicious circle that stands for the prison of time (lunar year) within which human beings live their lives.

In Figure 6.2, the downward spiral of swirling words gives the question mark a dynamism that is again related to life itself through the words. However, because it is a spiral and not, say, a downward linear arrow, it translates nicely into visual expression the cyclical structure of the narrative that inevitably moves towards the end and the end of Xiang-Lin's life.

In Figure 6.3, the wolf's mask is strikingly ominous, with the first letter setting the scene in the forest, and at the same time laying all the responsibility and the guilt for the tragedy in Xiang-Lin's mouth: 'I was really dumb.' The pictorial representations allow for the conflation of the world and Xiang-Lin herself in the very story that she tells. The wolf becomes a creation of the storyteller.

In Figure 6.4, the star provides a cosmological representation of the story which harks back to the idea that we are dealing with moon, sun and stars and their annual cycles. Again these representations effectively capture the larger questions of life and death posed by the Lu Xun story.

Finally, in Figure 6.5, the New Year's dish with chopsticks makes it very clear that the words spoken by the protagonists in the story are like many instruments of consumption, and even instruments of sacrifice, verbally represented by utterances and pictorially by chopsticks. In the same manner as the wolf ate up the boy and the gods ate the dish, the student explained, the villagers 'ate' Xiang-Lin's story and 'sacrificed' her.

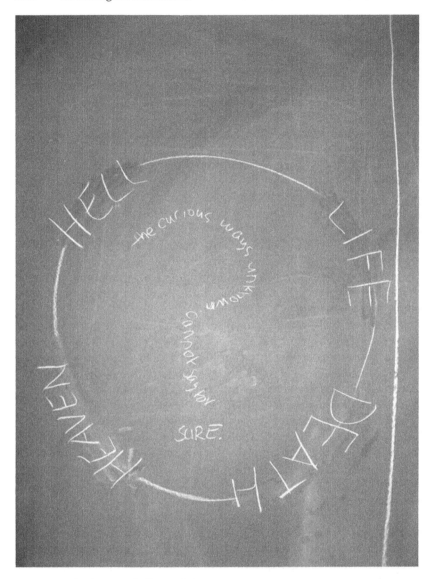

Figure 6.1 Student work: Example 1

Each transposition brought out the meaning potential of each form of representation and excluded others. For example, the visible shape of a question mark both illuminated the meaning of the story and narrowed it down. By narrowing it down, however, it opened other

Figure 6.2 Student work: Example 2

avenues of interpretation that were hidden behind the original story. Students got to understand that every linguistic translation, like their own cross-modal transpositions, is always a re-creation of another text, not just a deficient version of the original.

Figure 6.3 Student work: Example 3

6.3.5 Rekeying a text across historical contexts

Besides translation or transposition from one code or modality to another, multilingual practices can include rewritings in a different key, defined by Goffman as 'the set of conventions by which a given activity,

Figure 6.4 Student work: Example 4

one already meaningful in terms of some primary framework, is transformed into something patterned on this activity but seen by the participants to be something quite else' (1974: 44). In a fifth-semester German class – the bridge course to the upper division programme at the same university – students were asked to write a 300-word essay in

Figure 6.5 Student work: Example 5

prose or verse based on Heinrich Heine's poem 'Denk ich an Deutschland in der Nacht / so werde ich um den Schlaf gebracht' (When I think of Germany at night / I am deprived of sleep). In this poem, Heine contrasts his feelings with regard to Deutschland his homeland (*Heimat* = *die Mutter*) with Deutschland his fatherland (*Vaterland*): 'Nach

Deutschland lechzt' ich nicht so sehr / Wenn nicht die Mutter dorten wär' (I would not pine so much for Germany / were my mother not there). The prompt was:

Heinrich Heine expressed his loyalty to his German fatherland and his concern about his German homeland in the poem 'When I think of Germany at night'. Write about your relation to America / the United States in the form of a poem or an essay. Start with the words: 'When I think of America at night ...'

The teacher explained that the students might have a different relation to their *Vaterland*, the United States, which they feel pride for or anger against, than their *Heimat*, America, which they feel homesick for when they travel abroad. The teacher hoped that the students would play with the German frames *Vaterland* and *Heimat* to reflect on themselves as Americans. While all the students expressed a strong and unconditional love for their country or for the American dream that it represented, they had difficulty espousing Heine's position of self-imposed exile in France. The schematic distinction he makes (HOMELAND IS NOT FATHERLAND) seemed not only foreign but inapplicable to many of them.

One Californian student started with poised rationality: 'When I think of America at night – a very interesting concept and one that I would have never paid attention to if I had not been asked to do this assignment.' An immigrant from China wrote a eulogy in verse of his host country: 'When I think of America at night, / I am filled with pride and gratitude. / Although my heart doesn't always laugh, / My life is full of satisfaction.' A student from Texas equated love of country with obedience to its rules: 'I don't think of the USA at night, for the USA is my country, where I live. I love my country like my parents. I am a good son or citizen when I follow the rules that they give me, and likewise, when I see that they don't follow their and our rules, I must criticize them.' One student acknowledged ambivalence: 'When I think of America at night, I don't know what I should feel. It is no secret that this country is no longer as beautiful as it once was.' And another characterized the assignment as a very German assignment, writing in verse: 'When I think of America at night, / Then I think back to Germany. / Only from a German perspective / Is it possible for me to speak about America.' Class discussion led to questioning the questioner and the very positioning of the teacher who had chosen to give them this assignment.

6.3.6 Transcribing experience across perceptual modes

Finally, multilingual activities can include the exploration of the multisensory apprehension of various languages and their iconic and ideological value. In a freshman seminar on language and identity at the same university in the United States, students were given the following prompt: 'Write an essay (750w) about your linguistic experiences and heritage.' We examine here the essay of 19-year-old Judith, who was born in the Netherlands, moved to the United States at age seven and at the time was a freshman in college. Her essay was subsequently the object of an interview with the teacher/researcher. Composed in English by a non-native English speaker and multilingual writer, it starts like this:

The intersection: A language history
Finally, I have one of my own. I found a language of my own in Paris, of course. Paris, where only life changing things happen and most good ideas start. I'd first accessed it without understanding in a classroom. There it had belonged to no one, a lost language ill at home in the stuffy California air. But here, French was wedged comfortably between the cobblestones and my flowered dress. It was *mine* ...

Judith goes on to characterize her other languages: Spanish, 'spoken quickly and muttered like the wind'; Dutch, her mother tongue and the language of her parents; English, 'my outward voice'. The end of her essay summarizes the multiple sensory experiences provided by her various languages: 'Despite the outward Anglicism, I dream in tongues. I dream of drunken twilights and of overripe guavas and crinkled recipes and stacked notebooks. In all truth, I live at the intersection.'

After she wrote this essay, Judith (J) was interviewed by Claire Kramsch, teacher and researcher (R). Here are excerpts from this interview, which took place in English.

R: So how would you say in French: 'here, French was wedged comfortably between the cobblestones and my flowered dress. It was *mine* ...'?
J : er ... well ... 'ici, le francais ... no, la langue française était calée confortablement entre les pavés et ma robe à fleurs. Elle était *mienne* ...' (...)
R: and how is your relationship to Spanish?
J: Spanish didn't sort of invade my body the way that French did
R: and English?
J: English is important. I need it. Like, it's like I know I need it, kind of like you need broccoli. I need to eat broccoli, it's a vegetable, it's good for me. But like I don't always want it you know ...
R: it's good for you? (laughs)
J: yeah, I mean, if I can argue something well in English, if I can write something well in English, and I mean, that's what I was known for in [my high school] ... I just don't want to allow [English] to invade too much. I feel like I need to keep it at a distance ... in order to allow myself to ... stay a Dutch person in America, as opposed to an American person who occasionally visits the Netherlands and

was born there. I don't want to be an American born in the Netherlands. I want to be a Dutch girl in America.

Judith has an embodied relation to each of her languages. She 'dreams in tongues' – as if her body were possessed by a multilingual holy spirit. She talks about French 'invading her body'. She associates French with her first mature experiences and Spanish with the overripe guavas and the green mountains of Costa Rica. 'When I close my eyes and begin to think in Spanish, I think of green, lots of green', 'forests, earth, wind, and freedom just out of bounds, an enticing mystery'. And English is healthy food.

Living at the intersection is a metaphor for her multilingual self, but it is also a metaphor for the essay itself: the neat row of paragraphs dedicated to each of her languages and the punch line that juxtaposes metonymic equivalences, paratactically linked – 'drunken twilights, and overripe guavas, and crinkled recipes, and stacked notebooks'. No unified self in all of this, but a series of parallel lives, chiastic images (American in the Netherlands, Dutch in America) or pieces of a puzzle, cumulative and overlapping timescales of experiences: of body (French, Spanish) and mind (English), of her past (Dutch) and her future (English), of her lived inward voice and face (French) and her 'outward voice', or 'outer face' (English). In the same manner as she herself forms the link between all these metonymies, her French-speaking self is positioned at the intersection of the old and the new, Paris and Amsterdam: 'French was wedged comfortably between the cobblestones and my flowered dress.'

In fact, when asked to translate some of her writing into French, Judith's repair of 'le francais' to 'la langue française', with its switch from the masculine to the feminine gender, contributes to her possessive embrace of French and her identification with the French language. This move is one aspect of a synaesthetic relation to language that suffuses the whole essay. In synaesthesia research (e.g. Lvovich, 2012), synaesthesia refers not only to a transfer from the verbal to the visual mode – for example, Judith *sees* the Spanish language as green, just as Rimbaud saw vowels in colours (1871/1993) and Nabokov saw letters in various hues (1991: 74), but also to a transsemiotization of sight into feelings and emotions. For Judith, green is not just a colour but a feeling of earth, wind and freedom. Her languages offer a combination of various perceptual modes: the crinkled texture of Dutch recipes, the heaviness of English notebooks, the smell of overripe guavas, the sensation of the wind, the sight of a flowered dress wedged between the cobblestones – all evoked by the sound and feel of each linguistic code.

6.4 Discussion

The national *raison d'être* of foreign language study, with its ideology of one national language = one national literature = one national culture, no longer corresponds to the global reality of our times. This does not mean that it is not worthwhile to study standard national languages and cultures, only that the focus can no longer be merely on formal linguistic systems and their instantiation in monolingual conversations and monolingual texts. If, as Blommaert suggests, we consider the study of foreign languages to be the study of the multiple semiotic resources – grammatical, lexical, pragmatic, stylistic and discursive resources, which vary according to genre, medium and modality and are used by native and non-native speakers and writers to make meaning – then we need a different pedagogy. Pedagogies focused on static linguistic systems and rules of usage correspond to an era of modern nationalism. What our post-modern global communications era requires is a pedagogy focused on fluid relationships between different ways of meaning-making.

However, the national characteristics traditionally associated with native speakers have not disappeared just because the national native speaker has been discredited as the exclusive target of foreign language pedagogy. As we can see from the multilingual practices described above, national myths or stereotypes have become attached to the languages themselves. Languages in a sense have become emblems or condensation symbols that students apply to their learning experience. The Germanness of a German translation is changed into Japaneseness by drawing on cultural icons that evoke 'Japan' for an American reader's sensibility. The resonance of various languages in the subjectivity of a multilingual student like Judith takes on the stereotypical characteristics attached to national speakers themselves. She associated English with Anglo-Saxon pragmatism, Dutch with hominess, French with sexiness, Spanish with sensuousness. For foreign language study, such a mythification of language on the one hand opens up opportunities for creativity and hybridity on the part of the students, but on the other hand it can create difficulties for the translation teacher intent on teaching faithfulness to the original. The challenge is to channel students' imaginations out of exclusively national frames and to interrogate the frames themselves.

One way of doing this is not only to engage in but also to reflect on the multilingual practices that do away with the exclusive focus on the one code to bear meaning. By diversifying codes, modes, modalities and styles and systematically exploring their boundaries and their contact zones, we can raise students' awareness of the meaning-making processes at work in the construction of social and cultural experience – including the surreptitious use of stereotypes. Whether these are class stereotypes as in the translation of the Rowling text, age stereotypes as in St Exupéry's text, cultural stereotypes as in the Mexican ranchero song or national stereotypes as in the transposition of the Heine poem, multilingual practices open up opportunities to examine critically the subjective dimensions of multilingualism (Kramsch, 2009) and what is gained and lost in the process.

Notes

1. Rowling, J. K. and Fritz, K., *Harry Potter und der Stein der Weisen.*
2. For purposes of comparison, readers are encouraged to refer to Rowling J. K., *Harry Potter and the Philosopher's Stone.*
3. Unfortunately, due to copyright restrictions, we cannot reproduce our data here. In order fully to appreciate what the student accomplished with her different translations, we encourage readers to find and listen to both versions of the song, which are readily available (in several versions) on the Internet, using the artists' names and the song title as search terms. Furthermore, readers interested in seeing our data are encouraged to contact the authors directly.
4. Traditionally, borrowing has been employed to compensate for extralinguistic incompatibilities between languages, for example when a new technology is invented or a concept is unknown in a target language culture. It can also serve to add some of the 'flavour' of a source language culture into a translated text (Vinay & Darbelnet, 2004: 129), as when Russian words such as *datcha, apparatchik* or *intelligentsia* are preserved in a translation. It was in the spirit of this latter use of borrowing that the student translated the1980s Tigres del Norte version of her source text.
5. We present this activity here, even though it did not take place in a foreign language classroom, because it could easily be adapted to the teaching of foreign languages.

References

Anderson, B. (1983). *Imagined Communities: Reflections on the Origin and Spread of Nationalism.* London: Verso.

Auer, P. and Li Wei (eds.) (2007). *Handbook of Multilingualism and Multiculturalism.* Berlin: Mouton de Gruyter.

Blommaert, J. (2010). *The Sociolinguistics of Globalization.* Cambridge: Cambridge University Press.

Canagarajah, S. (2007). Lingua franca English, multilingual communities, and language acquisition. *The Modern Language Journal,* 91(5), 921–37.

Canagarajah, S. (2011). Codemeshing in academic writing: identifying teachable strategies of translanguaging. *The Modern Language Journal,* 95(3), 401–17.

Cenoz, J. and Gorter, D. (2011). Focus on multilingualism: a study in trilingual writing. Special issue of *The Modern Language Journal,* 95(3), 356–69.

Cook, V. J. (1999). Going beyond the native speaker in language teaching, *TESOL Quarterly,* 33(2), 185–209.

Cope, B. and Kalantzis, M. (eds.) (2000). *Multiliteracies.* London: Routledge.

Davies, A. (1991). *The Native Speaker in Applied Linguistics.* Edinburgh: Edinburgh University Press.

Firth, A. and Wagner, J. (1997). On discourse, communication, and (some) fundamental concepts in SLA research. *The Modern Language Journal,* **81,** 285–300.

García, O., Bartlett, L. and Kleifgen, J. (2007). From biliteracy to pluriliteracies. In P. Auer and Li Wei (eds.), *Handbook of Multilingualism and Multiculturalism* (pp. 207–28). Berlin: Mouton de Gruyter.

Goffman, E. (1974). *Frame Analysis.* New York: Harper & Row.

Heiser, K. A. (1912). Zur Einführung. *Japanische Märchen.* Straubing: Attenkofersche Verlagsbuchhandlung. Retrieved from http://gutenberg.spiegel.de/buch/2426/2 [Accessed 28 October 2013].

Herder, J. G. von (1772/1960). *Sprachphilosophische Schriften.* Hamburg: Felix Meiner Verlag.

Humboldt, W. von (1836/1988). *On Language: The Diversity of Human Language Structure and Its Influence on the Mental Development of Mankind,* trans. P. Heath. Cambridge: Cambridge University Press.

Kramsch, C. (1997). The privilege of the non-native speaker. *PMLA,* **112**(3), 359–69.

Kramsch, C. (2009). Grammar games and bilingual blends. *PMLA,* **124**(3), 887–95.

Kramsch, C. (2013). The translingual and transcultural imagination. In J. L. Plews and B. Schmenk (eds.), *Traditions and Transitions: Curricula for German Studies* (pp. 21–36). Waterloo, ON: Wilfrid Laurier University Press.

Lvovich, N. (2012). 'The Gift': synesthesia in translingual texts. *L2 Journal,* **4,** 214–29.

Makoni, S. and Pennycook, A. (2007). *Disinventing and Reconstructing Languages.* Clevedon: Multilingual Matters.

MLA AdHoc Committee on Foreign Languages (2007). Foreign language and higher education: new structures for a changed world. *Profession 2007,* 234–45.

Nabokov, V. (1991). *The Gift.* New York: Vintage International.

Rampton, B. (1990). Displacing the 'native speaker': expertise, affiliation and inheritance. *ELT Journal,* **44**(2), 97–101.

Rimbaud, A. (1871/1993). Voyelles. In S. Bernard and A. Guyaux (eds.), *Rimbaud Œuvres* (pp. 405–7). Paris: Classiques Garnier.

Rowling, J. K. (1997). *Harry Potter and the Sorcerer's Stone.* New York: Arthur A. Levine Books (Scholastic). [German edition: *Harry Potter und der Stein der Weisen,* trans. Klaus Fritz, Hamburg: Carlsen, 1998.]

Saussure, F. de (1916/1959). *Course in General Linguistics,* ed. C. Bally and A. Sechehaye, trans. W. Baskin. New York: McGraw-Hill.

Vinay, J. P. and Darbelnet, J. (1958/2004). A methodology for translation. In L. Venuti (ed.), *The Translation Studies Reader* (pp. 128–43). New York and London: Routledge.

Xun, L. (1990). New Year's sacrifice. *Diary of a Madman and Other Stories,* trans. W. A. Lyell. Honolulu: University of Hawai'i Press.

7 Language choices and ideologies in the bilingual classroom

Janet M. Fuller

7.1 Introduction

This chapter looks at the language choices made by children in a German–English bilingual school and the role they play in the construction of ideologies about language and the social categories of speakers of particular languages. This research is done within a social constructionist framework, meaning that social realities are not considered fixed but are discursively produced (Foucault, 1972: 49). Speaker identities are presented as socially constructed, as evidenced by the multiple and shifting identities individuals may perform (Kroskrity, 2000; Blackledge & Pavlenko, 2001; Bucholtz & Hall, 2005, 2008; Heller, 2007; Fuller, 2012). In this chapter, these identities will be shown to be part of a framework of language ideologies constructed by pre-teen speakers in a bilingual school. According to Errington (2000: 115), the term 'language ideology' is used for dealing with issues of use and structure relevant to their social contexts. However, as noted by many researchers (Gal, 1998; Woolard, 1998; Blackledge & Pavlenko, 2002; Kroskirty, 2004), language ideologies are rarely just about language, but are about the political systems in which they operate. Here, the connection between language and nationality is examined.

This approach to the study of language ideology focuses on how ways of speaking not only represent ideologies but also shape them. Specifically, I examine how the use of German, English and bilingual discourse are part of a construction of language ideologies. These data illustrate that there are multiple, and sometimes conflicting, ideologies which emerge in this setting. At the same time, hegemony is an important aspect of language ideology. Hegemony can be defined as power which is achieved through consent; asymmetries of power are naturalized and accepted across social groups, whether the members of those groups benefit from the hegemonic ideologies or not. There are clearly hegemonic ideologies which need to be made explicit and addressed in terms of their consequences for the education and social development of children in bilingual schooling.

A hegemonic language ideology, which is pervasive in many nations, including Germany, is normative monolingualism (Heller, 1999; Bauman & Briggs, 2003; Gal, 2006a, 2006b; Hansen-Thomas, 2007; Fuller, 2012). This ideology holds that monolingualism is the 'natural' state of being for a nation and the communities of individuals who reside within it. In Germany, there is a caveat for elite bilingualism; if the languages other than German which are spoken are prestigious – such as English or French – then speaking these languages is considered beneficial. However, in all cases, speakers of two languages should keep them strictly separate, which means that bilingual discourse is seen as deviant behaviour.

The perceived deviance of bilingual discourse is rooted in the link between languages and identity categories, and essentialist ideas about identity. If languages are thought to index a national identity – for example, speaking German indexes a German identity, speaking English indexes a US American one – and these identities are conceptualized as fixed, bounded and mutually exclusive categories, then speaking a mixture of German and English is seen as a challenge to not just a prescriptively acceptable way of speaking but also a prescriptively acceptable way of *being*. It is in this way that the language ideologies here are not just about languages but also about the boundaries of the ethnic and national groups they index.

The challenge to normative monolingualism shown in these data is an alternative ideology which values linguistic pluralism and creates valid identity categories that do not coincide with essentialist national identities. In this perspective, individuals may claim membership in two or more national categories; significantly, the membership is not based on grounds of 'ethnicity', or at least not solely, but rather on linguistic and social behaviour. Alternatively, speakers may identify with a broader identity category (e.g. European *Weltmensch* – citizen of the world), and/or position themselves in terms of the fusion of different national, cultural and ethnic backgrounds. In terms of language, this ideology values knowledge and experience with all languages, without a sole focus on socially powerful languages. Bilingual discourse may be a way of constructing such an identity and ideology.

This does not mean, of course, that German and English lose their value, although it may change the sociopragmatic meanings of these codes. In this analysis, I will show how, in the transnational context of one bilingual classroom, the associations of German and English as indices to national identities are not their primary social meanings.

What it means to be a German speaker or an English speaker is both discursively constructed and interactionally situated, which suggests that the meanings of these codes shift and develop, but the pattern of use does not form a picture of language as a symbol of national identity.

7.2 Data and setting

The school where these data were collected is the John F. Kennedy (JFK) School in Berlin, Germany, a German–American school which has been in existence since 1960. The researcher spent two days a week at the school from October 2005 to June 2006, participating in the classroom as a volunteer as well as observing and making recordings of the children in her role as a researcher.

The population this school serves has changed over the past few decades along with the population of Berlin. At its inception, there was a steady population of children from the United States whose parents were in the US military and were stationed in Berlin, and the other children at the school were German. As the population of US military families dwindled after reunification in 1989, the student body became increasingly international, not just German and American, with English speakers coming from a variety of countries and contexts, not just those who spoke English at home with their US family members. Most of the children at the JFK School had some personal connection to the English language, but the nature of these connections varied widely. Only a few of the children came from families in which both parents were German; for those that did, often their parents had themselves attended the JFK School or lived outside Germany, often in English-speaking countries. Sometimes the children had themselves lived in the United States, Scotland, India, South Africa, etc. and learned English there. Many of the children came from transnational families and had English as one of the languages spoken in the home. Still others were the offspring of diplomats and international businesspeople from all over the world who had attended other English-medium schools in other countries. For these children, English was destined to be the language of their education, although perhaps never their home language or the language of the wider community where they lived. Thus, the children had a diverse set of experiences with and connections to English. Similarly, their knowledge of German varied widely. Many had always lived in Germany and German was their dominant language; others had always lived in Germany but claimed another language as their dominant language. Many others had moved to Germany more recently and were in various stages of acquiring German.

The structure of the school rests on the categorization of the pupils into English Mother Tongue and German Mother Tongue groups; the English Mother Tongue children had German as their 'Partner Tongue', and vice versa. (Therefore, English Mother Tongue (EMT) and German Partner Tongue (GPT) refer to the same group of students, as does German Mother Tongue (GMT) and English Partner Tongue (EPT); to avoid confusion, however, I will refer to the children by their mother tongue designations.) Each class in the elementary grades is composed of children from both categories, and they do social studies, math, science, etc. as one group, in either English or German according to the dominant language of their classroom teacher. For language arts instruction in English and German, the children are separated according to Mother Tongue status. Because of their varied backgrounds, however, there were many children who were categorized as EMT who did not have English as their dominant language – in many cases they were dominant in German, but in a few instances it was a third language. The GMT half was equally diverse; although these children did tend to speak German as their dominant language, many of them had also learned another language in early childhood (English, Serbian, Romanian, Italian, etc.). Thus, while the children were divided into two discrete groups, their language proficiencies in both English and German formed a continuum.

The language ideology constructed through this organization involves elite bilingualism, but also the idea that individuals are, or at least should be, categorizable as having one 'mother tongue'. Ironically, because the goal of the programme is proficiency in both languages, this ideology involves the erasure of the idea that individuals might be equally proficient in both languages. It should be pointed out, however, that starting in the fifth grade (when most children are around the age of ten), some children were classified as 'Double Mother Tongue', so through this there was recognition of and value placed on high proficiency in both languages.

Another ideological issue embedded in this school structure had to do with what it meant to have a language as one's 'mother tongue'. There were some instances of children who spoke German as their home language and showed transfer from German in their English in terms of both phonology and grammar, but were classified as EMT because they had been educated in English before coming to the JFK School and had had little or no literacy training in German. One teacher described one of these children to me as 'having no native language' despite his performance of spoken German fulfilling any criteria I could imagine for being 'native'.

Overall, then, the structure of the school curriculum supported two aspects of language ideology. First, it supported an ideology of elite bilingualism as being asymmetrical in terms of the two languages; the norm is to have a 'mother tongue' and a 'partner tongue'. Second, a true 'mother tongue' involves not just oral competence but also literacy skills.

A further ideology perpetuated by the school, sometimes explicitly and often implicitly, was the ideology of the value of keeping languages strictly separate. In some classrooms, this was a strict rule, in others merely an expectation. However, there were no school-wide practices or events, either formal or informal, which endorsed bilingual discourse, except for translation from one language to another. As I will discuss below, however, the fourth-grade classroom I focus on in this chapter did have teachers who encouraged the use of both languages in a variety of ways.

The classroom to be discussed here was a fourth-grade classroom, containing children around the age of nine. There were two teachers over the course of the year for this group of students, because the original teacher left at the end of December and was replaced. Both of these teachers were anglophones from the United States; I will present more detailed information about each teacher individually below. The structure of the instruction was that this classroom teacher taught them all of their subjects (math, social studies, science) in English. This teacher was also responsible for the EMT instruction for the children in this class and another fourth-grade class, and the EPT instruction of the GMT children in these same two fourth-grade classes. Thus, my recordings include children who had this teacher as their main classroom teacher, but also children from the other classroom who came to have their English instruction. I do not have recordings from German instruction, as all of the children (both GMT and GPT) went to another classroom for German language arts.

Both of the teachers in this classroom embraced bilingualism. For the first half of the year, a male teacher I will call Mr Harvey was the teacher; he was in his second year of teaching at the JFK School and had been taking evening classes in German during his time in Berlin. Although his instruction was primarily in English, he often used German with the children and had no objection to their use of German to him or each other, as shown in Example 1 below. Here we see that Mr Harvey accepts an answer provided in German by repeating it with an emphatic *ja* 'yes', and then repeating this answer in English. Although he does retreat into the official language of instruction (not incidentally also his dominant language), the use of German is framed as acceptable linguistic behaviour. (See the Appendix for a key to the transcription conventions used throughout this chapter.)

Example 1

T = teacher, S = student
T: /The Huguenots came from (.) where please Thea./
S: /French. Ahhh **Frankreich. Frankreich. Ja.**/
     'France. France. Yes.'
T: /**Frankreich, ja** they came from France./
     'France, yes'   (4ATKS5x)[1]

Midway through the school year, Mr Harvey received and accepted a job offer in the United States. He was replaced by 'Ms Zeman', a female teacher who had worked in a Spanish–English bilingual programme in the United States and had also lived and worked in other countries outside the USA, but was not a speaker of German. Despite this limitation Ms Zeman was very open to the children using German when working together, even during English instruction. In our discussion of this, she told me that her philosophy was that if they are on-task, she did not care what language they were using. As the semester progressed, she learned some German and began using it with the children, as shown in Example 2. Although she only repeats one of the words used by the children, such utterances are an indication that she understands their German contributions and does not prohibit the use of that language.

Example 2

T = teacher, S1= first student, S2 = second student. The teacher is
    working on multiplication using flashcards with a group of chil-
    dren; she shows S1 a card with a problem on it.
T: Ok Joschke this one is for you.
S1: yeah
S2: oh **das ist einfach.**
    'oh, that's easy.'
T: sshh don't say **einfach** because it might not be for other people
    and that makes them feel bad.
    'easy'   (4MTKS4x)

Although the teacher is objecting to an utterance by the child in this example, the objection is not based on the choice of code (German), which she repeats, but on the content: she is requesting that the children don't say that certain problems are easy, so as not to discourage children who might be having difficulty with the problem. This acceptance of bilingual discourse by authority figures in the classroom contributes to the construction of language ideologies because it lends legitimacy to an ideology of linguistic pluralism. This allows the children to openly function as bilinguals in this space, which means that linguistic behaviour that challenges normative monolingualism becomes public.

Before turning to the data and how they show the construction of language ideologies through code choice, I should say a few words about my role in this classroom. I was introduced to the children as a researcher of bilingual children, and this aspect of my role was emphasized through the distribution of consent forms and subsequent recording in the classroom. The presence of the recording equipment was exciting for the children, and they would often ask to be recorded, or (infrequently) shy away from interactions which were being recorded. However, I was not constantly recording, and, regardless of whether a recorder was running, I was acting the part of a teacher's aide. There was a high level of parental volunteerism at the JFK School; in fact, there were often periods during which there were one or two other volunteers (parents of children in the classroom) present in the classroom at the same time as I. So, while the children did sometimes orient towards the recording equipment as something outside of their normal experience in the classroom, my presence was easily accepted as another volunteer. As an adult and a native speaker of English, I was an authority figure – one without the high level of authority possessed by the classroom teacher, but nonetheless someone they treated more like a teacher than a peer. But while my presence easily fitted into the usual educational context, the recording was outside of this, and in some instances the children clearly performed for the recorder. For instance, at the end of one recording, during which two boys had been going about their business as usual, suddenly one of the boys grabbed the recorder and, speaking directly into it, introduced himself and asked his friend '**Was ist Dein Name?**' (What is your name?). Thus, there is no consistent interpretation of the effect of my presence or, more importantly, the presence of the audio-recording equipment; different children oriented towards it or ignored it at different times and in different ways.

7.3 Language choice, classroom identities and language ideologies

As stated above, the hegemonic ideology in this setting was elite bilingualism, which is attained through bilingualism in languages that have social prestige, and also in keeping these languages separate to maintain their value. In the next section, I will discuss the many challenges to this ideology; here, I will present data that show how this ideology was reproduced in the classroom.

7.3.1 German as the peer code

The sociopragmatic meaning of German rested on its status as the language of the wider community. While German could be an index of national belonging, it was more likely a means of constructing peer-group membership in this setting. This meaning is constructed time and time again through switching to German for off-task discussion. There are two broad patterns here. First, when children are doing group work in English, German is often used to comment on and frame the English text they are producing. This is commonplace among both EMT and GMT children, as shown in Examples 3 and 4 respectively. In both of these examples, all of the talk is on-task, but English is used to provide suggestions for the text to be written, while German is used to discuss how they complete their assignment.

Example 3

Millie (M), Anna (A) and Brianna (B) (all EMT children) are working on a poster about swans; Anna is writing.

A: Trumpeter swans are white with black bills and black feet
B: They have orange feet
M: And they are so much bigger than any bird (.) he had ever seen before (.) okay! (.) they are (.) so much bigger than any- (.) than most birds
A: They are bigger than most /birds!/
M: /birds/
M: U:h Anna (.) **du hast einen Fehler gemacht, was hat Brianna gesagt**? (.) It says, like, their call sounds like a trumpeter swan (.) not they are call sounds like a trumpeter swan!
     'Uh Anna, you made a mistake, what did Brianna say?'
A: **Ok wie schreibt man das dann**, Brianna, what is it?
     'Okay, how do you write that then,'
B: Um, uh
A: **Hier** (.) **Ach so jetzt** 'Here (.) okay now'   (4MTKS2g)

Example 4

Max (M), Leon (L) and Friedrich (F) (all GMT children) are working on a poster for their project about foxes; they are beginning a new section about fox families.

M: **Also, ich schreib**
     'Okay, I'll write'
L: **Also**, families, (1) **schreib** families.
     'Okay, families, (1) write families.'

F: Foxes xxx xx xxx
M: **Wird** families **so geschrieben?**
     'Is this how you write "families"?'
L: Yeah
L: **Doch, glaub schon**
     'Yes, I think so'
M: **Okay, was soll ich hinschreiben?**
     'Okay, what should I write?'
F: **Keine Ahnung**
     'No idea'
M: Foxes just attack if they have a family
L: **Nein, das ist Unsinn. Das ist** weird. **Also, uhm**, Youngs, uhm,
     'No, that's nonsense. That's weird. Well, uhm, youngs, uhm,'
F: Fox, foxes (breed) eight to ten baby foxes.
L: In one birth   (4PTKS2b)

Second, when the children have conversations that are not about their school work, they also switch to German, as in Examples 5 (EMT) and 6 (GMT). In Example 5, the boys finish a task and move on to a personal conversation; in Example 6, we see some of the framing of the English task similar to that in the above examples in Thea's first utterance, but also a switch to German for off-task talk.

Example 5

M and A are working on a story they are writing together; as this excerpt begins they are finishing off the sections they have been working on.
M: Ka::y (.) Fini:shed.
A: (1) Oh ka:y
A: Let's see. (1) eh- (.) eh- Mine eh (.) down.(1) **Gestern hab ich was gekauft.**
     'I bought something yesterday.'
M: (1) **Was denn?**
     'What?'
A: **Ein Vide:o** (.) **und das Telefon** (.) **und dieses** /xxxx/
     'A video and a telephone and this xxx'   (5 MTKS 5b)

Example 6

Thea (T) and Anita (A) are working on a poster in English for their project about chocolate. Although much of the conversation is in English (possibly because I am sitting with them and participating in the conversation), at one point Thea laughs and shouts out **Der Joschke**

hat gepo:ppelt ('Joschke picked his nose'). The following conversation follows this by a few minutes.

T: **Nein, schreib einfach**, cocoa beans are used for money, for cocoa beans (.) you can buy uh:
      'No, write simply,'

A: From cocoa beans you can buy (produce)

T: From cocoa beans you can buy a:ll things Ha {laughs}

A: Four cocoa beans you

T: **Er hat schon wieder in der Nase gebohrt!**
      'He picked his nose again!'   (4PTKS2g)

What becomes clear through these excerpts is that peer talk is not only about solidarity; it also involves arguments, confrontation, taunts and teasing. Switching to German is drawing on the authority of German as the language of the wider community, the language for regular discourse – English has power as the language of school and as an international language, but this is not the kind of power that is drawn on when engaged in jockeying for position with one's peers. There is evidence for the power of German for confrontations from several examples of this behaviour from children who did not claim proficiency in German. A case in point is Eva, an EMT girl. Although Eva has lived in Berlin all her life and speaks fluent German, she explicitly identifies as an English speaker, and I heard her deny proficiency in German on a number of occasions. Despite this overt positioning of herself as uncomfortable with the German language, during this recording, which is only 22 minutes in length, she switches to German to disagree with her friend Anke (with whom she is working on math problems) or to confront other peers in no fewer than 12 exchanges. Her utterances include several outbursts to boys who try to mess with the recorder (**lass doch mal!** 'leave it alone!', **Nein, hör auf!** 'No, stop it!'). In addition to using German as a type of power code, she also uses German with Anke in utterances in which she is asking for help (**Was soll ich machen?** 'What should I do?) or complaining about how difficult math is (**Mann, aber ich weiss nicht wie das geht** 'Man, but I don't know how to do this' and **Scheisse! Warte, nein!** 'Shit! No, wait!'). This shows an overall pattern of tapping into the power of German as a peer code which is the most suitable way to negotiate relationships with one's classmates.

An important aspect of this use of German as a peer code is that it is not a construction of German national identity. Eva was not the only child who frequently used German with her peers, even in cases in which the peers had English as a home language, and she also discussed her own identities as explicitly and emphatically not German. So the ideology being constructed here is an interesting one; the German language is bleached of national meaning; there is a disconnect between language and nationality. Alternatively, it may be that nationality is not an important identity category in their worlds, a topic which will be taken up again below.

7.3.2 *The value of English*

English in this setting is sometimes used for peer interactions among children who identify as dominant in English. But while German draws on the power of its status as the peer code, which is linked to its status as the language of the wider community, English draws on its status as the language of their schooling. In this way, I have argued elsewhere, English is linked to membership in the educated elite because it is the key to their success in school (Fuller, 2012). This is most commonly seen in interactions which involve the teacher (or me in my role as a teacher's aide); in other words, in situations in which the children are performing their roles as good students rather than creating solidarity with their peers.

Examples 7 and 8 illustrate this. These examples are excerpts from a recording (also shown in Example 6) in which three GMT girls, Thea, Anita and Luci, were making a poster about their research on the history of chocolate. I was working closely with their group on this, helping them to organize their information and write it in English on the poster board. Although, of course, there was some discussion among the three girls and between one or more of the girls and other students in the class that was not about academic achievement, much of their behaviour was geared towards performing their roles as good students. They all make utterances which are displays of knowledge, and they compete for the opportunity to write on the poster, to determine what is to be included and to flaunt their own proficiency in English or mock another's lack of proficiency. For instance, at one point Anita is writing 'how chocolate spread through Europe' and says ***Du musst mir buchstabieren,*** *how* ('You have to spell [it] for me, how'), and Thea proceeded to spell the word by pronouncing the letters H – O – W first in German, then in English, and then shouting to any listening classmates, ***Anita weiss nicht wie man 'how' schreibt!*** ('Anita doesn't know how to write "how"!').

It is important to note not only that these three girls were categorized as GMT but also that they were among the few children in the class who did not have a native English-speaking parent and had never lived in an English-speaking country. While they were doing fine at using English for academic purposes, none of them had EMT speakers in their close friendship groups, and they used relatively little English in their peer interactions.

In Examples 7 and 8, we see how these girls use English to perform their student identities. Although there are some switches to German, they are valiant in their efforts to negotiate this task in English. Although this is undoubtedly in part due to my presence and status as an English-speaking authority, as well as to the fact that their language choices are being recorded, it is not a forced choice. They know that I speak German, and in many contexts are rebellious about language choice; thus, their choices must be interpreted as part of the identities they are constructing in this on-going interaction. Their use of English is not driven by their perceived need to use this language to communicate; they are playing the role of the good student, and that role is carried out in English.

Example 7

R = the researcher, T = Thea, A = Anita, L = Luci
R: So remember, you're supposed to be thinking about categories
S: Okay um
R: You were talking about
L: (Four) cocoa beans
R: which I think is very interesting /thing/
A: /cocoa beans?/
R: could be used to buy a pumpkin (.) what else (.) so (.) maybe one of your categories could be things that (1) you can use chocolate for. (.) you can make chocolate bars, you can make cocoa you can xxx (.) you can use it to tra:de for other things
T: Hey we can (.) we can write facts on the most famous (.) um white (.) um (.) ah chocolate houses where the (.) where the <u>whites</u> chocolate houses (.) **und dann, das die uhm, das auch** chocolate **zum trinken war**
     'and then, that the uhm, that chocolate was also for drinking'
A: **Ooh kann ich einfach das hinschreiben?**
     'Oh, can I just write that down?'
R: Let's just do that.
A: If you write (.) if you write this (.) you know what um how um choco/late/ is made like this.
A: /Yeah./   (4PTKS2g)

Example 8

R = the researcher, T = Thea, A = Anita
T: Yeah **du kannst** (2) you can (.) you can just write the travel that chocolate (.) or then, when the chocolate (1) went from Spain to Ital-
     'Yeah, you can'

R: Italy
T: Italy /to France/ to Dutch (.) and finally to Germany!
A: /to France/   (4PTKS2g)

These examples show that English, unsurprisingly, is closely linked to academic achievement and less integral to peer interactions. Although both languages can be used to negotiate identities and powerful stances, they differ in how they are used for such positioning.

7.4 Bilingual discourse and the ideology of diversity

In all of the examples given above, the ideologies reproduced with choices of either German or English include the strict separation of languages as part of elite bilingualism. Both English and German carry symbolic power, and their separation is key to their authority within this ideological frame.

Yet other ideologies are also made apparent in this classroom. There is clearly a place for bilingual discourse, in many forms, in this community of practice. Bilingual discourse challenges the ideology of normative monolingualism and creates an ideology of pluralism. Within this ideological frame, switching back and forth between languages is commonplace and part of the construction of in-group membership. Child (elite) bilingualism is what sets these kids apart from the mainstream German-speaking society. While there are one or two students in the classroom who speak little German, most of the children use both languages in a variety of ways. Despite varying levels of proficiency in the languages, the majority of the speakers alternate languages to position themselves advantageously with regard to the other interlocutors. As seen in some of the above examples, a switch to either German or English, depending on the context, can be a means of constructing a powerful position. This is also true of the use of German *and* English. One example of this can be seen in the interactions between Eva and her friend Anke in Examples 9 and 10, where they are working on math together. Bilingual discourse is used strategically in a variety of ways by both girls. In Example 9, something belonging to the girls has fallen on the floor, and some boys sitting near them are trying to grab it. Eva alternates between screaming at the boys to leave it alone in German and urging Anke to pick it up in English. Although the language choices are clearly related to the addressees, this is not a simple, straightforward matter of speaking German to those who prefer German and English to those who prefer English. Both of the boys sitting in front of Eva and Anke are EMT boys, and one of them, Connor, is not proficient in German; the other,

Roscoe, is a strong German speaker but speaks English and French at home and identifies as a more proficient speaker of those languages. Anke, on the other hand, is a GMT classmate. Although she speaks a lot of English with Eva and another EMT friend, Elyse, it is usually a mixture of English and German (as will be shown in Example 10). Thus, the code choices Eva makes here are about the contrast in the two languages and her own preferences; she uses German to mark the out-group members (i.e. pesky boys) and her preferred language, English, to address her friend. Without these switches, it would be unclear who should leave the item alone and who should pick it up; with these switches, her directives appear to make sense to the children, and Anke successfully retrieves the dropped item.

Example 9

Eva: **lass das!** get it! Pick it up, pick it up, Anke, **lass das** xxx Anke, Anke, pick it up!
   'leave it [alone!] … leave it [alone!]'

In the next example, we see that bilingual discourse is also used for power negotiations and positioning between the two girls. This excerpt begins with Anke chanting a bilingual sentence which is an insult about Eva; *Schwanz* literally means 'tail', but is slang for 'penis' and is also used as a derogatory term (usually to male addressees). Eva switches to German to ignore her and try to carry on with their math assignment. When this does not work, she switches to English and threatens to turn off the recorder if Anke does not behave. Anke follows her switch, capitulating in both code choice and content, as she agrees (albeit in a silly, frog-like voice) to cooperate. The girls then do discuss their math problem in German; since they have math instruction in English, this code choice is not about their familiarity with the subject in that language, but seems to be Eva's concession to Anke (who is better at math and is providing Eva with a lot of guidance through this assignment). Although Anke continues to sneak in an occasional insult, she does participate in the task. Thus, Eva's use of German here makes sense; while using English might call on the institutional power of the classroom to get Anke to stop being disruptive, if she wants Anke's help she needs to appeal to her as a peer, and in her dominant language. But, perhaps because these two friends have different dominant languages, the peer code is a bilingual discourse, not German. Both are used for disputes and agreements; this is seen most clearly in Anke's bilingual utterance *Eva is a* **Schwanz** and in the exchange in Example 11, a continuation of this conversation, during which the girls are both on-task and using both languages.

Example 10

A = Anke, E = Eva
A: /**Eva** is a **Schwanz**/ (.) **Eva** is a **Schwanz** (.) **Eva** is a /**Schwanz**/ {laughs}
    'Eva is a dick, Eva is a dick, Eva is a dick'
E: /(Patience)/ {shouting} **Okay okay jetzt muessen wir schauen das**
    wir das fertig machen xxxxxxxxx
    'Okay, okay, now we have to see that we get this done xxxx'
A: **Eva** is a **Schwanz** (.) **Eva** is a **Schwanz** {laughs}
    'Eva is a dick, Eva is a dick'
E: Anke Anke calm down, I'm going to turn it off
A: No don't don't don't
E: Then stop it!
A: (.) Okay {in frog-like voice}
E: **Uhm (.) Anke! (.) Also zum Beispiel Du weist xxx uhm sie:ben und**
    dann vier (.) mal (.) sieben mal sieben mal (2) Fuenf
    und dreizig (.) ist was?
    'Um, Anke! Well for example you know xxx uhm seven and then
    four times (.) seven times seven times (2) thirty-five (.)
    is what?'
A: **Nein nicht sieben mal fuenf und dreizig. Sieben geteilt durch**
    fuenf und dreizig wenn schon du Schwanz.
    'No not seven times thirty-five. If then seven divided by thirty-five,
    you dick.'
E: **Ja sieben geteilt durch sieben ist fuenf und dreizig. xxxxxxxx okay**
    macht jetzt macht jetzt schreib den (.) oder guck ob wir den haben
    'Yes, seven divided by seven is thirty-five. Xxxx Okay, that makes
    now that makes now, write that, or look if we have it'
A: **Du musst schreiben Dunkel Schwanz: Hallo (.) ah (.) ist fuenf**
    'You have to write, dark dick. Hey, that's five'   (4ATKS2g)

Example 11

A = Anke, E = Eva
A: Ja, that's what we're doing um (.) eleven (2) what's this ten ti:mes.
E: nine {shrieking} (.) ten times nine (.) **ist doch simple, nein.**
    'is really simple, no'
A: (**nein!**) {shrieking} **Das ist doch voll einfach**
    'no! That's totally easy'
E: eee:h
A: six times (.) **Oh ne das haben wir ja schon.**
    'Oh, we already have that one.'
E: /six times/ ten is **einfach**
    'easy'   (4ATKS2g)

As this example indicates, in some cases both languages are used not to create hierarchy but to construct solidarity. This was not, however, solely a pattern found with these two friends. Another example of this can be seen in a recording of four children, two boys and two girls, who were working in a group during math class. The project they were doing involved using different coloured pencils to illustrate fractions. Although there was some element of competition for the different coloured pencils, for the most part these negotiations were mild-mannered – they were not under time pressure, and everyone ultimately had to use all of the colours, so it was more a matter of timing the exchange than claiming scarce resources. As they took turns using the different coloured pencils, there was much offering and requesting, as shown in Examples 12–14.

Example 12

F = Friederik, M = Melody
F: How long you want **blau**?
       'blue'
M: Just two minutes.   (4ATKS2x)

Example 13

D = Daniel, F = Friederik, M = Melody
D: Next I need green.
F: **Du musst noch ein bisschen warten. Noch 'ne Minute.**
       'You have to wait a little bit. Just a minute.'
D: **Jetzt hat er blau.**
       'Now he has blue'
M: **Wer hat blau**?
       'Who has blue?'
F: **Ich brauchs doch gar nicht. (…) ahhh. Wie soll man zwei Sachen
       auf einmal anmalen.**
       'I don't even need it … ahhh. How are you supposed to draw on two
       things at a time?'
D: **Eins**
       'One'
F: **Hey ich brauch das nochmal xxx**
       'Hey, I need that again'
M: **Nee nee nee** you need another colour. Does anybody need another
       colour?
       'No no no …'   (4ATKS2x)

Example 14

D = Daniel, F = Friederik, M= Melody, V =Valerie
F: **Mann** (.) Does anyone need magenta?
       'Man'

M: **Nein**
    'No'
F: Magenta! I need blue. I need blue. I need, I need crayon blue.
D: I need blueberry blue.
V: I need blue.
F: I need blue {laughs}
D: I need blue
F: Oh man (.) I need green {laughs}
M: Ok
D: I just need pink and blue
F: Magenta   (4ATKS2x)

What is immediately striking about this conversation is that there is a great deal of back and forth between the two languages. This is particularly interesting because of the constellation of speakers in this group. Daniel, Friederik and Valerie are all GMT children, although Friederik and Valerie both have one US American, native-English-speaking parent. Melody is a relatively recent arrival in Berlin; she had lived there for only slightly over a year at the time of this recording. Thus, they form a fairly complete continuum, from Daniel, who has little experience with English outside of school, to Melody, who has not lived in Germany very long. Yet their linguistic negotiations move smoothly from language to language, with everyone speaking both codes. There is only one instance of construction of difference in terms of language proficiency, shown in Example 15. Here, Melody first corrects Friederik's use of the colour term *pink*, and then his pronunciation of *magenta*. Friederik responds 'who cares' to both of these corrections, a very idiomatic response. Even more significantly, however, in Example 14 above (chronologically after the exchange in Example 15), note that he does, actually, care and corrects Daniel's use of the colour term *pink* with *magenta*, pronounced with the medial [ʒ], as he was taught just minutes earlier by Melody.

Example 15

D = Daniel, F = Friederik, M= Melody, V =Valerie
F: Who needs blue?
M: I need blue.
F: Let's poker. Who needs pink?
D: No
F: Oh man. Oh great {laughs}
M: It's not pink it's magenta.
F: Who cares I call it pink.
V: Oh I need green.
    {laughs}

F: Oh come on so I mess with mag[g]enta.
M: mag[ʒ]enta
F: Who cares. {laughs}   (4ATKS2x)

An additional salient feature of this conversation is the frequent use of repetition, synchronizing the forms of utterances across speakers. When in Example 14 Frank says 'I need crayon blue', Diego echoes his construction in form with 'I need blueberry blue'; when in the subsequent few turns it is established that Frank, Diego and Melissa all need blue, they express this with exact repetitions of Frank's original 'I need blue' – no one says 'me too' or emphasizes the 'I' to show contrast; it is a perfect coordination of similarity. Language choice is part of the harmony constructed in this foursome, despite their differences in linguistic proficiency. The significance is that in the performance of cooperation, the children also performed bilingualism, all of them claiming both languages.

7.5 National identification

To return to a point made in the introduction, I suggest that bilingual discourse is a challenge to essentialized ideas about national identity categories. Fourteen of the children in this classroom filled out a questionnaire about their own multilingual practices, on which I also included a few questions about their own national identification and how they would define what it means to be German. Eight of the fourteen identified as something other than one national category – many of them as belonging to two nationalities (e.g. *German and American*), but one of them as *Weltmensch* 'citizen of the world'. It is significant, however, that the two nationalities claimed did not always correspond to the nationalities they assigned their parents; their identifications were not inherited but socially constructed. Four children claimed German–American status based on their attendance at a bilingual school; three of these children had parents they identified only as German. Another girl (Anna) identified as German, although her mother was US American. Yet another (Thea) identified as German–American because her maternal grandmother was from the USA and her maternal grandfather was from Germany – but she did not identify as Greek, the nationality she ascribed to her absentee father. Further, many of the children who had parents of two nationalities did not state the rationale for their own identification with those nationalities in essentialist terms, or at least not solely in those terms (e.g. 'because my father is German and my mother is American'). Instead, they tended to discuss their identification in terms of language – 'I consider myself German and American because I speak both languages' or 'More French and English than German because those are the languages I speak at home'. Similarly, some of the children who claimed German identity did so on the basis of speaking German, not because their parents were German.

We see, then, that dual-immersion bilingual education holds the potential to contribute to a rethinking of national identity in three ways. First, speaking a second language opens up the child's world; even if they do not travel beyond national borders, they identify with people and spaces outside their countries through their association with another language. Second, contact with children and teachers from different countries, even if they speak German with them, also shifts their identification. As shown so poignantly by Thea's identification with her mother's dual citizenship and not at all with her father's nationality, we see ourselves in terms of those around us; we do not necessarily identify with ethnic or national categories that are possible if they are not made relevant in our lives. Which brings me neatly to the third point: although nationality is potentially made more relevant in a school in which there is an international student body, I argue that it is also potentially made irrelevant. As suggested above, what is important about speaking German is not that it makes you sound German – more relevant is that it aligns you with the local youth culture. Contrasts in nationality can, and often do, create discrimination along national lines, but this diversity can also make it clear how irrelevant those categories are. These nine-year-olds really just want to do well on a class project, get the blue coloured pencil or make their friends laugh. They don't have to be German to do those things, although speaking German often helps.

Another part of the pluralistic ideology that is potentially fostered in a bilingual education programme is that languages other than the languages of instruction gain value, even if they are languages which are not prestigious in the wider society. I often witnessed children claiming languages that they did not master by any objective criteria; often these were home languages, but sometimes they were languages of countries they had visited. I could not always know the linguistic repertoires of the children aside from what they told me, but on several occasions a parent or teacher who knew the language would say, oh no, Eva doesn't really speak Polish, or Joschke really knows only a few words of Romanian. In other instances, the children would urge their peers to do things such as count to ten in Farsi, or translate something into Serbian. In my observation, no one ever mocked anyone for speaking a language that was not prestigious; to the contrary, knowledge of minority languages appeared to carry cultural cachet. It was not clear to me if the value of these languages was as a potential resource for communication, school achievement, travel or future employment, or if they were merely accessories that the well-dressed bilingual added to enhance the effect – but it's possible that these are the same thing. Instrumental value is possible only if there is a context in which speaking the language can become profitable, and that context exists only when the language is valued enough that people will speak it.

7.6 Conclusion

This research examines differing ideologies and practices in a bilingual education environment. The social setting of Berlin, Germany, is a multilingual city which has German as the everyday language for public interactions, but caters to speakers of prestigious international languages, especially English. The community at the John F. Kennedy School reinforces the prestige of English and the importance of German for everyday interaction, while adding an explicit norm that these two languages be kept strictly separate. This ideology is weakened in the classroom examined as the teachers are open to, and themselves participate in, bilingual discourse. Thus, the children have a variety of normative ideologies to draw on for their language choices – the value of German, the value of English, the value of elite bilingualism and the value of distinct, standard codes – but also are allowed to participate in the anti-normative practice of bilingual discourse. (Of course, children in other classrooms also use bilingual discourse, but it is not always endorsed by teachers, and is sometimes explicitly forbidden. See Fuller (2009) for an analysis of data from another classroom at this school.)

This analysis has shown how these children, drawing on normative ideologies associated with each particular language as a separate entity, enact positions which are socially powerful. However, these same children challenge these hegemonic ideologies through the use of bilingual discourse, which serves to both contest the ideology of normative monolingualism and to construct the speakers as transgressive with regard to essentialist identity categories.

This bilingual setting with an international cast of characters provides the children with an education in more than simply the grammars and literatures of their two languages. By the tender age of nine, they have learned to reflect with their language use the changing and fluctuating norms and social attitudes about language ideologies and social identities in contemporary Germany. Their stated identities are largely devoid of ethnonational sentiments, and their language use shows that they are open to a fluidity of associations with their languages. German may be the national language of Germany, but its status as the marker of youth culture in Berlin is often more salient; English is a prestigious international language and important for academic achievement, but also a language with which many have a personal relationship, and one which is not necessarily linked to experiences in a particular national context. This loosening of the association of language to national identity is part of an ideology in which national identity is seen as socially constructed and thus linked to social behaviour. The children's choices to use bilingual discourse are personal choices, with interactional motivations, but they are also a reflection and construction of language ideologies.

Appendix: Transcription key

A:	letter to indicate speaker
/between/	between slashes – overlap with the text between slashes in the next/preceding line
I'm (hungry)	words within the parentheses are unclear;
xxx	inaudible word
?	Rising intonation at the end of an utterance
.	falling intonation at the end of an utterance
!	animated intonation
Lass doch mal!	bold print: utterance in German
'what type …'	translation of utterance (into English)
{laughs}	words within curly brackets are descriptions of speech or actions
(.)	pause of less than one second
(1), (2), etc.	pause of 1, 2, etc. seconds
ba:d	colon indicates elongated vowel
[it], [ʒ]	words within square brackets are inserted to create coherence in translation; symbols within square brackets are inserted to indicate pronunciation of a segment

Note

1. Recordings are coded according to the grade (4), the children in the classroom (Mother Tongue, MT: Partner Tongue, PT; or All Tongue, AT), the school (John F. Kennedy School, KS) and the number of the recording in this category (1) and the presence of boys (b), girls (g) or both (x) in the group being recorded.

References

Bauman, R. and Briggs, C. L. (2003). Language, poetry and *Volk* in eighteenth-century Germany: Johann Gottfried Herder's construction of tradition. In R. Bauman and C. L. Briggs (eds.), *Voices of Modernity: Language Ideologies and the Politics of Inequality* (pp. 163–96). Cambridge: Cambridge University Press.

Blackledge, A. and Pavlenko, A. (2001). Negotiation of identities in multilingual contexts. *International Journal of Bilingualism*, 5, 243–57.

Blackledge, A. and Pavlenko, A. (2002). Introduction. *Multilingual*, 21, 121–40.

Bucholtz, M. and Hall, K. (2005). Identity and interaction: a sociocultural linguistic approach. *Discourse Studies*, 7, 585–614.

Bucholtz, M. and Hall, K. (2008). Finding identity: theory and data. *Multilingual*, 27, 151–63.

Errington, J. (2000). Ideology, *Journal of Linguistic Anthropology*, 9, 115–17.

Foucault, M. (1972). *The Archaeology of Knowledge and the Discourse of Language* (trans. A. M. Sheridan Smith). New York: Pantheon Books.

Fuller, J. (2009). 'Sam need gun go war': performances of non-standard English in the construction of identity. *Journal of Sociolinguistics*, 13, 659–69.

Fuller, J. (2012). *Bilingual Pre-teens: Competing Ideologies and Multiple Identities in the US and Germany*. New York: Routledge.

Gal, S. (1998). Multiplicity and contention among language ideologies: a commentary. In B. Schieffelen, K. Woolard and P. Kroskrity (eds.), *Language Ideologies: Practice and Theory* (pp. 317–22). Oxford: Oxford University Press.

Gal, S. (2006a). Contradictions of standard language in Europe: implications for the study of practices and publics. *Social Anthropology*, 14, 163–81.

Gal, S. (2006b). Migration; minorities and multilingualism: language ideologies in Europe. In C. Mar-Molinero and P. Stevenson (eds.), *Language Ideologies, Policies and Practices: Language and the Future of Europe* (pp. 13–27). New York: Palgrave Macmillan.

Hanson-Thomas, H. (2007). Language ideology, citizenship, and identity: the case of modern Germany. *Journal of Language and Politics*, 6, 249–64.

Heller, M. (1999). *Linguistic Minorities and Modernity: A Sociolinguistic Ethnography*. New York: Longman.

Heller, M. (2007). Bilingualism as ideology and practice. In M. Heller (ed.), *Bilingualism: A Social Approach* (pp. 1–21). New York: Palgrave Macmillan.

Kroskrity, P. (2000). Identity. *Journal of Linguistic Anthropology*, 9, 111–14.

Kroskrity, P. (2004). Language ideologies. In A. Duranti (ed.), *A Companion to Linguistic Anthropology* (pp. 496–517). Oxford: Blackwell.

Woolard, K. A. (1998). Introduction: language ideology as a field of inquiry. In B. Schieffelin, K. A. Woolard and P. Kroskrity (eds.), *Language Ideologies: Practice and Theory* (pp. 3–47). Oxford: Oxford University Press.

8 Communicative repertoires in the community language classroom: resources for negotiating authenticity

Angela Creese, Adrian Blackledge and Jaspreet Kaur Takhi

8.1 Introduction

Complementary schools (also known as 'community language schools', 'heritage language schools' or 'supplementary schools') are sites in which contrasting social values are intensively negotiated. In the discourses of teachers and students, questions about identity and belonging, and questions of authenticity (Shankar, 2008; Blommaert & Varis, 2011; see also Li Wei, this volume), routinely surface. These identities and authenticities are far from straightforward. In this chapter we investigate students' and teachers' negotiation of 'authenticity' in the complementary school classroom. We describe a broad range of identity positions brought into play in the negotiation of authenticity. Even in the tightly controlled and highly normative discursive practices of the language classroom, there is opportunity for a wide range of identity positioning. We examine the processes which make these identity positions available to students as they negotiate shifting allegiances to the social positions they index. Wortham (2004: 166) defines positioning as 'an event of identification, in which a recognizable category of identity is explicitly or implicitly applied to an individual in an event that takes place across seconds, minutes, or hours'. He describes how habitual and repeated ways of using language may be interpreted as predictable indicators of identity (Wortham, 2008).

Like definitions of 'ethnicity', authenticity is a 'muddy' and 'positional' concept (Reyes, 2010: 399). It can be understood only in context as a constructed, dynamic, shifting and situated practice. In this sense we view the negotiation of authenticity in the heritage language classroom as a creative process in which young people and their teachers consider, resist and enact social change. Blommaert and Varis (2011: 4) suggest that 'One has to "have" enough emblematic features in order to be ratified as an authentic member of an identity category.' They describe authenticity as a 'highly dynamic configuration of features' which requires 'constant adjustment, reinvention and amendment' (p. 4). In this chapter we consider classroom practices in the negotiation of authenticity in relation to a range of identity categories. Discussions of authenticity and repertoire are connected to Hymes's (1972) concept of 'appropriateness' in relation to his notion of communicative competence. Of the four factors which define communicative competence, it is 'whether (and to what degree) something is *appropriate* (adequate, happy, successful) in relation to a context in which it is used and evaluated' (Hymes, 1972: 281) which is relevant to our discussion. Hymes's definition of appropriateness is predicated on situated language use. As Hornberger (1989: 218) points out, 'this competence is by definition variable within individuals (from event to event), across individuals, and across speech communities'. Hornberger highlights the variability of appropriateness in individual agency. The notion of appropriateness appears to be undergoing something of a revival in discussions of authenticity, where the focus is on dynamic processes of social configuration. According to Blommaert and Varis (2011: 4), 'Competence [to use an old term] is competence in changing the parameters of identity categories, and in adjusting to such changes.' In the classroom represented in this chapter, authenticity is at least partly predicated on the teacher actively making connections with her students' multiple communities beyond the classroom. The teacher achieves this through linking appropriate language use to specific community contexts. Her pedagogic practices reflect the diversity of everyday voices in the multiple contexts and communities of the students' translocal worlds.

8.2 Teacher authenticity and pedagogy in heritage language education

Heller (2007: 8) proposes that utterances can best be understood as inherently heteroglossic; that is, 'a multiplicity of voices underlies linguistic variability in any given stretch of social performance'. Koven argues that bilingualism should be viewed as a complex form of identity work in which 'language choices are made for deliberate self-positioning relative to the heteroglossia available to bilinguals in their "sociolinguistic" universes' (2009: 344). Koven maintains that language choices can 'at least be partially explained and motivated by speakers' ideologically informed positioning and attitudes towards socially indexical forms in their two languages' (p. 344). In her study of French and Portuguese young women's forms of address, Koven claims that 'non-normative usage should not be viewed simply as a sign of incomplete competence, but the result of very complex self and other positioning in French and Portuguese sociolinguistic spaces' (p. 354). We might think of multilingual pedagogy in a similar way. Rather than consider heteroglossia and code-switching in complementary classrooms as non-normative or problematic, we can think of it as ideologically informed and strategic. A heteroglossic view of semiosis counters views of languages as hermetically sealed units (García, 2007) or separate, discrete entities or 'countable institutions' (Makoni & Pennycook, 2007: 2). Koven (2009: 363) argues that:

Sounding like an L1 monolingual may not be the goal of all bilinguals (Rampton, 1995, 2006). Instead of assuming ignorance as the explanation for particular bilingual usage, one should also attend to the multiple language ideologies with which bilinguals are confronted, in and across the contexts of both their languages. These ideologies inform and construe bilinguals' strategies.

In terms of pedagogy, there are dangers in insisting that students learn a normative standard variety which is out of sync with their communicative repertoires. Rymes (2010: 528) defines communicative repertoires as 'the collection of ways individuals use language and literacy and other means of communication (gestures, dress, posture, or accessories) to function effectively in the multiple communities in which they participate'. A teaching approach based on communicative repertoire focuses on the resources deployed by individuals in classrooms and is not limited by generalizations about communities, or analyses that seek to reproduce 'correctness' as a primary function of schooling. In her development of the concept of communicative repertoires, Rymes emphasizes individuals' language use and warns against a pedagogic approach that adopts an essentialized construct of a 'community' of speakers. This is in tune with Bauman and Briggs in their 'agent-centred view of performance' (1990: 69), which shifts the balance from a focus on the product of context to the process of contextualization. Rymes argues for a focus on 'communicative goals as repertoires emerge and recede' and a classroom pedagogy that builds on metalinguistic awareness (2010: 532). Cenoz and Gorter also refer to the notion of repertoires, in countering 'monolingual bias' in research and language teaching. They speak of drawing on 'the multilingual's total language repertoire' (2011: 341). Language which is 'authentic' is always contingent on the dynamic processes of social life.

García proposes a heteroglossic view of bilingualism which 'considers multiple language practices in interrelationship' (2009: 7). García suggests that language choice in multilingual speakers involves negotiation in every interaction as speakers 'decide who they want to be and choose their language practices accordingly' (2010: 524). She argues against monoglossic, linear and fixed ideologies of bilingualism and bilingual education, and for a dynamic and flexible bilingualism which centres on individual students' language practices. According to García, the role of educators is to notice learners' needs rather than demarcate lines between particular languages, as meaningful instructional practices support students' linguistic and cognitive growth (see also García et al., this volume).

Busch (forthcoming) also draws on the notion of linguistic repertoire and linguistic awareness in her research on heteroglossia and heterogeneity in the classroom. She argues that a heteroglossic approach highlights the fluid and flexible, rather than the stable and geographically fixed, use of language in the social spaces of the classroom. According to Busch, pedagogic spaces need to recognize the translocal communicative repertoires of young people and teachers and legitimate translanguaging as a meaning-making resource. Busch argues that schools 'must be reconceptualized as open spaces of potentialities, where the polyphony of voices, discourses and ways of speaking are seen as resource and asset' (forthcoming). Canagarajah (2007: 238) argues for developing a 'metalinguistic awareness' which develops the sensitivity to decode differences in dialects as students engage with a range of speakers and communities. He describes how teachers can create favourable circumstances for student negotiation of ideas, identity and arguments in their writing through 'codemeshing', which he describes as a dialogical pedagogy built from the ground up. However, Canagarajah also warns of the heavy censoring of translanguaging or codemeshing in literate contexts.

An ecological perspective on pedagogy in multilingual classrooms is another approach to valuing flexible bilingualism. An ecological perspective on multilingualism is 'essentially about opening up ideological and implementational space in the environment for as many languages as possible' (Hornberger, 2002: 30). Blackledge and Creese (2010; also Creese & Blackledge, 2010) argue for a pedagogy which maps onto the linguistic diversity of young people's lives outside of the classroom. They illustrate how translanguaging and flexible bilingualism act as a pedagogic resource to engage a complex audience of students, other teachers and parents. Translanguaging practices are therefore aimed at language teaching and learning and also provide a way to connect to different proficiencies, affiliations and heritages of multiple communities beyond the classroom (Leung et al., 1999). Connecting the classroom to different aspects of social practice beyond the classroom is also touched on by Low and Sarkar (forthcoming). They suggest that the 'poetics of the everyday practices' should be made relevant to classroom practices and illustrate how multilingual Montreal hip-hop can be used in schooling. They develop Glissant's concept of 'oraliture' (Glissant, 1989, in Low & Sarkar, forthcoming) in which writing is infused with the characteristics of oral expression in such forms as 'meandering, repetition, onomatopoeia and generative word-work'. Citing the research of Dyson, Low and Sarkar argue that pedagogy should include 'an ear for the diversity of everyday voices ... and an alertness to opportunities for performance' (Dyson, 2005: 150, in Low & Sarkar, forthcoming).

In this chapter we describe flexible bilingualism as a classroom practice which indexes a positive attitude towards local bilingual practices in Birmingham, UK. We argue that some of these practices authenticate teacher identity and serve as an emblematic template of what constitutes authenticity in the Panjabi classroom.

8.3 A Panjabi complementary school in Birmingham, England

The research we report here is part of a larger research project funded by Humanities in the European Research Area (HERA-JRP-CD-FP-051).[1] The project aimed to investigate the range of language and literacy practices of multilingual young people in four European settings, to explore the cultural and social significance of these practices, and to investigate how their language and literacy practices are used to negotiate inheritance and identities. In Copenhagen researchers spent a year observing in a large mainstream school with a multilingual student constituency; in Stockholm researchers conducted detailed investigations in two bilingual schools (Swedish/Finnish and Swedish/Spanish); in Tilburg researchers were immersed in a Chinese complementary school. The focus of the present chapter, though, is research conducted in a complementary school in Birmingham.

Angela Creese and Jaspreet Kaur Takhi spent five months observing in all classes in the school. After the initial five months of observation across all classes in the school, one class on each site was identified for closer observation. In negotiation with the teachers of these classes, two students were identified as 'key participants', for focused observation. After further observations in these two classrooms, the students, teachers and teaching assistants were issued with digital voice recorders so that they could audio-record themselves during class time. The participants were also asked to record themselves outside of the classroom to capture their own linguistic repertoires (as well as those of their families and friends) at home and in other environments. The researchers interviewed 15 key stakeholders in the schools, including

the key participant teachers and administrators and the key participant students and their parents. In this chapter we draw on a range of
data sets, including interview transcripts, classroom recordings and
field notes of observations.

The school in this study operates on Saturdays and is additional to
mainstream schooling. It was set up 'to provide more quality teaching in Panjabi than was being offered in Birmingham at the time'
(field notes). The school has charity status and was established
in 2004 by a group of successful local Birmingham businessmen.
One of its sites is a bespoke building converted for the purpose of
schooling, while the second uses the classrooms of a local mainstream secondary school on Saturdays. Across the two sites there are
approximately 15 teachers and teaching assistants teaching
200 pupils, ranging from the ages of 5 to 18 years. The teachers do
not have official teaching qualifications, but do have a GCSE and an
A-Level[2] qualification in Panjabi. The teaching assistants are typically college and university students. Those involved in setting up
and running the school speak of 'a school that has exactly the same
rules and procedures as a mainstream school'. The school principal
speaks of 'excellence, high enrolment, over-subscription, waiting
lists, word-of-mouth successful recruitment, organized teaching and
administrative procedures'.

In this chapter we discuss the Saturday class housed in the secondary school, and focus on the teacher, Hema. Outside the complementary school classroom, Hema worked as a classroom assistant in the
same mainstream secondary school which the complementary school
borrowed for its Saturday classes. Hema had worked for the past
16 years in this mainstream school. She came from India to the UK to
get married 16 years ago. She has a Master's degree in Economics, also
obtained in India, and a qualification for teaching adults which she
achieved in Birmingham. In her interview Hema looks back over her
16 years in the UK:

> but when I was first here I was in a bit of difficulty because
> our English to us, the pronunciation here and over there was very
> different   (Hema interview)

Pronunciation presented Hema with particular problems on arrival,
and she points to her 'Indian' pronunciation of English words as an
index of distinction which marked her out from her peers. She told us
that she gradually became attuned to these differences, pointing to a
period of particular difficulty when she first arrived in England. In the
interview Hema describes her daily life as 'multilingual' and mentions

proficiency in English, Hindi and Panjabi. She also describes 'mixing' as common practice:

> both languages yeah both languages we mix them yes when they [her family and students] don't understand and we don't have words in Panjabi to describe to them we then describe them in English (Hema interview)

Hema points to the pragmatic and communicative function of language here. In order to create meaning, whatever signs engage and connect to the interlocutors are used. However, Hema is passionate about the importance of preserving Panjabi and describes its significance to her life and identity:

> I think our language is extremely important ... if you don't know your language then what will you do? And secondly if you have your roots, if a tree doesn't have roots then how big will that tree grow? Because you won't have any self-confidence because you won't know who you are. Without an identity then what will you do? (Hema interview)

A range of ideologies is at play here, as Hema expresses views about language separation and mixing, language proficiency, pragmatic competence and difficulties in pronunciation. We now turn to look at her bilingual practices in the classroom.

8.4 Establishing teacher legitimacy and authenticity in the Panjabi complementary school classroom

A feature of Hema's class is her insistence on correctness in relation to particular features of Panjabi. These include, amongst others, an insistence on subject–verb agreement, pragmatically appropriate greetings and correct pronunciation. In Hema's class, students are asked to recite particular sounds many times and to look for distinctions across sounds.

> She tells them off (gently) for not distinguishing sounds. 'Look at me. Take your tongue to the top. OK, now say this 5 times. Come on, all together.' (field notes)

> One girl asks why are there so many 'g's in Panjabi. This makes Hema laugh. 'I don't know' she says, 'it's just the way it is'. (field notes)

Hema insists on pronunciation which reflects a Standard Panjabi norm. She uses herself as a pronunciation model to achieve this while also referring to other authentic sources available to students:

> Come on, pronunciation. Just think how your Bibi <*grandmother*> would say it   (field notes)

Hema proposes that the (generalized) grandmother is a source of correct pronunciation, and an authentic model. This is a strategy that Hema commonly uses in class. The next example is a transcript of a classroom recording in which Hema is typically conducting a dictation exercise, requiring the students to write the Panjabi texts as she recites it. Hema constructs the classroom assistant, Narinder, as a model of authentic pronunciation. Narinder had arrived in the UK from India more recently than Hema: one year ago, as opposed to Hema's 16 years. We pick up the recording at the point where it occurs to Hema that she could draw on Narinder as a model.

Hema: [reading to the class and in an aside to Narinder:] do you want to do this?
Narinder: kithayak? <*whereabouts?*>
Hema: yeah stress dekay word bolnay ok? <*yeah stress the word, with emphasis ok?*> [whispers:] saaday <*our*>
Narinder: [to children:] saaday ghar <*our house*> de vich <*in it*>
Hema: [to Narinder:] yeah saaDay so they they hear the sound
Narinder: ok [reads slowly:] saaDay ghar <*our house*> de <*of*> laagay <*near*> ek <*a vaddi sarakh hai <*a big road is*>
Hema: [to class:] ok listen to me, ok, when somebody's talking you … you look people's lips, like how they're pronouncing this, ok? Miss said 'saaDay' <*our*> when you pronounce this d where you are taking your tongue? where I'm taking my tongue? sAAday, so which dadda <*d sound*> you need? All of you got dadda <*d sound*> wrong. saaDay
Narinder: [to Hema] repeat kardaa? <*shall I repeat it?*>
Hema: sAADay <*our*>
Narinder: sAADay ghar de laagay ek vadi sarakh hai <*near our house there is a big road*>
Hema: ok when I'm saying saaDay <*our*> my tongue is going the top, yeah, so which dadda <*d sound*> I need to put? you need to write saaDHay or saaDay <*our*>?
Kirsty: saaDay <*our*>
Hema: so which dadda <*d sound*> you need?

Kirsty: is it that one?
Hema: it's like a three with a loop that's why I told Miss to do this
            so you can see the difference how she's pronouncing it and
            how you are writing

In this extract Hema insists on Standard Panjabi from her students. Their ability to distinguish between different /d/ (dadda) sounds is central to the pedagogic exercise. This is not an area where the teacher appears willing to compromise on linguistic accuracy. The difference in the phoneme /d/ with and without aspiration is a distinction at the heart of her teaching point. Hema teaches the students to pay attention to these nuanced differences as signs conveying meaning. Hema uses the sound contrast to point to two words with different meanings: 'SaaDay', which means 'our', and 'SaaDHay', which means 'half past' [the hour]. Hema makes her teaching point by constructing both Narinder and herself as authentic 'native speakers' able to make the sound distinction. Hema asks Narinder to emphasize key sounds so that the students can hear the distinction between them and imitate them orally. Her introduction of Narinder at this point evokes Narinder as the authentic model of Standard Panjabi pronunciation. In deploying Narinder in this way, she reminds the students of Narinder's newly arrived status as a good model to imitate as they practise their Panjabi pronunciation. Hema positions 'Miss' as the authority in making sound distinctions. In two-teacher classrooms, the dynamics of teacher role and interaction foreground power relations and institutional discourses more obviously than in single-teacher classrooms (Creese, 2005). In the interaction here, Hema's positioning of Narinder as the newly arrived native speaker serves to remind students of a Standard Panjabi linked to the Panjab. However, Hema also presents herself as a model for good and correct pronunciation, even if she does not represent her model as closely linked to the Panjab in the same way.

It is notable in this interaction that Hema refers not only to the sound but to the embodiment of correct, or standard, pronunciation. She instructs the students to watch the shape and movement of Narinder's and her own mouth as each of them pronounces the /d/ and /dh/ sounds: 'Take your tongue to the top', 'you look people's lips', 'where I'm taking my tongue?', 'my tongue is going the top, yeah?' She positions both Narinder and herself as teachers who not only sound authentic but also embody authentic pronunciation, moving their tongues and lips in an authentic way. That is, their historical body (Scollon & Scollon, 2004), or their bodily hexis (Bourdieu, 2008), is assumed to equip them with the cultural capital to produce authentic pronunciation of Panjabi. This authenticity appears to be linked to their status as native speakers, and to the students' (perceived) status as non-native speakers. Hema tells the students that because they failed to watch the way she and Narinder move their lips and tongues, they made mistakes in their written dictation: 'all of you got dadda wrong'.

The ability to make distinctions between the different phonemes serves as an emblematic template of authenticity here. There are norms of appropriateness in play. An ability to make the contrast between the two parallel terms /d/ and /d h/ is demanded of the students by Hema because articulating standard pronunciation is a requirement for the students to pass their examination. However, this pedagogic exercise is far more than this. Hema's insistence on correctness might be attributed to a variety of factors. First, phoneme differences denote differences in referential meanings. Second, inability to hear difference might contribute to further writing and representation errors. Third, incorrect pronunciation in Panjabi indexes a distancing from the Panjab and Panjabi heritages, which participants are constructed as sharing. Hema's inclusion of Narinder at this point in the lesson to model the 'fresh' (Talmy, 2004) version of these sounds points to the importance Hema gives to pronunciation as emblematic of 'being' Panjabi. Through pronunciation practice, the construction of a shared Panjabi heritage is performed.

8.5 Multilingual classroom ecologies

In our previous work on complementary schools, we have described multilingual pedagogies which deploy signs beyond language boundaries in the teaching and learning of community languages (Creese & Blackledge, 2010, 2011). These sites establish a classroom ecology that explicitly seeks student engagement through their bilingualism. Regular and routine use is made of bilingual strategies in complementary school classrooms, through translanguaging, transliteration and translation (Creese & Blackledge, 2010). These usual and mundane practices attract little commentary from participants themselves. However, in the next example Hema, rather unusually, addresses the class directly about the integration and separation of languages. She asks them to reflect on the kinds of decisions bilinguals are asked to make in life beyond the classroom. Hema has just been doing a pronunciation and translation exercise with the class, which prompts questions from the students about borrowings from English into Panjabi and how to translate them. She responds to these questions with a brief narrative:

I will share one thing with you. Last week I was doing a translation for somebody. Er, it was a Gurdwara <*Sikh temple*> and there was a leaflet. A couple of lines only I had to translate for some, er babaji <*grandfather*>, like bazurgh <*elderly person*> yeah? Elderly person. Er and the word was 'community', yeah? And, I was doing the translation and I said 'samhudai' <*community*> yeah? Community means samhudai. He couldn't understand! Ah then I tried to make this word more easier. No! Then I was thinking 'hunh mein ehnoo ki dasaa?' <*what shall I tell him now?*> 'what shall I tell him now?' Then I said shall I say the word 'community'? I said 'community'. It was fine! [laughter] [He] did understand, because some words like, they are so familiar right? The people, the people living with those words, right? He easily understood what I'm talking about. 'Community haa puth, tu community kehna si, community kehna si menoo!' <*yes child, you should have said community, should have said community to me!*> I said ok. I was 'uncleji <*uncle*> I was doing word to word translation'. Ok? Some words they are more easier to understand if you say them in English. Ok? (classroom audio-recording)

In Hema's dramatic mini-narrative, she tells her students about a recent incident in which she had been called upon to translate some written text from English into Panjabi for an elder at the Gurdwara. The first-person pronoun is used performatively to connect her to wider circulating discourses about community life and questions of language use, as she presupposes shared reference points in the rendition of the story. Assumptions are made about the common ground she shares with her audience: the need for a translation service, and religious referents such as the Gurdwara. Hema uses 'I' to position herself relative to different identities, discourses and ideologies. She gives voice to debates including topics of translation and language change. She evokes discourses of respect, using honorifics and kinship terms, and articulates her students' voices by raising their questions and concerns. She negotiates a path which puts her on a shared footing with her students and their multiple communities, and positions herself as a representative of other voices in the Panjabi community. Her not-so-new native-speaker identity allows her to index a wide range of identity positions across multiple communities, ideologies and social practices.

In telling the story, Hema uses several narrative devices, including direct reported speech, indirect reported speech, scene-setting and narrative commentary. Bauman and Briggs (1990) propose that reported speech enables performers to draw on multiple speech events, voices and points of view. A key feature of reported speech is the relation between the reporting and represented voices. In the representation of speech events is the potential for 'interaction between narrated and narrating participants' (Agha, 2005: 50). The narrated participants in Hema's story are the 'babaji' <*grandfather*>, or 'bazurgh' <*elderly person*>, and herself. Her reference to the older man in terms of kinship and respect suggests a positive orientation of the narrator to her character. When Hema reports that the elder was not able to understand the Panjabi word 'samhudai', her commentary ('He couldn't understand!') expresses not a negative evaluation, but surprise. Hema's surprise appears to be based on a presupposition, which she shares with her students, that the babaji would be able to understand the Panjabi term. Now Hema reports her own thought processes (or the thought processes of her own character) as she struggles to complete the translation task effectively: 'Then I was thinking hunh mein ehnoo ki dasaa? what shall I tell him now?' It is notable here, and elsewhere in the brief narrative, that Hema does not let go of her role as a language teacher, several times using translation as a pedagogic strategy. She continues to report her (character's) thought process: 'Then I said "shall I say the word community"?' In the story Hema's character is represented as one who is uncertain about how to proceed, but willing to negotiate her way through the 'translation zone' (Apter, 2005) at the Gurdwara. Hema's narrative continues to report the outcome of the negotiation: 'I said "community". It was fine!' Her story is of translation from English to Panjabi to English, as it turns out that the best translation (in this time and place) of 'community' is not 'samhudai' but 'community'. Hema's narrative commentary on the interaction concludes that the elder was easily able to understand her because people are 'living with' these words, and they become familiar. Hema concludes her story by once again reporting the speech of the two characters in the story:

> 'Community haa puth, tu community kehna si, community kehna si menoo' <*yes child, you should have said community, should have said community to me*> I said OK. I was 'uncleji <*uncle*> I was doing word to word translation'.

Hema does not deploy a reporting verb in reporting the babaji's point. Voloshinov suggests that in some instances reported speech may be represented in such a way that it merges with the representing speech: 'the omission of the reporting verb indicates the identification of the narrator with his character' (1973: 151). The absence of the reporting verb in quoting the babaji here contributes to Hema's teaching point: she should have said 'community' rather than 'samhudai' because it is legitimate to deploy linguistic signs from different 'languages' flexibly and dynamically. The represented voice of Hema's character is finally almost apologetic, as she recognizes that her attempt to do 'word for word translation' was not appropriate in this situation.

Hema makes connections to different timescales, social practices and communities. She makes a point of endorsing older people's contributions, particularly within families. We have seen this in the narrative about her experience of translating in the Gurdwara, and earlier in her mention of the grandmother generation for modelling pronunciation. The next example is a further instance of Hema's connecting the domain of the classroom with the domain of the home. The class are practising the long /i/ sound in Panjabi 'bihari' words. In a typical language classroom task, Hema is collecting examples of words making this sound. One of the students, Pavan, offers the word 'leeray', meaning 'cloth', or 'rags', which at first Hema thinks she has misheard.

Hema:	next one?
Pavan:	leeray <*pieces of cloth/rags*>
Hema:	which one?
Pavan:	leeray
Hema:	leader?
Pavan:	leeray
Hema:	leader as in leader?
Pavan:	leeray
Kirsty:	leeray, Miss he's saying 'leeray', clothes
Hema:	leeRAY?
Kirsty:	yeah
Hema:	leeRAY, leeray is clothes, I haven't heard this word for ages
Kirsty:	my grandma says it
Hema:	[to Pavan:] where did you learn this word from?
Pavan:	from my bibi <*paternal grandmother*>
Hema:	your bibi? your bibi as well? Yeah, leeray is really traditional word for clothes, ok, really old traditional word, leeray. Now we say 'kaprey' <*clothes*> ok? Good word, well done, yeah carry on (classroom audio-recording)

The student Pavan has learned the word 'leeray' from his grandmother. Another student, Kirsty, also recognizes the word from her grandmother. Hema praises both children for bringing this word into the classroom. Although she lets them know there is an alternative which is more contemporary and more standard ('kaprey'), she praises the children for making these connections between home and school. In doing so she endorses the language of their homes, families and heritages and legitimizes these resources as authentic for learning Standard Panjabi. This point is reminiscent of Gonzalez et al.'s concept of 'funds of knowledge', which are 'historically accumulated and culturally developed bodies of knowledge and skills essential for household or individual functioning and well-being' (2005: 72). The relevance of home knowledge in the classroom is endorsed by Hema, and she uses her own background knowledge to make these connections. This is in keeping with Martin-Jones and Saxena's study (2003) which describes how bilingual teaching assistants in a UK primary school made connections between home and school literacies. Hema is skilful in moving across boundaries and making connections through her own mobility, histories and multilingualism. Our field notes provide many accounts of her speaking to students about a number of topics of interest to her students. These include: a discussion of social networking and digital technologies; a gentle berating of the boys for spending too much time on games at the computer; discussing make-up and accessories with groups of girls in the break; enquiring about weddings in students' families; plans for when the students leave school; and a reminder that their Panjabi will be useful when they qualify as doctors and dentists. Hema is a reflective teacher – making connections through her pedagogy to her students' lives. She expects a similar level of reflection from her students. Examples from field notes record an incident in Hema's A-level class. The students have been reading a text on 'caste', which Hema goes on to discuss with them.

> Hema asks one of the girls what she thinks of the text. The girl says, 'I highly agree.' This makes some of the children laugh. However, Hema isn't happy with the answer and explains the text has some positive things about friendship but also negative things about rich people only being friends with rich people, and not with the poor. I think the children with less proficiency in Panjabi think they are expected to only agree with the friendship stuff in the text, and don't understand how strongly Hema feels about this ... Hema feels very strongly about this.
>
> Suddenly Hema turns to me and asks me if I have heard of 'castes'. I am taken aback but say 'yes'. She explains that in the Panjabi community there are people who are still very interested in caste and only want to be friends with people from a similar caste. She says it's not the children's fault, but some parents. She tells the class that in the 'multicultural West' these questions are not relevant. We should be respecting all people and not decide on friendship about money. (field notes)

This field note points to other contexts beyond the classroom. Transnationally connected between the Panjab and Birmingham, we are taken into family homes where, according to Hema, old prejudices are being reproduced. Hema makes an explicit argument against the relevance of caste in Birmingham and demands that her students think critically about references to 'caste' in their texts. For Hema, it is not appropriate to endorse such a text. Authenticity in the classroom requires an orientation to the 'multicultural West'.

Hema establishes her 'authenticity' as a representative of her students, and as a flexible bilingual, in touch with the kinds of decisions bilingual people, young and old, are facing in Birmingham. She negotiates a path that puts her on a shared footing with her students and their multiple communities, as well as positioning herself as a representative of other voices in the Birmingham communities in which she participates. Her identity allows her to index a wide range of identity positions across multiple communities, ideologies and social practices.

8.6 Conclusion

Negotiation of identities and belonging may depend on being able to call upon resources that are 'authentic' in certain contexts. Identity discourses and practices can be described as discursive orientations towards sets of features that are seen (or can be seen) as emblematic of particular identities (Blommaert & Varis, 2011: 6). Identity practices include discursive orientations towards sets of emblematic resources. Hema's flexible bilingualism, her knowledge of Birmingham life and its varied and multiple domains of practice create a set of resources which proves authentic in the classroom. Her bilingualism resonates with that of her students. These authenticities and identities are far from straightforward. They are not fixed; rather, they are fast-moving, 'organised as a patchwork of different specific objects and directions of action' (Blommaert & Varis, 2011: 1), and inclined to shift their position in the blink of an eye. Teachers, assistants and young people were involved in a process of evaluating, aligning with and distancing themselves from the 'perpetual semiotic reorientations of identity work' (Blommaert, 2012: 6). Blommaert and Varis point out that discourses in which people identify themselves and others include 'a bewildering range of objects towards which people express affinity, attachment, belonging; or rejection, disgust, disapproval' (2011: 4).

What are the implications of this for language, diversity and education? First, we have seen that a multiplicity of voices exists in the Panjabi heritage language classroom, and these point to the multiple and emergent communities to which people belong. The teacher and students took up a range of positionings relative to a variety of identity positions made available to them in the classroom. Hema proved skilful in her movement along a continuum of identities. She used her own personal mobility, history and professional knowledge to foreground and background different social identities and made these relevant to the young people through a heteroglossic approach to pedagogy, the selection of curriculum tasks, the narratives she told and the personal interactions she had with individuals, groups and the whole class of students. At times this involved foregrounding identities connected to sounding like a Standard Panjabi speaker through pronunciation practice. Processes of identification were established through reference to older family members and their use of 'traditional' words and pronunciation. The deployment of the newly arrived teaching assistant to index contemporary language practices in India was also made relevant to students. At other times, Hema highlighted Birmingham voices and spoke of sounding like a Birmingham bilingual cognisant of local norms. Lessons involved considering the appropriateness of language use in a range of contexts beyond the classroom and developing a metalinguistic awareness of language use in Birmingham's bilingual communities.

Second, such an analysis asks how multiple voices are represented. While we would argue that teaching and learning in our urban communities should emphasize the multiple competencies of multilingual learners, such an approach does not in itself guarantee critical engagement with localities, histories and identities. There may be much to learn from a heteroglossic orientation to language teaching which incorporates multilingualism and goes beyond it, to ensure that teachers like Hema bring into play linguistic signs and voices which index students' localities, social histories, circumstances and identities (Bailey, 2012).

Notes

1. The project 'Investigating discourses of inheritance and identities in four multilingual European settings' is financially supported by the HERA Joint Research Programme (www.heranet.info), which is co-funded by AHRC, AKA, DASTI, ETF, FNR, FWF, HAZU, IRCHSS, MHEST, NWO, RANNIS, RCN, VR and The European Community FP7 2007–2013 under the Socio-economic Sciences and Humanities programme. The research team was as follows: Adrian Blackledge, Jan Blommaert, Angela Creese, Liva Hyttel-Sørensen, Carla Jonsson, Jens Normann Jørgensen, Kasper Juffermans, Sjaak Kroon, Jarmo Lainio, Jinling Li, Marilyn Martin-Jones, Anu Muhonen, Lamies Nassri and Jaspreet Kaur Takhi.
2. The General Certificate in Secondary Education is taken at the age of 16 nationally in England. Advanced (A) level examinations are taken by young people at 18.

References

Agha, A. (2005). Voice, footing, enregisterment. *Journal of Linguistic Anthropology*, 15(1), 38–59.

Apter, E. (2005). *The Translation Zone: A New Comparative Literature.* Princeton, NJ: Princeton University Press.

Bailey, B. (2012). *Heteroglossia.* In M. Martin-Jones, A. Blackledge and A. Creese (eds.), *The Routledge Handbook of Multilingualism* (pp. 499–507). London: Routledge.

Bauman, R. and Briggs, C. (1990). Poetics and performance as critical perspectives on language and social life. *Annual Review of Anthropology*, 19, 59–88.

Blackledge, A. and Creese, A. (2010). *Multilingualism: A Critical Perspective.* London: Continuum.

Blommaert, J. (2012). Complexity, accent and conviviality: concluding comments. *Tilburg Papers in Culture Studies, 26.* Tilburg: Tilburg University.

Blommaert, J. and Varis, P. (2011). Enough is enough: the heuristics of authenticity in superdiversity. *Tilburg Papers in Culture Studies, 2.* Tilburg: Tilburg University.

Bourdieu, P. (2008). *The Bachelors' Ball.* Cambridge: Polity Press.

Busch, B. (forthcoming). Building on heteroglossia and heterogeneity: the experience of a multilingual classroom. In A. Creese and A. Blackledge (eds.), *Heteroglossia as Practice and Pedagogy.* Berlin: Springer.

Canagarajah, A. S. (2007). Lingua franca English, multilingual communities, and language acquisition. *The Modern Language Journal*, 91, 921–37.

Cenoz, J. and Gorter, D. (2011). A holistic approach to multilingual education: introduction. *The Modern Language Journal*, 95(3), 339–43.

Creese, A. (2005). *Teacher Collaboration and Talk in Multilingual Classrooms.* Clevedon: Multilingual Matters.

Creese, A. and Blackledge, A. (2010). Translanguaging in the bilingual classroom: a pedagogy for learning and teaching. *The Modern Language Journal*, 94, 103–15.

Creese, A. and Blackledge, A. (2011). Separate and flexible bilingualism in complementary schools: multiple language practices in interrelationship. *Journal of Pragmatics*, 43(5), 1196–208.

Dyson, A. H. (2005). Crafting 'The humble prose of living': rethinking oral/written relations in the echoes of spoken word. *English Education*, 37(2), 149–64.

García, O. (2007). Foreword. In S. Makoni and A. Pennycook (eds.), *Disinventing and Reconstituting Languages* (pp. xi–xv). Clevedon: Multilingual Matters.

García, O. (2009). *Bilingual Education in the 21st Century.* Oxford: Wiley-Blackwell.

García, O. (2010). Languaging and ethnifying. In Joshua A. Fishman and O. García (eds.), *Handbook of Language and Ethnic Identity: Disciplinary and Regional Perspectives,* Vol. I (pp. 519–34). Oxford: Oxford University Press.

González, N., Moll, L. C. and Amanti, C. (eds.) (2005). *Funds of Knowledge: Theorizing Practices in Households, Communites, and Classrooms.* Mahwah, NJ: Lawrence Erlbaum Associates.

Heller, M. (ed.) (2007). *Bilingualism: A Social Approach.* Basingstoke: Palgrave Macmillan.

Hornberger, N. H. (1989). Continua of biliteracy. *Review of Educational Research*, 59(3), 271–96.

Hornberger, N. H. (2002). Multilingual language policies and the continua of biliteracy: an ecological approach, *Language Policy*, 1, 27–51.

Hymes, D. H. (1972). On communicative competence. In J. B. Pride and J. Holmes (eds.), *Sociolinguistics* (pp. 269–93). London: Penguin.

Koven, M. (2007). *Selves in Two Languages: Bilinguals' Verbal Enactments of Identity in French and Portuguese.* Amsterdam: John Benjamins.

Koven, M. (2009). Managing relationships and identities through forms of address: what French-Portuguese bilinguals call their parents in each language. *Language and Communication*, 29, 343–65.

Leung, C., Harris, R. and Rampton, B. (1999). The idealized native speaker, reified ethnicities and classroom realities. *TESOL Quarterly*, 31(3), 543–60.

Low, B. and Sarkar, M. (forthcoming). Translanguaging in the multilingual Montreal hip-hop community: everyday poetics as counter to the myths of the monolingual classroom. In A. Creese and A. Blackledge (eds.), *Heteroglossia as Practice and Pedagogy.* Berlin: Springer.

Makoni, S. and Pennycook, A. (eds.) (2007). Disinventing and reconstituting languages. In S. Makoni and A. Pennycook (eds.), *Disinventing and Reconstituting Languages* (pp. 1–41). Clevedon: Multilingual Matters.

Martin-Jones, M. and M. Saxena, M. (2003). Bilingual resources and 'funds of knowledge' for teaching and learning in multi-ethnic classrooms in Britain. In A. Creese and P. Martin (eds.), *Multilingual Classroom Ecologies* (pp. 61–76). Clevedon: Multilingual Matters.

Reyes, A. (2010). Language and ethnicity. In N. H. Hornberger and S. L. McKay (eds.), *Sociolinguistics and Language Education* (pp. 398–426). Clevedon: Multilingual Matters.

Rymes, B. R. (2010). Classroom discourse analysis: a focus on communicative repertoires. In N. H. Hornberger and S. L. McKay (eds.), *Sociolinguistics and Language Education* (pp. 528–46). Clevedon: Multilingual Matters.

Shankar, S. (2008). *Desi Land: Teen Culture, Class, and Success in Silicon Valley.* Durham, NC/London: Duke University Press.

Scollon, R. and Scollon, S. W. (2004). *Nexus Analysis. Discourse and the Emerging Internet.* London: Routledge.

Talmy, S. (2004). Forever FOB: the cultural production of ESL in a High School. *Pragmatics*, 14 (2/3), 149–72.

Voloshinov, V. N. (1973). *Marxism and the Philosophy of Language*, trans. L. Matejka and I. R. Titunik. First published 1929. London/New York: Seminar Press.

Wortham, S. (2004). From good student to outcast: the emergence of a classroom identity, *ETHOS*, 32(2), 164–87.

Wortham, S. (2008). The objectification of identity across events. *Linguistics and Education*, 19, 294–311.

9 Complementary classrooms for multilingual minority ethnic children as a translanguaging space

Li Wei

9.1 Introduction

The term 'translanguaging' has recently been taken up by many researchers of multilingualism as an encompassing term for a variety of multilingual practices, traditionally termed as code-switching, code-mixing, borrowing and crossing, which are commonplace amongst multilingual language users. It has served as a corrective of the still widespread perception that such practices are somehow out of the ordinary, abnormal or deviant, by highlighting the positive and creative dimensions of the practices (see a review in García & Li Wei, 2014). In this chapter, I will examine the translanguaging practices of children of immigrant background in a specific socio-educational context as evidence of their creativity, criticality and multicompetence. The group of children I am focusing on in this chapter are those of Chinese ethnic origin in Britain. They are best described as transnationals: most of them are British-born, but many are of immigrant background, that is, their parents were born outside Britain; some of them have lived in other parts of the world. The specific context that I am studying is that of complementary schools, a voluntary education provision made available by minority ethnic, usually immigrant, communities in Britain to support their children's learning and use of the ethnic languages. Through a detailed analysis of classroom exchanges amongst the pupils and their teachers, I want to argue that translanguaging has a transformative capacity, as it creates a social space for the multilingual language user by bringing together different dimensions of their personal history, experience and environment, their attitude, belief and ideology, their cognitive and physical capacity into one coordinated and meaningful performance, thereby making it into a lived experience. I have called this space 'translanguaging space', a space for the act of translanguaging as well as a space created through translanguaging (Li Wei, 2011). As we will see through the examples of the pupils', and their teachers', alternation between languages and between modes of communication (e.g. speaking and writing), the complementary schools for minority ethnic children in Britain provide just such a translanguaging space. Skills, knowledge and identities are acquired and developed through the act of translanguaging.

The chapter is structured as follows: I begin with a brief discussion of the various uses of the term 'translanguaging' in multilingual research and the links between my particular take on the concept and other concepts such as multicompetence, symbolic competence, creativity and criticality. I will then outline the structure and current situation of the Chinese complementary schools in the UK. The main part of the chapter examines in detail examples of translanguaging practices by the Chinese pupils, and their teachers, in the Chinese complementary school classrooms, highlighting the transformative nature of translanguaging in terms of both knowledge acquisition and identity development. The chapter concludes with a summary of the key findings and arguments and a discussion of their implications.

9.2 Translanguaging space

The term 'translanguaging' is often attributed to Cen Williams (1994, 1996) who first used it to describe a pedagogical practice in bilingual classrooms where the input (e.g. reading and listening) is in one language and the output (e.g. speaking and writing) in another language. Baker (2006) discusses a range of potential advantages of translanguaging in the bilingual classroom in developing the learner's academic language skills in both languages. García (2009: 45) extended the notion of translanguaging to refer to 'multiple discursive practices in which bilinguals engage in order to make sense of their bilingual worlds'. As the chapters by Creese et al. and García et al. in this volume show, translanguaging continues to be regarded as a meaningful and creative pedagogical approach in multilingual classrooms (see also Creese & Blackledge, 2010; Canagarajah, 2011; Cenoz & Gorter, 2011).

My use of the term 'translanguaging' has a different origin; it builds on the psycholinguistic notion of 'languaging', which refers to the process of using language to gain knowledge, to make sense, to articulate one's thought and to communicate about using language (e.g. Lado, 1979; Hall, 1996; Smagorinsky, 1998; Swain, 2006; Maschler, 2009). In this process, 'language serves as a vehicle through which thinking is articulated and transformed into an artifactual form' (Swain, 2006: 97). It is also connected to A. L. Becker's attempt to move away from language as a noun, or something that has been accomplished, to language as a verb and an on-going process, or languaging (1988: 25; see also Becker, 1991a, 1991b). For me, translanguaging is both going between different linguistic structures and systems, including different modalities (e.g. speaking, writing, signing), and going beyond them. It includes the full range of linguistic performances of multilingual language users for purposes that transcend the combination of structures, the alternation between systems, the transmission of information and the representation of values, identities and relationships. As has been pointed out earlier, the act of translanguaging is transformative in nature; it brings together different dimensions of multilingual speakers' linguistic, cognitive and social skills, their knowledge and experience of the social world and their attitudes and beliefs, and in doing so, it develops and transforms their skills, knowledge, experience, attitudes and beliefs, thus creating a new identity for the multilingual speaker (Li Wei, 2011. See also García & Li Wei, 2014).

My approach to translanguaging embraces a number of related concepts. First, it connects with the notions of creativity and criticality. Whilst the notions of creativity and criticality have received some attention in applied linguistics broadly (see articles in the special issue of *Applied Linguistics*, edited by Swann and Maybin, 2007; Brumfit et al. 2005), they have not been dealt with in any systematic way with regard to multilingual practices. As in my previous publications, creativity here refers to the ability to choose between following and flouting the rules and norms of behaviour, including the use of language, and to push and break boundaries between the old and the new, the conventional and the original, and the acceptable and the challenging (see also Li Wei & Wu, 2009; Li Wei, 2011). An important prerequisite for linguistic creativity is knowledge of the linguistic system. This may be linked to Chomsky's notion of linguistic competence. However, for the multilingual, it is crucial to consider this knowledge in a holistic way, not just as one of the languages in the multilingual language user's linguistic repertoire, which would be only a subsystem for the user. A holistic conceptualization of the knowledge of the multilingual language user also needs to account for all the languages he or she knows, as well as knowledge of the norms for use of the languages in context and of how the different languages may interact in producing well-formed, contextually appropriate mixed-code utterances. The knowledge of appropriate use of multilingual resources in context also provides the foundation for criticality – the ability to use evidence appropriately, systematically and insightfully to inform considered views of cultural, social and linguistic phenomena, to question and problematize received wisdom, and to express views adequately through reasoned responses to situations. The two concepts – creativity and criticality – are intrinsically linked: one cannot push or break boundaries (i.e. being creative) without being critical, and the best expression of one's criticality is one's creativity.

My approach to translanguaging is also linked to Cook's notion of *multicompetence* (e.g. 1991). Multicompetence as a theoretical concept is developed in the context of second language (L2) learning to reflect the totality of linguistic knowledge in one mind. It starts from the point that the mind of the L2 user is different from that of the monolingual speaker and aims to capture the L2 user's state of mind by investigating how he or she puts to use knowledge of more than one language and how the different linguistic systems interact and impact on the language user's mind. The concept of multicompetence is particularly useful in describing and understanding translanguaging practices. As a distinctive and defining feature of being bilingual or multilingual, translanguaging requires the knowledge of and competence in all the languages involved, plus the involvement of higher-level executive systems to manage across the languages, as ample research evidence has confirmed. Furthermore, translanguaging is not simply a combination and mixture of different linguistic structures but also a creative strategy by the language user. A multicompetence approach enables us to investigate the structural, cognitive and sociocultural dimensions of translanguaging in an integrated and holistic way. It also has the added value of revealing the multilingual language users' creativity and criticality that are manifest in their translanguaging practices. One of my aims in the present chapter is to show that translanguaging is good evidence of the multilingual minority ethnic children's multicompetence, their knowledge of the deeper linguistic and social meanings of the languages they speak, their awareness of the historical trajectories of their community and their positions in it, and their ability to change the dynamics of the social relationships with others and to make an impact on their immediate environment.

By focusing on the transformative dimension of translanguaging, my approach also embraces the notion of symbolic competence, as developed by Kramsch and her associates (e.g. Kramsch, 2006; Kramsch & Whiteside, 2008; see also Kramsch & Huffmaster, this volume). Kramsch and Whiteside (2008: 664) pointed out:

Social actors in multilingual settings seem to activate more than a communicative competence that would enable them to communicate accurately, effectively, and appropriately with one another. They seem to display a particularly acute ability to play with various linguistic codes and with the various spatial and temporal resonances of these codes. We call this competence 'symbolic competence'.

Symbolic competence is defined as 'the ability not only to approximate or appropriate for oneself someone else's language, but to shape the very context in which the language is learned and used' (Kramsch & Whiteside, 2008: 664). Extending Bourdieu's notion of *sens pratique*, which is exercised by a *habitus* that structures the very field it is structured by in a quest for symbolic survival (Bourdieu, 1997/2000), Kramsch and Whiteside (2008) argue that a multilingual *sens pratique* multiplies the possibilities of meaning offered by the various codes in presence. As they suggested (p. 664): 'In today's global and migratory world, distinction might not come so much from the ownership of one social or linguistic patrimony (e.g., Mexican or Chinese culture, English language) as much as it comes from the ability to play a game of distinction on the margins of established patrimonies.'

9.3 Chinese complementary schools in the UK

As has been mentioned above, complementary schools in Britain are voluntary, community organizations for children from immigrant or minority ethnic backgrounds whose parents may speak languages other than English at home (see also Creese et al., this volume). They are similar to the heritage language schools in the USA and the community language schools in Australia and elsewhere. Most of them are open at weekends, and the pupils go to regular mainstream schools from Monday to Friday. A particular focus of the complementary schools is on the teaching of literacy in the ethnic languages. Li Wei (2006) discussed the history and current state of complementary schools in Britain. These schools have been part of a major sociopolitical and educational movement in the UK for nearly half a century, and have attracted public debates vis-à-vis government's involvement in educational management and challenged the dominant ideology of uniculturalism in the country. Yet, their own policies and practices have rarely been questioned (cf. Li Wei & Wu, 2009). For instance, how successful have the complementary schools been in achieving their stated objective of maintaining the linguistic knowledge and cultural identity amongst the British-born generations? What kind of literacy is fostered in the complementary schools? What is the 'cultural identity' that the schools and communities wish to maintain? Do parents and children share the same idea and vision about their identities? With regard to pedagogy and classroom management, it is obvious and understandable that the complementary schools want to insist on using specific community languages in this particular domain. Nevertheless, in addition to the practical difficulty of maintaining a strict 'no English' policy in the schools, the long-term consequence of such compartmentalization of community languages is an issue of concern.

My particular focus in this chapter is on how Chinese pupils in complementary schools engage in translanguaging as a symbolic and creative resource in a supposedly Chinese-only environment. The Chinese are one of the longest-established immigrant communities in the UK. The current Chinese community in the country is developed from post-war migrants, who began to arrive in Britain in the 1950s. The vast majority of the post-war Chinese immigrants were from Hong Kong. They were Cantonese and/or Hakka speakers. Many of them were peasants and labourers, who left an urbanizing Hong Kong to seek a better living in the UK. They have been engaged in largely family-based catering businesses and other service industries. The Chinese now form the third-largest immigrant community in Britain, after those of Afro-Caribbean and Indian subcontinent origin. Over a quarter of them are now British-born. A more detailed account of the sociolinguistic situation of the Chinese community in the UK can be found in Li Wei (2007).

There were informal reports of 'home schooling' in the 1950s and 1960s, that is, of children in Chinese families in cities such as London, Liverpool and Manchester, where there were significant numbers of Chinese residents, being taught by their parents and others at home (You, 2006). The very first 'Chinese schools' emerged on the basis of such collectives of families, providing private education to their children. The reasons for the emergence of such schools were complex. There is no doubt that racial discrimination played a role. However, the fact that the vast majority of the Chinese were, and still are, engaged in service industries has led to scattered settlements right across the country. It is often said that any town or village in Britain with around 2,000 residents will have at least one family-run Chinese takeaway. The Chinese children of these families would have little or no contact with other Chinese children if there were no Chinese complementary school.

The establishment of the Chinese schools must be seen as a major achievement of the community in their determination to support themselves. It also reflects a major failure of the mainstream schools to provide the necessary support to the Chinese children. According to the UK Federation of Chinese Schools and the UK Association for the Promotion of Chinese Education, the two largest national organizations for Chinese complementary schools, there are over 200 Chinese complementary schools in the UK. They are located in major urban centres. Many families have to travel for hours to send their children to the schools. They receive little support from the local education authorities. They are almost entirely self-financed. Parents pay fees to send the children, and local Chinese businesses offer sponsorships and other support (e.g. paying for the hire of premises and facilities).

Many of the schools use teaching materials provided free of charge by voluntary organizations in mainland China, Hong Kong and Taiwan. The teachers are mainly enthusiastic parents and university students from China. In the last ten years, a pattern has emerged. There are now four types of Chinese schools: (1) for Cantonese-speaking children from Hong Kong immigrant families; (2) for Cantonese-speaking children of Hong Kong immigrant families with particular religious affiliations, that is, run by the church; (3) for Mandarin-speaking children from mainland China; and (4) for Mandarin-speaking children of Buddhist families, mainly from Taiwan. Most of the schools run classes over the weekend for up to three hours. Parents play a crucial role in the schools – parents pay, parents govern and parents teach. A typical Chinese complementary school in the UK looks like this: it rents its premises from a local school or education centre. There is a temporary reception desk at the entrance for parents to speak to the teachers about any issues of inter-est. A shop is available for children to buy snacks and drinks. Space is provided for staff to have tea and coffee during the break and to have meetings. The children are grouped according to proficiency in Chinese. There are traditional Chinese dance, arts and sports sessions before or after the language and literacy sessions. Many schools also provide English language lessons for parents.

9.4 Translanguaging practices

The examples that I examine now come from a series of sociolinguistic ethnographic studies of the Chinese complementary schools in differ-ent cities in England, including, in particular, Newcastle, Manchester and London. Both Cantonese and Mandarin schools have been included in these studies. One of the facts of the current situation of the Chinese commentary schools in the UK is that all of the Cantonese schools also teach Mandarin, yet none of the Mandarin schools teach Cantonese. I have suggested elsewhere that this is a sign of the chang-ing hierarchies amongst varieties of the Chinese language as a result of the rising politico-economic power of mainland China (see Li Wei & Zhu Hua, 2010a, 2010b).

We followed the same approach in our study of all the Chinese com-plementary schools. Extensive ethnographic observations were made. After initial meetings with the administrators in each school to explain the purpose of the research project, information sheets were distributed to teachers, parents and pupils, and permissions were sought for further data collection. We were allowed access to observe classroom interaction and to collect data in a range of settings, including break time and formal school events such as prize-giving ceremonies. A selection of teachers, administrators, parents and pupils were interviewed, and recordings, both audio and video, were made in the classroom as well as during break time. Data analysis followed a broadly Interactional Sociolinguistics approach, where linguistic features of conversational data are interpreted in relation to the context of the interaction as well as the identities of the participants, with a particular focus on the process of meaning-making (Gumperz, 1982). In what follows, I focus specifically on the pupils' translanguaging practices that involve, in particular, simultaneous use of and switching between speech and writing. All of the examples are taken from the transcripts of audio-recorded interactions. Examples are given in standard Chinese and English orthography. The Chinese text is followed by a pinyin transliteration – the romanized rendition of the pronunciation of the Chinese characters – in brackets. The English gloss and translation are given in single quote marks either after or underneath the Chinese transcript.

The first example I want to analyse is taken from an exchange recorded in a Cantonese school in London. The class consists of twelve 14- to 15-year-olds. The teacher is from mainland China. She studied in Guangzhou (Canton) for a number of years and speaks good Cantonese. However, she normally speaks Mandarin with her friends, as her native Chinese dialect is different from both Cantonese and Mandarin, and she claims that she does not know many people in London who can speak her dialect. She is also a fluent speaker of English and is completing her postgraduate degree in education at a London college. She has set the class a task of writing a 100-character story in Chinese which must contain some dialogues. The pupils are working on their own but occasionally ask each other for help. Unlike some other teachers in Chinese complementary schools who seem to prefer the pupils doing their work silently and independently, this teacher does not mind the pupils talking in class and encourages them to solve any problems amongst themselves. The pupils sit around tables in groups of three and four.

Example 1

B1: How do you say 唔該 (*m guai*)?
G1: 唔該啦 (*m guai la*).
B1 : No, how do you write it?
G1: You can't.
B2 writes down 五塊 (*m faai*, meaning 'five dollars')

Laugh.

G1: That's five dollars (.) money.

B2: Yes.

G1: Yes.

T: What's going on?

B1: 唔該生 (*m guai sang*), how do you write 唔該 (*m guai*)?
'Excuse me, teacher.'

Laugh.

B2: 唔該生唔該 (*m guai sang m guai*).
'Excuse me teacher excuse me.'

T: You can't.

B1: What do you mean you can't?

T: 冇啦 (*mou la*). 对不住 (*dui m jiu*).
'There isn't. Excuse me/Sorry.'

Teacher writes down 对不住 and pronounces it *dui m jiu*.

G2: But is it the same?

T: 係啦 (*hai la*). It's more formal.
Yes.

B1: So you say 唔該 (*m guai*) and write this [pointing at the characters
the teacher has written].

T: Yes.

Silence. Pupils looking confused.

T: When do you want to say it?

B1: What do you mean?

T: I mean you say it differently for different things.

Silence.

G1: Oh so you can say 唔該 (*m guai*) when you want to call somebody,
and 对不住 (*dui mu jiu*) when you are sorry.

T: No you don't say it. You write it.

Silence.

G2: 好难啊 (*ho nan a*).
'So hard.'

T: I mean you write 請問 (*cheng man*) if you want to ask a question. Or
对不住 (*dui mu jiu*) if you want to say Sorry or Excuse me.

G1: What about 唔該 (*m guai*)?

B1: You don't write 唔該 (*m guai*).

Puzzled.

T: It's Cantonese.

G1: So you don't write Cantonese.

T: That's right.

B2: Cool.

B1: Crap.

All laugh.

Teacher says B1's name.

G1: Do we have to write Mandarin for everything then?

T: OK. Five minutes, OK?

The extract begins with one of the boys, B1, asking the girl sitting next to him, G1, how to write the characters for the Cantonese phrase for 'Excuse me', which he wants to use to construct a dialogue in his story. He mistakenly asks 'how do you say?' rather than 'how do you write?' He evidently knows how to say the phrase in Cantonese. So G1 responds by repeating the phrase B1 has said himself plus a Cantonese particle, *la*, indicating affirmation. B1 corrects himself and asks G1 how to write the characters. G1 says 'You can't.' The Cantonese phrase *m guai* is a colloquial expression that is rarely written. Regional varieties of Chinese, of which Cantonese is a major one, have many unique words and phrases that usually exist in spoken form only. Sometimes people invent written characters for such words and phrases or use characters that have similar pronunciations to approximate them. Even highly literate adult writers of Chinese face the challenge of knowing how to represent the regional and colloquial words and phrases in the written form. Cantonese is amongst the few regional varieties of Chinese that have an elaborate set of written characters for the dialectal expressions. However, this kind of advanced knowledge of register differences is rarely taught in the heritage language learning context. G1, however, does seem to be aware of the fact that *m guai* is a colloquial Cantonese expression that doesn't normally get written. Another boy, B2, joins in the discussion by writing down two characters that have a very similar pronunciation as the phrase *m guai*. However, the words he has written mean 'five dollars'. It is very likely that he has seen the expression in a Chinese shop or restaurant or even the Chinese school he is attending. It is not entirely clear what his intention is when he writes out the words. He appears to know that the words he has written down are not *m guai*, as when G1 points it out, he accepts it. It may be that it is his solution to the problem of representing colloquial Cantonese phrases, namely, finding an approximate that he knows. However, it may be that he simply wants to make fun of the task he has been asked to do.

It is at this point that the teacher comes over to the table and asks what is happening. B1 asks the question to the teacher. The question contains the very phrase, *m guai*, or 'Excuse me', that he is asking for help with. The word, *sang*, is shortened for *sinsang*, literally 'born before' (the speaker). It tends to be used as an address term for teachers or anyone more senior than the speaker, though it is more often used for a male addressee than a female one. The other pupils laugh, probably because they think B1 has used the wrong address term, but also possibly because the way B1 constructs the question, with *m guai* used twice, sounds funny. Indeed, B2 highlights the fact that there is a repetition in B1's question in his turn. The teacher's answer is exactly the same as G1's in her previous reply. B1 asks the teacher to clarify. The teacher uses an equally colloquial Cantonese expression in her elliptic reply, *mou la*, literally 'have no', meaning there is no written form for *m guai*. She then gives another Chinese expression for 'Excuse me', *dui m jiu*. *Dui m jiu* is more formal and exists in Mandarin and therefore has a written form that is commonly used. She writes it out and pronounces it in Cantonese. However, another girl at the same table, G2, asks the teacher whether the two phrases are the same. The teachers says yes and explains that *dui m jiu* is more formal. In fact, the two phrases are not the same in terms of meaning and usage. *Dui m jiu* is more apologetic, whereas *m guai* has no such connotation. B1 tries to clarify the usage with the teacher, but all the pupils look rather confused. The teacher then asks exactly what the pupils want to express and explains that different phrases are used in different contexts. After a short pause, G1 offers her explanation and seeks the teacher's confirmation. However, the teacher's response, 'you don't say it. You write it', confuses them even more. G2 moans 'So hard'. The teacher offers further explanation of the usage of different expressions, introducing a new phrase 請問 (*cheng man*, or 'please can I ask'). The real question the pupils have always had is how to write, and use, *m guai*. So G1 asks again. This time B1, who asked the question originally, offers his understanding that you do not write the phrase *m guai* at all. The discussion then changes its focus when the teacher says, following B1's turn, that *m guai* cannot be written because it is a Cantonese phrase. G1's utterance 'So you don't write Cantonese' can be seen as a challenge to the teacher's explanation. The pronoun she uses, 'you', could mean either everyone or the teacher herself specifically. The two boys seem to react differently; B2 probably feels that at last he understands the difference in usage, while B1 thinks that it is bad that one cannot write Cantonese. However, it is B1's reaction and his rejection of B2's apparent acceptance of the teacher's explanation that gets the laugh from the others. G1 further challenges the teacher by asking if everything has to be written in Mandarin. The teacher puts a stop to the discussion by turning to the whole class and warning them that they have only five minutes to finish the task.

Two issues emerge from this example that interest me in particular. First, we can see that translanguaging is commonplace amongst the pupils and the teacher. They move seemingly freely between languages and between speaking and writing. They are genuinely engaged in learning and problem-solving, and use translanguaging as a resource to facilitate that process. Second, and perhaps more important, is the gradual realization by the children of the status differential between different varieties of Chinese through the exchange. What started as an apparently simple question about writing two characters has turned into a discussion of the legitimacy of the language they speak and hence their linguistic and ethnic identity. As mentioned before, all Cantonese schools in Britain nowadays offer Mandarin classes to both children and their parents, whereas no Mandarin school teaches Cantonese. Mandarin is being actively promoted in the Chinese community in Britain as a new Chinese lingua franca to connect with mainland China and is fast gaining currency, at least in formal settings. Official visits by the Chinese embassy staff to the local Chinese community organizations are always conducted in Mandarin, and cultural events such as Chinese New Year celebrations are increasingly done in Mandarin as well. Mandarin has also replaced Cantonese in much of the satellite television and other entertainment media in Europe. Many Cantonese-speaking parents realize the pragmatic potential of Mandarin and encourage their children to learn it at the Chinese school. Yet, enthusiasm for Mandarin is by no means universal in the Chinese diaspora. There are groups who feel a strong affinity to Cantonese and nostalgia for Hong Kong. They see the spread of Mandarin as another example of the increasing power and influence of mainland China. Even among people who are not directly linked to Hong Kong, there are those who see the spread of Mandarin as a threat to Cantonese cultural heritage. Of course, the fact that many colloquial Cantonese words and phrases have no written form has nothing to do with the changing hierarchy and sociopolitical values amongst the different varieties of the Chinese language, and Cantonese is certainly not the only regional variety of Chinese that lacks written form for its special expressions. Nevertheless, when the community one belongs to is already undergoing dramatic changes, a realization that one's native tongue cannot be written must add to their feeling 'crap'.

That said, the teachers and the pupils in the Cantonese schools in Britain do write special characters to represent their language. Some of the notices in the Chinese complementary schools are typical examples of translanguaging between Cantonese characters, standard Chinese and English. The sticker in Figure 9.1 was placed on the wall of a toilet in one of the Cantonese schools. It says 'No Water. Go to 1F [1st floor]', where *no* is written in a colloquial Cantonese character 冇 whose standard Chinese equivalent would be two character 没有, *water* is written in standard Chinese and the rest in English.

However, the teachers often emphasize that the Cantonese characters are 'informal' and would not allow the pupils to use them in their homework or examination papers. The pupils, on the other hand, have been observed using Cantonese characters in their school work,

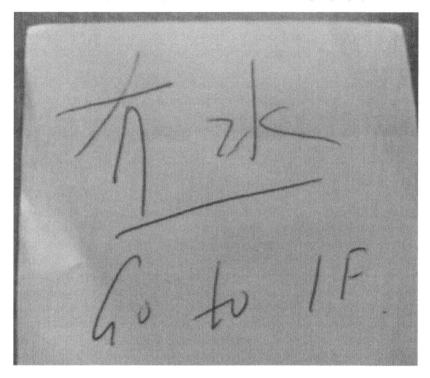

Figure 9.1 Handwritten sign in Chinese school

probably without knowing what the Mandarin equivalent was. Sometimes, their writing is clearly influenced by the Cantonese pronunciation, and they simply use approximates that they think they know. For example, in a piece of homework that we have seen, a boy in one of the Cantonese schools wrote 睇 *tai* (look) whose Mandarin equivalent is 看 *kan*. Another boy wrote 天日 *tin-yat* (tomorrow) when the Cantonese characters would be 聽日 *ting-yat* and the Mandarin equivalent 明天 *ming-tian*. In this latter case, it is more likely that the boy used a simpler character to approximate the pronunciation rather than mistaking one character from the Mandarin expression.

What these examples show is that teachers and pupils do use Cantonese characters wherever and whenever they can. They are making a functional difference in terms of the contexts in which different writing systems – Cantonese or Mandarin – should be used. This functional difference is making them realize that there is a more significant differential in terms of the symbolic value of the writing systems. The wider sociopolitical changes in the community they live in have been brought home to them in what seems to be a rather mundane manner. But the impact is nonetheless deep and thought-provoking.

We turn now to another example of translanguaging in the Chinese complementary school classroom. Example 2 is taken from a recording of a discussion in a Mandarin school in London. The pupils are mainly 15- to 17-year- olds. Most of them have done GCSE (General Certificate in Secondary Education) Chinese and are preparing to do A-level Chinese, which will qualify them for higher education entry. The topic of the discussion is the well-known poem, 'Dayan River, My Wet-Nurse' (大堰河—我的保姆), by the renowned Chinese poet and artist Ai Qing (1910–1996), father of the dissident artist Ai Weiwei. Using well-known literary works in language teaching is common practice in many different cultures. Chinese schools, both in China and in the Chinese diasporas, tend to use a lot of ancient poems and fables. This particular poem, however, is a piece of modern literature. The poem is in some sense biographical, as it speaks from someone who was brought up by a wet-nurse, who was later imprisoned for his patriotic beliefs and actions, and who vowed in the poem to change the world and to pay back what the wet-nurse has done for him. Ai Qing was given up at birth by his parents and brought up by peasants in the countryside, but he later became an artist and poet. This poem was written in the winter of 1932. Earlier that year, Ai Qing came back to China from France, after studying fine art there, and joined the League of Left-Wing Artists, a Shanghai-based group of communist sympathizers against the foreign colonization of China. He was arrested and imprisoned by the Kuomintang authorities, along with 12 other activists, for 'attempting to overthrow the government'. This poem was written in prison. It has been widely regarded in China as a patriotic epic poem and approved for use in secondary school textbooks on Chinese language and literature by the mainland Chinese government. The fact that such a poem is used in teaching in a Chinese complementary school in Britain is in itself remarkable. The pupils in the school know very little about Chinese history. They are generally aware that mainland China and Taiwan are separated by two different political systems, but they know very little about the civil wars that the Communist Party and the Kuomintang fought. The teacher, when teaching the poem, gives little background information on the time when the poem was written. It is simply taken as an example of patriotism that artists show towards China the motherland. Interestingly, some of the pupils are aware of the poet's son, Ai Weiwei, who had an exhibition of sunflower seeds at the Tate Modern in London in 2010.

At the time this discussion took place, Ai Weiwei's arrest in China for alleged tax evasion had been in the news, and many of the pupils had heard about it.

Example 2

T: So, 你看了这首诗后, 你首先注意到的是什么？或者说, 你的第一感觉、首先反映的是什么？
      'So, when you read the poem what do you notice first? In other words, what is your first feeling or reaction?'

G1:   He loves his wet-nurse.

T: Yeah. That's right. What else? 还有什么？ ('what else?')

B1:   It's kind of graphic.

T: What?

Some pupils giggle.

B2:   You mean PORNO-graphic.

B1:   Shut up.

G1:   It's true actually. It's got a lot of … naked … nakedness I suppose.

B1:   Yeah.

T: What? Where? [comes over to B1]

B1:   There [pointing to lines that mention lips, cheeks and breasts]
      呈给吻过我的唇 ('Dedicated to your lips that kissed me')
      呈给你泥黑的温柔的脸颜 ('Dedicated to your cheeks, warm and soft, the colour of earth')
      呈给你养育了我的乳房 ('Dedicated to your breasts that suckled me')

B2:   Are you supposed to discuss that?

B3:   Not in class.

B1:   She [pointing to the teacher] asked.

Some giggle.

G2:   Is he religious?

T: Religious? Where?

G2:   He says '咒语' ('condemnation'). 还有 '赞美诗', '灵魂','天堂', '地狱' ('also praise, spirit, heaven, hell').
      坐在辉煌的结彩的堂上 ('Sitting in a resplendent hall bedecked with silk')
      ......
      你的乳儿是在狱里 ('Your foster-child is in jail')
      ......
      我是在写着给予这不公道的世界的咒语 ('I write condemnations of this unjust World')
      ......
      写着一首呈给你的赞美诗 ('Writing a poem of praise, dedicated to you')
      呈给你黄土下紫色的灵魂 ('Dedicated to your spirit, purple under the brown soil')

G1: Mm. It's only 堂 ('hall') though.
T: That's good.
B3: Is that why he was arrested?
B1: No he wasn't arrested. His son was arrested.
G1: He was. He was too.
B2: Yeah. If you are religious, you will be arrested in China.
T: That's not true. If you are against the government.
G1: But I thought Ai Weiwei didn't pay tax.
T: Who are you talking about? We are talking about Ai Qing, his father, not Ai Weiwei.
B1: Is sunflower a religious symbol in Chinese?
G1: What?
T: All right. Pay attention. 大堰的堰不是这个雁 ('The *yan* 堰 in Dayan is not this *yan* 雁').
G2: What about (finger spelling), like swallow?
T: No. That's *yan* (She writes 燕).

When the teacher asks the class for their reaction to reading the poem, G1 offers what might be termed surface reading, that is, an obvious, literary interpretation. B1, on the other hand, comments on the references to certain body parts and describes it as 'graphic'. The other pupils can see what he is referring to as they giggle. B2 teases him by saying 'You mean PORNO-graphic.' The teacher comes over to B1 and asks what part of the poem he is talking about. As G1 points out the references, correctly, G2 asks whether they should be talking about it, and B3 adds 'Not in class'. B1 protests that it is the teacher who asked the question and he is merely responding to the teacher. At this point, G2 offers another observation by asking whether the poet is religious. The teacher seems intrigued by the question and asks G2 to clarify. G2 refers to some key words in the poem that do have religious connotations, although she mistakes 堂 (*tang*) 'hall' for 天堂 (*tian tang*) 'heaven' and 狱 (*yu*) 'jail' for 地狱 (*di yu*) 'hell'. In both of the mistaken cases, she reads the monosyllabic words for disyllabic words. It later transpired that the girl is a Cantonese first language speaker, and Cantonese has more monosyllabic words than Mandarin. Besides these minor technical details, her reading is an interesting one. And the teacher accepts it. B3 then asks if being religious is the reason that the poet was arrested. B1 tries to correct B3 by pointing out that it is the son, Ai Weiwei, who has been arrested. G1 defends B3 by saying that Ai Qing, too, was arrested. This seemingly factual discussion indicates that these pupils are fully aware of what's going on around them as well as in the wider society. They have a good level of political awareness. When B2 makes the statement that one gets arrested for being religious, the teacher corrects him and says that one would get arrested for being against the government, not for being religious. G1 then offers her contribution by repeating what she must have heard from the news that Ai Weiwei was arrested for tax evasion. The teacher tries to refocus on the poem and the poet, not the poet's son. However, B1 asks, possibly tongue-in-cheek, if sunflower is a religious symbol, still making connections with Ai Weiwei's arrest. The teacher has to stop them and directs their attention to the writing of the characters.

The fact that this discussion of religion and arrest, either of the poet or his artist son, takes place around reading of what is supposed to be a patriotic poem is significant. It is unlikely that the teacher had intended to have such a discussion; rather, she wanted to give the pupils a sense of nationalism by teaching them a poem that was written at a time when China was being invaded by foreign powers and the government in power at the time was corrupt and powerless. Yet, the pupils bring with them their own social experience and understanding of the world and their knowledge, albeit limited, of contemporary China into the reading of the poem. They are not passive learners, but active participants in the learning process. They make honest contributions to the discussion, which in fact helps to raise it to a higher level. Translanguaging is an integral part of the discussion and contributes positively to the learning process.

One further example of pupils bringing their own cultural experience into the learning through translanguaging is an exchange that was also triggered by the reading of a modern poem. The poem is by Xu Zhimo 徐志摩 (1897–1931), a Romantic poet who studied in both the USA and the UK. It was England, especially Cambridge, that he loved most. And in 1928, after his last visit to Cambridge, he wrote his best-known poem 'Goodbye Again to Cambridge', which is now inscribed on a white marble at the back of King's College, Cambridge. The exchange in Example 3 took place after the teacher had read aloud the poem to the class, fourteen 13- to 14-year-old pupils in a Mandarin school in London. The teacher then explains that 康桥 *Kang Qiao* is the old Chinese translation for Cambridge. This is, in fact, not wholly correct. Many English names, for places, people and objects, are transliterated into Chinese according to Cantonese pronunciation, rather than Mandarin or Putonghua pronunciation. The standard Chinese name for Cambridge is *Jian Qiao*. The word 剑 is pronounced 'Kam' in Cantonese. So, Kang Qiao, as the poet had it, was once used by some speakers of Chinese for Cambridge. However, the difference between the two Chinese versions is not old versus new, but rather a dialectal difference. This has caused an interesting discussion of Chinese names for foreign places in the class.

Example 3

B1: Oxford is *Niu Jin* 意译不是音译.
'Oxford is *Niu Jin*, meaning translation not sound translation.'

T: 对。你还挺明白的。
'Correct. You are quite knowledgeable.'

B1: 我爸牛津毕业的。
'My dad is an Oxford graduate.'

B2: 那新西兰又是意译又是音译。
'But New Zealand (*Xin Xilan*) is both meaning translation and sound translation.'

T: 嗯。新是 New.
'Um. *Xin* is New.'

B2: 我 uncle 在新西兰。
'My uncle lives in New Zealand.'

B1: 那纽约呢？
'What about New York?'

G1: That's pronunciation.

B1: But it's 约克 *Yue Ke*, isn't it?

G1: So you want it 纽约克.
'So you want it *Niu Yue Ke*.'

B2: 新约克.
'*Xin* (New) *Yue Ke*.'

T: 对呀。是那个意思。
'Correct, that's the meaning.'

G1: 可是是纽约.
'But it is *Niu Ye*.'

T: 你们去过纽约吗？
'Have you been to New York?'
Several pupils: 去过 ('Have been').

T: Wow, 都去过啊！
'Wow, you have all been there!'

G1: 老师,那新加坡呢？
'Teacher, what about Singapore?'

T: 新加坡是音译。
'Singapore (*Xin Jia Po*) is sound translation.'

G2: 也有人叫星加坡.
'Some people call it *Xing Jia Po*.'

T: 那也是音译.
'It is also sound translation.'

B2: 老师, 她妈是新加坡人 [pointing to G2].
'Teacher, her mom is Singaporean.'

T: 是吗？
'Is that right?'

G2 nods.

T: 你们看看中国的名字英文里有哪些音译哪些意译？

'Can you tell me which English names for Chinese places are sound translations and which are meaning translations?'

B1: I know Yellow River.

T: 对, 是意译。
'Correct, it's meaning translation.'

G1: Yangtze River.

T: 对, 音译。
'Correct, it's sound translation.'

B1: I thought it was 长江 (*Chang Jiang*), Long River.

T: 是。但是也叫扬子江。
'Yes. But it is also called Yangtze River.'

Place names have been translated in various ways in Chinese, some with sound transliteration and others being renditions of meaning. Similarly, some Chinese place names have been translated into English with meaning renditions, such as the Yellow River, while others, such as the Yangtze River, are sound transliterations. The different forms often cause frustrations and difficulties for learners. However, that does not seem to be the case for the pupils in this particular class. In fact, the pupils in this example seem to be very knowledgeable with the various translated names. Nevertheless, what we see here is not simply the pupils showing off what they know in terms of translation between Chinese and English but also the places they have been to and their global connections. Their transnational and transcultural identity is performed vividly through what appears to be mundane classroom discussions of technical details of sound and meaning translation.

9.5 Summary and conclusions

As has been said at the beginning of this chapter, despite the commonplace occurrence of multilingual practices in our everyday life, there is a pervasive belief in society, bilingual and monolingual alike, that languages are best kept separate, discrete and pure; mixing and switching between languages are seen as interference or trespassing which may have a detrimental effect on both individual language users and the communities they live in. Multilingual practices by children especially are often frowned upon or taken as indications of deficits in their linguistic, cognitive and social capacities: they mix and switch between languages because they don't know any of their languages well enough to keep them separate. I have tried to show, through the analysis of translanguaging practices in the Chinese complementary school classrooms, that far from being evidence of deficit of any kind, the multilingual, transnational children are highly skilled in their language use. Moreover, they have an acute awareness of what they can do and what they can't do with the linguistic resources they have, and are able to utilize all the resources appropriately and effectively. Thus, translanguaging is evidence of the children's multicompetence, creativity and criticality.

But more importantly, I have tried to show that translanguaging enables the children to bring together not only their multiple linguistic and cognitive skills but also their knowledge and experience of the social world, especially their awareness of history and the trajectory of the community they belong to and their positions in it, and their attitudes and beliefs. Furthermore, translanguaging has a transformative effect in terms of both the information or facts that children learn and acquire as information and their sense of belonging, position and identity. When the pupils in Example 1 realize that their native language cannot be fully written down or accepted in formal contexts, they also become aware of the impact of globalization on their community's position in a new, changing world and their own sociocultural identity. When the pupils in Example 2 raise issues of religion and arrests in China, they are also revealing their political awareness and understanding of different values systems. And when the pupils in Example 3 show off what they know of the different translations of world place names, they are also demonstrating their transnational and transcultural identities.

Translanguaging has been shown to be an effective pedagogical practice in bilingual and multilingual education. What I have tried to do in this chapter is to demonstrate that the value of translanguaging goes far beyond pedagogy and learning. It can have a fundamental impact on the development of identity, social relationships and values amongst its users. It creates a lived experience and a social space for multilinguals to perform and transform their identity, attitudes and values.

References

Baker, C. (2006). *Foundations of Bilingual Education and Bilingualism* (4th edn). Clevedon: Multilingual Matters.

Becker, A. L. (1988). Language in particular: a lecture. In D. Tannen (ed.), *Linguistics in Context* (pp. 17–35). Norwood, NJ: Ablex.

Becker, A. L. (1991a). A short essay on languaging. In F. Steiner (ed.), *Research and Reflexivity* (pp. 226–34). Newbury Park, CA: Sage.

Becker, A. L. (1991b). Language and languaging. *Language and Communication*, 11(2), 33–5.

Brumfit, C. Myles, F., Mitchell, R., Johnston, B. and Ford, P. (2005). Modern languages and the development of criticality. *International Journal of Applied Linguistics*, 15(2), 145–68.

Canagarajah, S. (2011). Translanguaging in the classroom: emerging issues for research and pedagogy. *Applied Linguistics Review*, 2, 1–27.

Cenoz, J. and Gorter, D. (2011). Focus on multilingualism: a study of trilingual writing. *The Modern Language Journal*, 95(3), 356–69.

Cook, V. J. (1991). The poverty-of-the-stimulus argument and multi-competence. *Second Language Research*, 7, 103–17.

Creese, A. and Blackledge, A. (2010). Translanguaging in the bilingual classroom: a pedagogy for learning and teaching? *The Modern Language Journal*, 94, 103–15.

García, O. (2009). *Bilingual Education in the 21st Century*. Oxford: Blackwell.

García, O. and Li Wei (2014). *Translanguaging: Language, Bilingualism, Education*. Basingstoke: Palgrave Macmillan.

Gumperz, J. J. (1982). *Discourse Strategies*. Cambridge: Cambridge University Press.

Hall, I. M. (1996). Languaging: the linguistics of psychotherapy. PhD dissertation, The Union Institute. Dissertation Abstracts International A, 57 (11) 4717.

Kramsch, C. (2006). From communicative competence to symbolic competence. *The Modern Language Journal*, 90, 249–52.

Kramsch, C. and Whiteside, A. (2008). Language ecology in multilingual settings: towards a theory of symbolic competence. *Applied Linguistics*, 29, 645–71.

Lado, R. (1979). Thinking and 'languaging': a psycholinguistic model of performance and learning. *Sophia Linguistica*, 12, 3–24.

Li, Wei. (2006). Complementary schools: past, present and future. *Language and Education*, 20, 76–83.

Li, Wei. (2007). Chinese. In D. Britain (ed.), *Language of the British Isles* (pp. 308–25). Cambridge: Cambridge University Press.

Li, Wei. (2011). Moment analysis and translanguaging space. *Journal of Pragmatics*, 43, 1222–35.

Li, Wei and Wu, C. J. (2009). Polite Chinese children revisited: creativity and the use of code-switching in the Chinese complementary school classroom. *International Journal of Bilingual Education and Bilingualism*, 12, 193–211.

Li, Wei and Zhu, Hua (2010a). Changing hierarchies in Chinese language education for the British Chinese learners. In L. Tsung and K. Cruickshank (eds.), *Teaching and Learning Chinese in Global Contexts: Multimodality and Literacy in the New Media Age* (pp. 11–27.). London: Continuum.

Li, Wei and Zhu, Hua (2010b). Voices from the diaspora: changing hierarchies and dynamics of Chinese multilingualism. *International Journal of the Sociology of Language*, 205, 155–71.

Maschler, Y. (2009). *Metalanguage in Interaction: Hebrew Discourse Markers*. Amsterdam: John Benjamins.

Smagorinsky, P. (1998). Thinking and speech and protocol analysis. *Mind, Culture and Activity*, 5, 157–77.

Swain, M. (2006). Languaging, agency and collaboration in advanced second language learning. In H. Byrnes (ed.), *Advanced Language Learning: The Contributions of Halliday and Vygotsky* (pp. 95–108). London: Continuum.

Swann, J. and Maybin, J. (eds.) (2007). Language creativity in everyday contexts. Special issue of *Applied Linguistics*, 28(4).

Williams, C. (1994). Arfarniado Ddulliau Dysguac Addysguyng Nghyddestun Addysg Uwchradd Ddwyieithog. Unpublished PhD thesis, University of Wales Bangor.

Williams, C. (1996). Secondary education: teaching in the bilingual situation. In C. Williams, G. Lewis and C. Baker (eds.), *The Language Policy: Taking Stock*. (pp. 63–78). Llangefni, Wales: CAI.

You, H. (2006). *Chinese Community in the UK 2006* [in Chinese]. London: Mei & Ken.

10 Constructing in-between spaces to 'do' bilingualism: a tale of two high schools in one city

Ofelia García, Nelson Flores and
Heather Homonoff Woodley

10.1 Introduction

As technology and migration have gone global, multilingualism has become more familiar. It is interesting, however, that our greater awareness of multiple language practices has no correspondence at the societal level, even when educational programmes are organized for immigrants. In the United States, the greater language diversity has led some schools to shed traditional models of bilingual education that had been organized to educate especially the most numerous language-minority group – Spanish-speaking Latinos. This has meant that the bilingual education programmes of the past – both developmental programmes and transitional bilingual education programmes – have been increasingly abandoned, while programmes in which instruction is in English only (self-contained English as a Second Language programmes) have grown. At the same time, however, there are more schools that are being organized to teach two language groups in two languages, leading to the growth of the so-called 'dual language' bilingual programmes. What's going on? Are we societally on board with monolingualism or multilingualism? And what is happening in these supposedly monolingual English as a Second Language programmes and bilingual dual language programmes?

This chapter takes the position that language in US education has been, and continues to be, a site of struggle over power and identity. In the twentieth century, the tension was between those who wanted to have bilingual education options and those who insisted that schooling should be in English only. Although this struggle between supporters and critics of bilingual education continues, the tension today is between those who see *bilingualism as a commodity* that they must *have* as two separate languages, and those who *do bilingualism as bilingual Americans*. These two positions, of course, result in different stances towards types of education and pedagogy, as well as theories of what language and bilingualism are. Those who want to *have bilingualism* because of its societal and market value, most often Anglos who come from monolingual households, insist on programmes that strictly separate languages and insist on bilingualism being two separate languages. That is, bilingualism for them is additive (Lambert, 1975) and linear. Those who *do bilingualism* in the United States, most often bilingual themselves, show a more flexible attitude towards bilingual language use and understand bilingualism as one complex language repertoire. For these people, bilingualism is dynamic (García, 2009) and enacted through translanguaging,[1] that is, the flexible use of linguistic resources by bilinguals in order to make sense of their complex worlds (García, 2009; Blackledge & Creese, 2010; Creese & Blackledge, 2010; Hornberger & Link, 2012; Lewis et al., 2012a, 2012b; García & Li Wei, 2014; see also Creese et al., this volume).

At the same time, because the language separation / two languages idea has been 'normalized' in the imaginations of many, including language-minoritized communities, and because that position in the past had given US Latinos a measure of cultural autonomy in education, there is some fear among many Latino educators that support of a more dynamic bilingualism, rather than separate English and Spanish spaces, will result in stamping out bilingual education and losing protection for Spanish. This chapter considers the tensions between three positions: (1) a 'monolingual' position that insists that immigrant students be taught in English so that they 'have' English, (2) a 'dual' position of wanting to 'have' English and Spanish and (3) an integrative dynamic one that normalizes 'doing' bilingualism as an American. We present a multi-sited ethnographic-based case study (Hannerz, 2003) that shows how these tensions have been negotiated in two high schools for emergent bilinguals[2] that have been organized to educate, for the most part, Latino immigrants. The schools have been able to construct in-between spaces that allow them the flexibility to get their students to 'do' bilingualism as US Latinos, while simultaneously following official positions of English-only and separation of languages.

The two schools are autonomous and yet are located in the same school building in the borough of the Bronx, New York City. The year-long ethnographic studies of the language education policies in the two schools (2010–2011) were conducted by the three authors.[3] The ethnographic studies included a full day of observations of classes every two weeks, as well as interviews with the educators, over the academic year. Many have called attention to the power of ethnography as a lens to ground studies of language policy (Hornberger & Johnson, 2007;

McCarty, 2010), including not only language management decisions, enacted by the state and other authoritative bodies, but also and most importantly, the language ideologies and language practices of the local community (Spolsky, 2004). Our study will show that language education policy is interpreted, implemented and resisted differently in the two schools (Johnson, 2009; Menken & García, 2010), leading educators in both schools to construct in-between spaces that transgress the English as a Second Language or dual language policy that the schools officially follow.

Our multi-sited ethnographic case studies extend the work of James Collins (2011), who asked the questions 'Who gets to define what counts as language?' (p. 129), 'What are languages?' (p. 131) and 'How is language in the world?' (p. 132), a world organized into tiered, hierarchical power relations as well as 'local' speech communities. The questions that we explore in this chapter through our case studies can then be formulated as follows:

- How do educators in two schools for emergent bilingual adolescents who are newcomers to the USA negotiate official school policies of English only and language separation? How do educators and students perform their language practices?
- What ideologies about bilingualism and education of language minorities are manifested through the analysis of classroom discourse?

Ricento and Hornberger (1996) have talked about 'unpeeling the onion' of language education policy. The multi-sited case studies in this chapter look at what happens in schools at the level of community of practice. But beyond the school itself, an ethnographic study of language education policy must consider the forces that are created at the nation-state level and the global level. Thus, we start this chapter by reviewing the language education policies and ideologies that have been in place in the USA since the twentieth century. Following a Bakhtinian (1981) approach, we bring in voices at different timescales and from different communities in order to show that language education policy operates at different levels simultaneously.

10.2 'Having' bilingualism or 'doing' bilingualism?

Language education, steeped in the idea that one must acquire/learn/ have a language, has had a long history of separation – separation of students by language levels to keep input comprehensible, and of languages in teaching to focus attention on the 'target' language (Howatt,

1984; Yu, 2000). Yet as language education has entered the mainstream school system, especially to teach language-minoritized students, the concepts of separate distinct levels of proficiency, as well as separation of language practices, have started to be questioned (Fitts, 2006; Cummins, 2007; García, 2009; García & Leiva, 2014; Kibler, 2010; Martínez, 2010; Canagarajah, 2011; Li Wei, 2011; Palmer & Martínez, 2013; Sayer, 2012; see also Creese et al.; Kramsch & Huffmaster; and Li Wei, this volume). This questioning has to do with more and more students using language and 'doing' their bilingualism differently from how educators expect. The history of the language education of US Latinos serves as the backdrop for the analysis of how separating languages so that some privileged students can 'have' one of them or two of them has coexisted in tension with the bilingual performances of language-minoritized students.

During the many years of racial segregation in the United States, even though Mexicans were considered 'white' under state segregation laws, they were segregated through local practice (Donato et al., 1991). The US Supreme Court declared racial segregation unconstitutional in 1954 in *Brown* vs. *Board of Education*, but language categories functioned differently from racial ones. For example, whereas it was clear that racial segregation excluded students from the equal educational opportunity guaranteed under the Civil Rights Act of 1964, integration for bilingual Mexican students often meant 'submersion' in English-only education and educational failure.

During this time, language education followed the Direct Method, as well as the Audio-lingual Method. Both methods advocated against the use of translation and of the student's language. Following this approach, the English as a Second Language programmes that were developed in the 1950s and 1960s ignored and minimized the use of the students' home languages. But in the wake of the civil rights era, and as a result of federal funding that became available through the Bilingual Education Act (1968), as well as the Supreme Court's decision in *Lau* vs. *Nichols* (1974) upholding language-minoritized students' rights to an education they understood, schools started to develop bilingual education programmes. As bilingual education came into being, pedagogies that supported complete language separation became contested. Latino teachers were now in charge of the education of their own children, making it possible to use the fluid bilingual ways of speaking in the Latino community to educate in ways that affirmed the children's complex identities. In many cases, the school leadership and Anglo educators simply did not care about these students and were happy to leave their education in the hands of Latino educators who knew them best. However, others started to fear that

Latino children would continue to 'do' Spanish, alongside English, when a shift to English had been expected of all immigrants in the past.

The Bilingual Education Act was reauthorized for the last time in 1994. In exchange for lifting the quota on English-only programmes that could be funded through bilingual education funds, a different kind of bilingual education programme, one that was not simply transitional, was embraced by all – the two-way immersion programmes. These programmes (often called 'dual language' education) saw Spanish and English as something to be dually 'had', by Anglos as well as Latinos.[4] In drawing tight boundaries around the two languages, and identifying half of the students as 'native speakers' of English, and the other half as 'native speakers' of Spanish, the Latino students' ethnolinguistic identity, as well as that of the Anglo students, was defined as static. On the one hand, Spanish speakers were marked as 'non-native second-language' speakers of English, ensuring that only Anglos held authoritative English. On the other, the Spanish used and taught through complete separation from English had little to do with the bilingual practices of US Latinos. All students needed to 'have' English for standardized tests, and although in dual language bilingual programmes they were encouraged to perform English *and* Spanish throughout the first six years of schools, they were never to 'do' bilingualism. That is, these dual language programmes saw the two languages as separate and ignored the translanguaging of bilingual communities.

As other kinds of bilingual education programmes came under attack, 'sheltered English' or 'structured immersion' programmes, modelled on the immersion programmes in Canada that had been developed for language majority anglophone children, were developed. These programmes use English only. It is interesting to note that these English-only programmes have reappropriated the same 'immersion methodology' that dual language bilingual programmes follow, although they use it to undermine the goal of bilingualism. The methodology carefully 'shelters', or brackets, one language from the other, while language use is slower and more simplified, with guarded vocabulary, shorter sentences and visuals or modelling of lesson and graphic organizers for support.

As transitional bilingual education programmes started to be dismantled with a mandate to educate Latino students in English only, another change was taking place. The ethnolinguistic categories that had been made possible by power relations associated with colonization and nation-state ideologies started to be blurred (Makoni & Pennycook, 2007), and new subjectivities were created. Ethnolinguistic groups started to 'bleed' into each other. Latinos in the United States were now more heterogeneous than ever. On the one hand, Mexicans, Puerto Ricans and Cubans were now joined by many from Central America and South America and, on the East Coast especially, by Dominicans. The educational failure of Latinos was now no longer just that of the first generation who needed to learn English, but also of second- and third-generation Latinos who were further along the bilingual continuum, and many who were even English monolingual. On the other hand, the increased social integration had led to more contact between non-Latinos and Latinos, with many children who identified as US Latinos having parents of different ethnicities and language proficiencies. Finally, many Latinos now spoke languages other than either English or Spanish at home, as more speakers of indigenous Latin American languages joined the growing ranks of US Latinos. All of a sudden, dual language bilingual programmes that were supposed to be 'two-way' programmes realized they could no longer categorize children as one or the other. Latinos showed a complexity of language use that could not be categorized as simply Spanish or English. At the same time, increased immigration from many different contexts also meant that the school population was now not simply just English-speaking and Spanish-speaking, but consisted of speakers of many languages other than English. English speakers could not be assumed to be white Anglos as they had been in the past (an assumption that in and of itself ignored the English usage of people of colour, and most notably of African Americans, throughout US history); instead, English-speaking East Indians, West Indians, Africans were now numerous and visible, and features of African-American English were widely heard. Many of these speakers were themselves bilingual. Bilingualism, as it had been previously understood, started to be challenged not only by the monolingual perspective but also by a more complex multilingual perspective.

Faced by the backlash against bilingualism now coming from a monolingual positionality, as well as from a multilingual one that found bilingualism insufficient, Latino educators, anxious to carve out a space where their children could be educated through English and Spanish, mounted the only wagon that was available to them – that of dual language programmes. However, in their increasingly segregated neighbourhoods, two-way bilingual education programmes were not always possible. Under the guise of 'dual language', many Latino educators instituted bilingual education programmes, now called 'one-way dual language' programmes. In these bilingual programmes, Latino students with different language profiles and generational and national differences were educated. In return, however, Latinos gave up the greater language fluidity that had been prevalent in other types of bilingual education programmes. In both developmental mainte- nance programmes and transitional bilingual education programmes, Latino educators had used a bilingual vernacular which included lin- guistic borrowings as well as 'code-switching' (Jacobson, 1983). Although many language scholars have argued that these everyday language practices of bilinguals are normative and intelligent expres- sions of bilingualism (Poplack, 1980; Zentella, 1997; MacSwan, 2000), these practices have been racialized and stigmatized (Martínez, 2010; Rosa, 2010), and rendered as 'corrupted' language, as 'Spanglish'. The 'dual language' separation arrangement instead was supposed to generate 'parallel monolingualisms' (Heller, 1999). But in becoming 'dual language learners', Latino children have given up 'doing' bilingualism as bilingual US Latinos, capable of sustaining these complex language practices as Americans.

The case studies that we present below are of two small schools that focus on the education of Latino emergent bilinguals and that are located in one building.[5] The two schools serve only 'newcomers', that is, students who have been in the United States for less than two years at the time of admission. Furthermore, the two schools have had remarkable success in educating these students and have above-aver- age graduation rates. As we will see, both show the traces of the tension between three language ideologies – (1) an English-only monolingual ideology, (2) an additive bilingual ideology of 'having' English sepa- rately from Spanish and (3) a dynamic bilingual ideology of 'doing' bilingualism as performances of bilingual US Latinos. The case studies show that in order to exist and be successful, these two schools have had to take up an official discourse of English-only, and of separation of English from Spanish. In reality, however, our data show that both schools are distinguished by a flexibility of language use, by what we call translanguaging practices, which make possible the development of bilingualism and bilingual US identities while advancing concepts of equality and social justice that question the superiority of English- only. In the sections below, we first offer a description of both schools, before analysing the ideologies about bilingualism and education that are manifested in the classroom discourse.

10.3 The two schools: a description

Both of our schools are located in an old school building that was for- merly a large comprehensive high school in the borough of the Bronx – in 2007 the borough with the highest rate of poverty in the city (27%), the highest rate of single-parenthood (60%) and the lowest number of college-educated residents (17%) (Block, 2009). In 2009, 32% of the residents of the Bronx were foreign-born, 56% spoke languages other than English at home and 45% spoke Spanish at home (US Census Bureau, 2009). The sense of urban decay is obvious at the school building's entrance. To enter the school you must go through metal detectors, and security guards often frisk students as they walk in.

One high school, which we will call the Latin American Intercontinental School, is located on parts of the first and second floors of the building. The school belongs to a network of high schools that were founded precisely to educate immigrants who are new to English. The original network model required that students spoke home languages other than English. Yet this particular school was organized to work with only Spanish-speaking immigrants and is, for purposes of State accountability,[6] an English as a Second Language programme. The other school, the High School of Global Practices, located on parts of the fourth and fifth floor of the same school building, is also for State accountability purposes an English as a Second Language programme, although it also indicates to the State that it has a 'dual language' bilingual programme. When it started ten years ago, all students were Spanish speakers; however, the recent arrival in the Bronx of many immigrants who do not speak Spanish has led to the growing linguistic diversity of the school. Whereas the first school has evolved from a model that required that the newcomers had different languages to one that now includes only Spanish speakers, the other school has moved in the opposite direction, now including immigrant students who speak languages other than Spanish. Both schools report to New York State that they have 'English as a Second Language' programmes. However, data gathered during one year of observation in the schools reveal that their enactment of a teaching 'model', as either English as a Second Language or 'dual language', their pedagogies and the discursive practices within the schools do not respond neatly to traditional definitions. Both schools show the insufficiencies of educational 'models' and of traditional descriptions of language use in schools with language diversity.

10.3.1 Latin American Intercontinental School

At the time of the study, the school was in its third year of existence. As mentioned above, the student population is 100% Spanish-speaking and all are emergent bilinguals; that is, all are officially designated 'English Language Learners'. The majority of the students are from the Caribbean, particularly from the Dominican Republic, and 100% of the students are eligible for free and reduced lunch because of low income. Despite the fact that all students are Spanish-speaking, about 20% of the total student body enters school with very low Spanish literacy levels and have experienced interrupted formal education for more than two years. Students are organized into two academies – the junior academy mixes ninth and tenth graders, and the senior academy combines eleventh and twelfth graders. Students are not separated into levels for English classes or other content classes. All classrooms have tables instead of traditional desks to facilitate the collaborative group work that lies at the core of the school's approach to learning. The school prides itself on teaching language through content, interdisciplinary planning, project-based learning and rigorous portfolio presentations that students are expected to complete every semester.

10.3.2 High School of Global Practices

The High School of Global Practices was opened ten years ago. Students entering this school are also categorized as 'English Language Learners' by the NYC Department of Education. About 98% of the school population is eligible for free or reduced lunch. The student population of the school is about 90% Spanish-speaking, most are from the Dominican Republic, and some classes are composed entirely of Spanish speakers. However, there are increasing numbers of students from Bangladesh, various West African countries (most from Guinea, with some from Togo, Burkina Faso, Senegal, Mali and the Ivory Coast) and Arab countries, especially Yemen and Morocco. The students who speak languages other than Spanish are predominantly Muslim. Twenty percent of the students in the school are categorized as having interrupted formal education and come with very low home language literacy levels.

In the case of the two schools in our study, the official policy of English-only and language separation does not reflect the diversity of discourses found in the schools.

The next section analyses how it is that both schools have been able to negotiate the official stories through the complex discursive practices that educators have adopted in educating these language-minority students.

10.4 Official and unofficial stories on bilingualism and education

Officially for State accountability purposes, as we have said, the schools have traditional English as a Second Language programmes, and one school has a very small dual language bilingual programme. However, our year-long ethnographic study revealed that this official policy had little to do with the ideologies that many educators in the school held about bilingualism and education, or with the language practices in which teachers and students engaged. We have chosen to describe the classroom interactions of five teachers who are responsible for supposedly different linguistic spaces within the schools. At the Latin American Intercontinental School, we describe interactions between three teachers in their allegedly 'English', 'bilingual' and 'Spanish' classroom, and their students. At the High School of Global Practices, we offer an account of interactions between a teacher and students in a classroom that was said to be the 'Spanish' component of the 'dual language' programme, as well as of interactions of a teacher and students in an 'English' classroom. We analyse how these classrooms become in reality 'translanguaging spaces' (Li Wei, 2011; see also Li Wei, this volume), spaces where 'a new discourse is being produced by a new trans-subject' (García & Leiva, 2014). A translanguaging space refers not to the use of two separate languages or even to the shift of one language to the other. A theory of translanguaging posits that from the perspective of bilinguals, what we have is one linguistic repertoire with features that bilingual speakers use which have been socially assigned to one or another language (García & Li Wei, 2014). Translanguaging is rooted in the belief that bilinguals select language features from one linguistic repertoire and soft assemble their language practices in ways that fit their particular sociolinguistic situation (García & Li Wei, 2014). By positioning the discourse 'between' two languages that are no longer static or linked to one national identity, translanguaging then generates alternative representations and enunciations (García, 2009; García and Leiva, 2014). We turn now to how this happens in the two schools.

10.4.1 Latin American Intercontinental School

On paper and for State accountability purposes, this school is officially designated as an English as a Second Language programme, which technically speaking indicates an English-only approach to teaching and learning. Yet, despite the name of its official programme model, fluid bilingual practices are present as a tool for meaning-making in all classes observed. The school has even officially sanctioned that the math class be taught in Spanish. Below we describe the construction of three different translanguaging spaces in the school in what have been traditionally an English Language Arts class, an officially 'bilingual' math class and a Native Language Arts class.

TRANSLANGUAGING IN ENGLISH LANGUAGE ARTS

Although officially an English class, this class is taught by a teacher whose home language is Italian, and who thus leverages her knowledge of Italian in order to communicate with her Spanish-speaking students. This allows her to develop strong affective bonds with her students while advancing their learning. As one student put it:

> Oh, Angela, la Miss Angela. O sea ella no sabe español, pero ella hace el intento de ayudar … o sea, esa clase no más corresponde en inglés … pero ella hace el intento con nosotros … ayudarnos, o sea si una cosa está en inglés, ella trata de traducir más o menos en español para ir aprendiendo más o menos lo que dicen.
>
> [Oh, Angela, Miss Angela. She doesn't know Spanish but she tries to help … I mean this class is just in English … but she tries with us … to help us, I mean if something is in English, she tries to translate more or less in Spanish to keep learning more or less what is said.]

We describe here a lesson that involved reading the play *Twelve Angry Men*. Although the text is in English, the lesson is an example of how a translanguaging space is created by the teacher. To contextualize the reading of the play, students watch a short clip from the movie of the play in English with Spanish subtitles first, then in English without subtitles. Students are provided with the script of certain sections written in English, with Spanish translations. Students then engage in a writing activity analysing what the judge said, using the script that has been provided. Not only does Angela use written texts in Spanish (both the subtitles and the script) to help students understand the English of the text, but she also draws on their increased content understanding of the plot to help them discuss the text. During the discussion, students participate using their entire language repertoire, including Spanish language practices. Angela ensures that all students understand the meanings in the text. She asks such things as: 'Qué significa x?' 'How do you say y?' 'Can you tell us in Spanish in your own words what it means?' But beyond this, Angela points often to cognates in the text. For example, at one point she has written a sentence on the blackboard that includes the word *verdict*. Pointing to the word, she tells them: 'This one is also close to Spanish.' And she sometimes uses her understanding of Italian to avoid confusions that would steer students in the wrong direction:

Angela: Who is the defendant?
Student 1: *El defensor!*

Angela: The defendant is not the lawyer.
Student 2:   *El defendido*. The person that is accused.

Two things happen in this exchange that would not happen in an English-only approach. First, Angela is able to use her receptive skills in Spanish to clarify a student's misunderstanding of the meaning of the word *defendant*. Second, after having negotiated meaning in Spanish, a student is then able to explain the meaning of the word in English. The student's Spanish is used to facilitate rather than hinder English language development.

In effect, through the teacher's leveraging of fluid languaging in this classroom discourse, students are learning to use their entire semiotic repertoire to make meaning in the classroom and to develop language practices that are socially regarded as standard English. Students are being taught how to 'do' bilingualism, and not simply to 'have' English, in addition to, and separately from, Spanish.

TRANSLANGUAGING IN 'BILINGUAL' MATH CLASS

While translanguaging was used in classes where English was the official language of instruction, it was also utilized in math classes which were officially designated as 'bilingual'. A bilingual classroom can mean different things to different people. For some, it means a classroom in which a language other than English is solely used; for others, it means the use of two languages. For this teacher, bilingualism in instruction meant the creation of a space in which translanguaging is used to leverage the students' emergent bilingualism, as well as their background and content knowledge.

In the following lesson, Yolanda, born and raised in the Dominican Republic, demonstrates how translanguaging facilitates her students' learning as well as a US bilingual identity. After about 20 minutes of a lesson in which Yolanda is teaching a lesson on the math concept of 'perimeter' using both Spanish and English fluidly, it became obvious to her that the students still did not understand the concept. She immediately says to them:

> Nosotros somos del campo. Voy a poner un ejemplo. Ud. tiene una casita bien bella, un patio. Y Ud. sabe que el área de su casa va a ser todo su terreno, el espacio que ocupa las tierras en que está tu casa.

> Pero si vienen los animales del vecino, entonces Ud. decide poner una cerca, ¿Dónde se pone la cerca?
> (Different students call out answers)

Sí. Alrededor.

Entonces Ud. va a comprar en la ferretería el material que va a comprar para cercar su terreno. La mayoría de las casas tienen 15 metros × 12 metros si están en el pueblo. ¿Cuántos metros van a necesitar para cercar su casa?

[We're from the countryside. I'm going to give you an example. You have a very pretty house, with a backyard. And you know that the area of your house is going to be all of your land, the space that occupies the land in which your house is.

But the neighbor's animals come, and so you decide that you have to fence your property. Where are you going to put the fence?

(Different students call out answers)

Yes. Around.

Then you go to the hardware store to buy the material that you're going to buy to fence your property. Most houses have 15 × 12 meters if they are in the countryside. How many meters are you going to need to fence your house?]

Yolanda uses Spanish to appeal to the students' cultural experiences, especially rural ones, which makes it easier to understand mathematic concepts. When asking students to draw figures in order to contextualize the mathematical problem they're solving, she tells them: 'Yo pensaría en mi patiecito, en la mata de guayaba' (I would think of my little backyard, of my guava tree). The *mata de guayaba*, as well as their home language practices in Latin America, are always present in the students' world. Yolanda does with language the same thing that she does with culture; that is, she treats the entire repertoire of linguistic and cultural practices (not just those from the school domain) as very important for students' sense-making.

Yolanda focuses on building the students' languaging and their bilingual repertoire. This is evident when one day, teaching about correlations, she asks students to write a sentence in Spanish on the blackboard. But seeing students' hesitation and the incomplete sentences they write, she asks:

¿Quién me dice qué es una oración? Porque veo que la mayoría de sus oraciones no tienen sentido completo. Una oración tiene que tener un verbo, un sustantivo, un sujeto y un predicado.

[Who can tell me what is a sentence? Because I see that most of your sentences do not have a full meaning. A sentence has to have a verb, a noun, a subject and a predicate.]

Yolanda does not focus simply on English language development, but on the development of language practices, and especially standard language practices for academic functions. Both English and Spanish standard language practices need to be developed, and these can only emerge in interrelationship. For these students, understanding sentence structure, regardless of language, is most important.

Although Spanish was frequently used in this 'bilingual' math classroom, Yolanda is also mindful of the students' development of English, again focusing on the development of the students' bilingual repertoire. The discourse that follows takes place during the first minutes of the lesson on perimeter (English translations in square brackets):

Teacher: OK, *¿quién quiere leer cuál es el Do Now?*[7]
              [Who wants to read the Do Now?]
(Calls on a student who reads it in English)
Teacher: *¿Quién más quiere leer?*
              [Who else wants to read?]
(Calls on another student who reads it in English)
Teacher: *Todos diciendo …* (they all read chorally from the blackboard)
              [Everyone saying …]
Teacher: *¿Quién quiere traducirlo en español?*
              [Who wants to translate it into Spanish?]
Student: *¿Qué es la diferencia entre perímetro y área?*
              [What is the difference between perimeter and area?]
Teacher: *Repitan*: What is the difference between perimeter and area?
              [Repeat]
Teacher: *¿Cuál palabra es nueva para Uds. aquí?*
              [What word is new for you here?]
Students: Perimeter (chorally).
Teacher: *Así es*, perimeter, *perímetro.*
              [That's it.]

In this brief exchange Yolanda is speaking Spanish, although she has students read in English, repeat the written English on the blackboard, translate into Spanish and use their metalinguistic skills to identify new words. She finally repeats the term she's teaching in English and Spanish.

Another day, Yolanda is teaching about correlations. Although she's teaching in Spanish, she has the students write a sentence in their book in English. She points out the differences in pronoun use between English and Spanish:

> *En inglés no se omite el sujeto. Por favor Ud tiene que tener* 'he', 'she', 'it'.

[In English you don't omit the subject. Please, you have to have 'he', 'she', 'it'.]

And she then asks the class:

¿Quién me puede empezar esa oración en inglés? Vamos a ver, ¿quién me quiere empezar en inglés?

[Who can start that sentence in English? Let's see, who wants to start in English?]

At the end of class, after the students have understood the mathematical concept, she says:

Ahora tienen que elaborar una pequeña oración en inglés, una pequeña oracioncita en inglés. ¿Qué relación existe entre las calorías y los gramos de grasa? Por favor, una oracioncita pequeñita.

[Now you have to elaborate a small sentence in English, a little sentence in English. What relationship is there between calories and grams of fat? Please, a little sentence.]

At times during the lesson, Yolanda provides terms in English for the concepts she is teaching in Spanish. She says, for example: 'Una línea recta, en inglés se dice "straight line".'

What Yolanda stresses the most is that students could use their entire linguistic repertoire to demonstrate their mathematical knowledge. No one is wrong, and no way of saying anything is wrong. During this lesson, she tells them:

Aquí nadie se equivoca. ¿Quién quiere decir algo?

[No one here is wrong. Who wants to say something?]

And when students do not speak up, she adds:

Uds. saben que pueden usar inglés, spanglish o español, ¿verdad que sí?

[You know that you can use English, Spanglish, or Spanish, right?]

Yolanda knows that it is important for students to understand mathematics, and that to do so their entire cultural and linguistic repertoire has to be mined. In so doing, Yolanda is developing a sense of 'doing' bilingualism as US bilingual Latinos – capable of building on their home language practices to develop school literacy.

TRANSLANGUAGING AND NATIVE LANGUAGE ARTS

In this school, all students also have one class in Spanish that is tra-ditionally referred to as Native Language Arts (NLA). But in this school, 'native' has lost the association of 'first', with the teacher constructing a translanguaging space in order to build a bilingual identity that considers bilingualism itself to be 'first', and all lan-guage practices, including those associated with English, capable of becoming 'native'.

The NLA class is not simply a 'scaffold' for English learning. One NLA teacher describes the role of her course as follows:

> So my main goal is to help 100% of my students, to help them achieve, to help them succeed; not only in Spanish, but also in their other classes; for example, writing essays, and interpreting litera-ture and analyzing. Those are skills that can be used in any other class and we can definitely teach them that in Spanish. As long as they have the skill, making the transfer is a lot easier; so that's my main goal, just helping them succeed, and do well, and graduate.

Spanish is not simply a separate subject matter for these students. It is a way of making the entire cognitive and linguistic repertoire of students more complex as it is used for all tasks, including academic ones, as well as for tasks that require English-only performances. To achieve this, NLA teachers meet with English teachers twice a week to co-plan instruction. As one NLA teacher explained:

> We meet with the English teachers twice a week, because they do like the fluency, the reading and writing fluency in English. And we focus on literary elements and literary techniques and more on the literature aspects of the language.

This teacher understands that together the English and Spanish NLA teachers are building the students' integrated language reper-toire, consisting of complex language practices that sometimes require students to perform in one or another language, but make up one bilingual repertoire that US Latinos can use.

This school does not see itself as offering a bilingual education pro-gramme. However, through translanguaging, bilingualism in educa-tion is deployed, ensuring that these immigrant students develop a sense of being bilingual Americans who have the advantage of a broader linguistic repertoire than those who speak English only. We turn now to our second school, which, despite being located in the same school building, has other ways of negotiating the official language policy.

10.4.2 High School of Global Practices

Because this school was originally planned for Spanish speakers only, the school has a 'Spanish' feel. Most announcements and postings in the school are in Spanish, and the secretaries and guidance counsellors all speak Spanish. The majority of teachers speak Spanish, and many use it as a pedagogical tool within classes that are technically English-only. Despite the choice of the school administration to offer an English as a Second Language programme, the school built translanguaging spaces from the beginning. That is, translanguaging has been used as an informal pedagogy to ensure Latino students' understanding of content and development of English literacy, as well as the sustainability of Spanish, a language all adolescents speak. But with the arrival of students with languages other than Spanish, translanguaging practices have had to be extended to encompass these other languages. In 2008, the school decided to safeguard a space for Spanish only, by developing what they call a 'dual language' programme.

The students in this dual language bilingual programme take some of their courses in English and some content courses in Spanish. But the programme does not show the rigidity of most traditional dual language programmes in which a strict percentage of the content is taught specifically through only one language or the other. Rather, in this school's dual language bilingual programme students are guaranteed that some content be taught through the medium of Spanish, although, as we will see, these are also translanguaging spaces.

Below we describe how the construction of these different translanguaging spaces occurs in a content class supposedly taught in Spanish in the dual language programme, as well as in what, officially, is an English class. As we will see, both teachers are building a space where the hierarchies that exist between English and Spanish are dissolved, and where new bilingual identities of US Latinos emerge.

TRANSLANGUAGING IN THE DUAL LANGUAGE PROGRAMME:
HISTORY IN SPANISH

Although Ms Rojas's[8] history class is technically designated as a Spanish language content area class, this teacher uses translanguaging in ways that develop students' sense of 'doing' bilingualism, as well as their ability to use language in the complex ways that are being required by the new common core State standards that have been adopted in the USA. On the day of this lesson, Ms Rojas wanted to explore legislation and policies surrounding race and interracial marriages in the history of the United States. As she explained, there are few resources for such topics in Spanish that relate to this age group. Therefore, she found an article in a teen publication that was in English. Groups of students read the text in English, and together they discussed the meaning of the text in Spanish. They often annotated the English text with 'glosses', using words from Spanish, and at times used i-Pads and Google Translate. This was followed by a whole-class discussion, supposedly 'in Spanish,' that focused on interracial marriage and race-based laws in the United States. As the students shared their views, perspectives and questions in Spanish, they used English freely to cite evidence from the English language text. To support their positions, they read aloud passages from the article in English.

The class then moved on to a writing exercise. The focusing question for the free-writing exercise was: 'How big a role does race play in your life? How does it affect your views of yourself and your place in the world?' At this point, Ms Rojas gave students the freedom to choose any language of their choice for writing. She explained that this activity was 'about the content' and 'making connections', and that it was important that students be allowed their full range of expression. Figures 10.1, 10.2 and 10.3 show the ways in which three girls first reacted to the question. Their answers were subsequently used to expand the writing.

The first entry in Figure 10.1 and the last one in Figure 10.3 are written in Spanish, whereas the second one is written in English. But the language choice has little to do with the content and intent, since the first and third entries, written in Spanish, refer to the United States, whereas the second entry, written in English, refers to a Latin American context. In Spanish, the first entry talks about mixtures of races, including those that make up 'mi comunidad', presumably a Latino one, in the United States. The third entry, also written in Spanish, shows meta-linguistic awareness, pointing to the title/question that is written in English, and providing a translation into Spanish. But then, in Spanish, the student refers to 'white people' being dominant in the USA and to the racial prejudice that others may show towards those that come from Latin America. In contrast, the entry in English goes back to her 'country', her 'family' and her 'origins'. And through English she expresses the fact that people from Spain enslaved people from Africa and Asia 'to make them work hard'. This student is starting to develop a critical consciousness, understanding that it was enslavement that was responsible for people that 'started to mix each other and in this way create new races'. It is precisely this sense of mixture that is creating new ways of performing language through translanguaging; that is, neither Spanish nor English, but 'new'. This is the same concept

Ms
3/16/2011

How big a role does race play in your
life? How does it affect your view of
yourself and your place in the world?
Explai?

La raza es el color de piel que proviene
de mezclas, entre personas de diferente paises.
En mi vida la raza siempre ha sido muy interesante
e importante ya que hay una gran cantidad de personas en
mi comunidad. Estados Unidos contiene una gran cantidad
de personas que son mexclada entre paises
y hacen lo que se llama "raza."

Figure 10.1 Student work: Example 1

Sra.

And answer: How big a role does race play
in your life? How does it affed your view of
yourself and your place in the world? explain.

When I was reading this article I went
back to my country, my family and my origins. I started
to think about the different races that conform
my country from a long time ago when spain
began to bring people from Africa, and Asia to
make them work hard. However, later they started
to mix each other and in this way create new
races.

Figure 10.2 Student work: Example 2

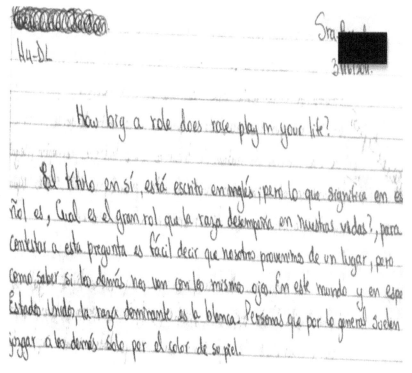

Figure 10.3 Student work: Example 3

contained in the writings of the Cuban anthropologist Fernando Ortiz (2002/1940) who introduced the concept of *transculturación* to refer to the complex and multidirectional process in cultural formation, always different from the source. *Transculturación* dissolves solid cultural and racial differences while it creates new realities. In the same way, translanguaging creates a new reality because neither English nor Spanish is seen as static or dominant, but rather operates within a dynamic network of cultural and linguistic transformations. Translanguaging encourages a recombination of linguistic features that precisely questions the linguistic dominance of English over the Spanish of Latin American immigrants. Coronil (1995: xxix–xxx) explains that the concept of *transculturación* 'breathes life into reified categories, bringing into the open concealed exchanges among peoples and releasing histories buried within fixed identities'. For the first time, these students, in developing a US Latino bilingual identity, are able to express their histories of racial and linguistic subjugation by 'releasing' their tongues, developing an 'other tongue' and engaging in 'border thinking' (Mignolo, 2000: 1). This border thinking, this 'thinking *between* two languages and their historical relations' (p. 74, our italics), requires 'an other tongue' as a way to crack the global designs of the United States. Through translanguaging, the students are situated in a space where alternative representations and enunciations can be generated because buried histories are released and alternative, and conflicting, knowledges are produced. The Latino educator and students in this class have 'appropriated' the 'dual language', spaces transforming them into 'translanguaging' spaces. As we will see, language is also approached the same way when the class is in English.

TRANSLANGUAGING IN AN ENGLISH CLASS

As in the English class described above in the Latin American Intercontinental School, translanguaging is also a common practice in this English class where most of the students are Spanish speakers, but some are not. Because Ms Dinos, the teacher in this class, speaks Spanish, Spanish use is common between students and teacher. The teacher explains:

> Especially at the lower level, bilingualism in quick translation helps to make connections, helps students to learn vocabulary, gives students background, and helps them to feel more supported by teachers and peers. It makes a thoroughly interesting language class with constant comparing and contrasting of languages.

She also uses Spanish when working one on one with students or in small groups to clarify a concept, word or question. When asked about this practice when there are students in her class who do not speak Spanish, she expressed her desire to put her bilingualism to good use in an instructional sense. She said:

> If I have 35 kids, and 33 speak Spanish, and if I explain in Spanish, it might not be fair to the few, but it's also not fair to the majority to not speak Spanish. So then I can explain in Spanish, and then work closely with the two or three who don't … If I feel a non-Spanish speaker doesn't understand something, I'll have a student who shares a language to translate or help, and also ask the student to tell me the words so I can learn, and help.

Students' language practices are used by this teacher not only to facilitate comprehension of the lesson but also as a way for students to act as experts in the classroom, and as language teachers of their home language for the teacher and other students. As Ms Dinos explains:

> My Bengali speaker, we had something written on the board in dif-
> ferent languages, simple things, 'Good morning', 'I love you', 'Thank
> you'. The Bengali speaker said the phrases and the whole class
> repeated them, then when he was done, the whole class clapped.
> It's a small step, but an important one in our enjoyment of diversity.

It turns out that it is this teacher's experience with translanguaging that allows her to extend herself to accommodate the bilingualism of others. She has developed the practice of pointing out cognates between English and Spanish, but building on the Latin roots of the second-most-known language among the students, French, spoken by many of the multilingual West African students, she now also does this for French. The teacher has also changed the way in which translanguaging is used in the classroom, to ensure that everyone is included. Whereas before she would often translanguage herself in whole-group lessons, now she calls on students with different language backgrounds to translanguage for clarification or meaning, but does not do it herself.

Ms Dinos uses 'language groups' where students of similar home languages work independently together, thus giving space for students to translanguage while working with English text or material. For many, these groupings are organized around an additional language, not necessarily a home language. For example, in one class, students from Guinea, Togo and Senegal worked together in French to create a semantic map written in English. For these students, home languages include Fulani, Kotokoli and Wolof, yet all were schooled in French in their home country, thus making this language common for them and a useful tool to make meaning of new content in English.

Finally, Ms Dinos encourages students to use their home languages independently. For example, she has encouraged students to create personal bilingual dictionaries, by writing down the word they do not know in English and using Google Translate or a bilingual dictionary to supply a definition. This enables all students to have a resource for future reference.

In this school, as in the first one, the teachers are building 'a space for the act of translanguaging as well as a space created through translanguaging' (Li Wei, 2011: 1223). The result is the ability to negotiate the official language policy of English-only and language separation in a way that affirms the rights of language-minoritized students by building on their language practices and dynamic bilingualism.

10.5 Conclusion

Putting alongside each other the national ideologies and official school language policy about English and bilingualism as a commodity to 'have', and the classroom discourse as enacted by teachers and students, this chapter reveals the negotiations that take place in schools that construct in-between spaces of promise for immigrant students. Although both schools are in the same school building and have an English as a Second Language programme exclusively for newcomers, as well as a student body with the same socioeconomic characteristics, their constructions of translanguaging spaces vary because of their different histories and constituencies. Both schools, however, understand that for these emergent bilingual youths to succeed in the four years of a US high school, more is needed than English-only and dual language practices that keep languages separate. Under the guise of an English as a Second Language 'official' designation for their programmes, these schools have built flexible translanguaging spaces capable of constructing and adjusting to new US bilingual subjectivities. Within these translanguaging spaces, it is then possible for educators and teachers to enact a process of social and subjectivity transformations capable of resisting the asymmetries of power that a dominant language or two separate 'language codes' have created in the past.

Notes

1. The term 'translanguaging' was first coined in Welsh (*trawsieithu*) by Cen Williams (1994) to refer to a pedagogical practice where students are asked to alternate languages for the purposes of reading and writing or for receptive or productive use; for example, students might be asked to read in English and write in Welsh and vice versa (Baker, 2006).
2. Following García and Kleifgen (2010), we use the term 'emergent bilingual', rather than the more accepted US term 'English Language Learner', to emphasize what these students can do and their potential, rather than what they lack. The term also emphasizes that bilingualism is at the center of the learning of English, because the use of the students' existing language practices are key in its development and because bilingualism should be the end product in the acquisition of an additional language.
3. Flores and García were involved in one school, whereas Woodley and García were involved in the second school. We are grateful to the administration, the teachers and the students in both schools for the time they granted us. All names of schools and teachers are pseudonyms.
4. For critiques of dual language programmes because of their dualistic designs, see especially Fitts (2006), McCollum (2000) and Valdés (1997).
5. In New York City, under mayoral control, many large comprehensive secondary schools were broken up into small schools of fewer than 500 students.
6. The New York State Education Department requires schools that educate emergent bilinguals to indicate whether their programmes for these students are English as a Second Language programmes or bilingual programmes. Each of these two types of programmes has specific requirements.

7. In New York City schools, teachers are required to have on the blackboard a 'Do Now', which is a short activity that students must do when they first come into a class, after they change teachers and subjects. It is meant to get students to settle down, take out their notebooks and pencils, and focus on the new content.
8. Unlike the first school where students called teachers by their first name, in this school only last names of teachers are used. Names selected here follow this practice.

References

Bakhtin, M. (1981). *Dialogic Imagination: Four Essays*. Austin: University of Texas Press.

Blackledge, A. and Creese, A. (2010). *Multilingualism*. London: Continuum.

Bloch, D. (2009). Census says African, Hispanic immigrants flocking to Bronx Boro. *The Daily News* (3 February 2009). Retrieved from www.nydailynews. com/new-york/bronx/census-african-hispanic-immigrants-flocking-bronx-boro-article-1.388678

Canagarajah, S. (2011). Codemeshing in academic writing: identifying teachable strategies of translanguaging. *The Modern Language Journal*, 95(3), 40–117.

Collins, J. (2011). Language, globalization, and the state: issues for the new policy studies. In T. L. McCarty (ed.), *Ethnography and Language Policy* (pp. 128–36). New York / London: Routledge.

Coronil, F. (1995). Transculturation and the politics of theory: countering the center, Cuban counterpoint. Introduction to *Cuban Counterpoint: Tobacco and Sugar* [1940], by F. Ortiz, trans. H. de Onis (pp. ix–lv). Durham, NC: Duke University Press.

Creese, A. and Blackledge, A. (2010). Translanguaging in the bilingual classroom: a pedagogy for learning and teaching?' *The Modern Language Journal*, 94(1), 103–15.

Cummins, J. (2007). Rethinking monolingual instructional strategies in multilingual classrooms. *Canadian Journal of Applied Linguistics*, 10(2), 221–40.

Donato, R., Menchaca, M. and Valencia, R. R. (1991). Segregation, desegregation, and integration of Chicano students: problems and prospects. In R. Valencia (ed.), *Chicano School Failure and Success: Research and Policy Agendas for the 1990s* (pp. 27–63). London: Falmer.

Fitts, S. (2006). Reconstructing the status quo: linguistic interaction in a dual-language school. *Bilingual Research Journal*, 29(2), 337–65.

García, O. (2009). *Bilingual Education in the 21st Century: A Global Perspective*. Malden, MA and Oxford: Blackwell-Wiley.

García, O. and Kleifgen, J. (2010). *Educating Emergent Bilinguals: Policies, Programs and Practices for English Language Learners*. New York: Teachers College Press.

García, O. and Leiva, C. (2014). Theorizing and enacting translanguaging for social justice. In A. Blackledge and A. Creese (eds.), *Heteroglossia as Practice and Pedagogy* (pp. 199–216). New York: Springer.

García, O. and Li Wei (2014). *Translanguaging: Language, Bilingualism and Education*. Basingstoke: Palgrave Macmillan.

Hannerz, U. (2003). Beint there ... and there ... and there! Reflections on multi-site ethnography. *Ethnography*, 4(2), 201–16.

Heller, M. (1999). *Linguistic Minorities and Modernity: A Sociolinguistic Ethnography*. London: Longman.

Hornberger, N. H. and Cassels Johnson, D. (2007). Slicing the onion ethnographically: layers and spaces in multilingual language education policy and practice. *TESOL Quarterly*, 41(3), 509–32.

Hornberger, N. and Link, H. (2012). Translanguaging and transnational literacies in multilingual classrooms: a bilingual lens. *International Journal of Bilingual Education and Bilingualism*, 15(3), 261–78.

Howatt, A. (1984). *A History of English Language Teaching*. Oxford: Oxford University Press.

Jacobson, R. (1983). Can two languages be developed concurrently? Recent developments in bilingual methodology. In H. B. Altman and M. G. McClure (eds.), *Proceedings of the 18th Southern Conference on Language Teaching* (pp. 110–31). Atlanta, GA: Southern Conference on Language Teaching, Spelman College.

Johnson, D. C. (2010). Implementational and ideological spaces in bilingual education language policy. *International Journal of Bilingual Education and Bilingualism*, 13(1), 61–79.

Kibler, A. (2010). Writing through two languages: first language expertise in a language minority classroom. *Journal of Second Language Writing*, 19, 121–42.

Lambert, W. (1975). Culture and language as factors in learning and education. In A. Wolfgang (ed.), *Education of Immigrant Students* (pp. 55–83). Toronto: Ontario Institute for Studies in Education.

Lewis, G., Jones, B. and Baker, C. (2012a). Translanguaging: developing its conceptualisation and contextualisation. *Educational Research and Evaluation*, 18(7), 655–70.

Lewis, G., Jones, B. and Baker, C. (2012b). Translanguaging: origins and development from school to street and beyond. *Educational Research and Evaluation*, 18(7), 641–54.

Li, Wei (2011). Moment analysis and translanguaging space: discursive construction of identities by multilingual Chinese youth in Britain. *Journal of Pragmatics*, 43, 1222–35.

MacSwan, J. (2000). The architecture of the bilingual language faculty: evidence from intrasentential code switching. *Bilingualism: Language and Cognition*, 3, 37–54.

Makoni, S. and Pennycook, A. (2007). *Disinventing and Reconstituting Languages*. Clevedon: Multilingual Matters.

Martínez, R. A. (2010). Spanglish as a literacy tool: toward an understanding of the potential role of Spanish–English code-switching in the development of academic literacy. *Research in the Teaching of English*, 45(2), 124–49.

McCarty, T. L. (ed.) (2010). *Ethnography and Language Policy*. New York / London: Routledge.

McCollum, P. (2000). Learning to value English: cultural capital in a two-way bilingual program. *Bilingual Research Journal*, 23, 113–34.

Menken, K. and García, O. (eds.) (2010). *Negotiating Language Policies in Schools: Educators as Policymakers.* New York: Routledge.

Mignolo, W. (2000). *Local Histories / Global Designs: Coloniality, Subaltern Knowledges, and Border Thinking.* Princeton, NJ: Princeton University Press.

Ortiz, F. (2002/1940). *Contrapunteo cubano del tabaco y el azúcar [Tobacco and Sugar: A Cuban Counterpoint].* Madrid: Cátedra.

Palmer, D. and Martínez, R. A. (2013). Teacher agency in bilingual spaces: a fresh look at preparing teachers to educate Latina/o bilingual children. *Review of Research in Education,* 37, 269–97.

Poplack, S. (1980). Sometimes I start a sentence in Spanish y termino en español: toward a typology of code-switching. *Linguistics,* 18, 581–618.

Ricento, T. K. and Hornberger, N. H. (1996). Unpeeling the onion: language planning and policy and the ELT professional. *TESOL Quarterly,* 30(3), 401–27.

Rosa, J. D. (2010). Looking like a language, sounding like a race: making Latin@ panethnicity and managing American anxieties. Unpublished PhD thesis, University of Chicago.

Sayer, P. (2012). Translanguaging, TexMex, and bilingual pedagogy: emergent bilinguals learning through the vernacular. *TESOL Quarterly.* doi:10.1002/tesq.53

Spolsky, B. (2004). *Language Policy.* Cambridge: Cambridge University Press.

US Census Bureau (2009). American Community Survey. Retrieved from www.census.gov/acs/www/data_documentation/2009_release/

Valdés, G. (1997). Dual language immersion programs: a cautionary note concerning the eduction of language-minority students. *Harvard Educational Review,* 67(3), 391–429.

Williams, C. (1994). Arfarniad o Ddulliau Dysgu ac Addysgu yng Nghyd-destun Addysg Uwchradd Ddwyieithog. Unpublished PhD thesis, University of Wales, Bangor.

Yu, W. (2000). Direct method. In M. Byram (ed.), *Routledge Encyclopedia of Language Teaching and Learning* (pp. 176–8). New York: Routledge.

Zentella, A. C. (1997). *Growing Up Bilingual: Puerto Rican Children in New York.* Malden, MA: Blackwell.

11 Becoming multilingual and being multilingual: some thoughts

David Block

11.1 From 'language learning' and 'language use' to 'becoming multilingual' and 'being multilingual'

There is a long-standing issue in second language acquisition (SLA) and educational bilingualism studies of how to describe individuals in terms of their language-mediated identities. In Block (2003), I discuss a distinction made by researchers such as Susan Gass (1998) between language 'learners' and language 'users', the argument being, in effect, that researchers can and should distinguish between individuals when they are in language learning mode and when they are in language using mode. In making this distinction, Gass was making a programmatic statement about SLA as a field of inquiry in the larger field of what she called 'second language studies'. She was also responding to Alan Firth and Johannes Wagner's (1997) prescient and oft-cited call for a broadening of SLA to take on frameworks and methodologies used in discourse analysis. She stated her position as follows:

> the goal of my work (and the work of others within the input/interaction framework ...) has never been to understand language use per se ... but rather to understand what types of interaction might bring about what types of changes in linguistic knowledge ... Nevertheless, it is true that in order to examine these changes, one must consider language use in context. But in some sense this is trivial; the emphasis in input and interaction studies is on the *language* used and not on the act of communication. This may appear to be a small difference, but to misunderstand the emphasis and the research questions ... can result ... in fundamental misinterpretations and naïve criticism. In fact, the result is the proverbial (and not very useful) comparison between apples and oranges. (Gass, 1998: 84)

This perspective, eminently linguistic at the expense of a broader view of SLA which would include communication writ large, is represented in Figure 11.1 below.

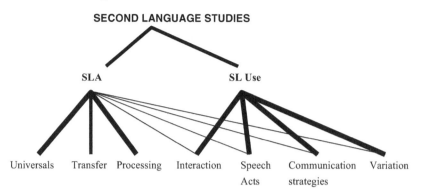

Figure 11.1 A characterization of research in second language studies (Block, 2003: 117; based on Gass, 2000: 54)

In this case, SLA is understood as 'linguistic-cognitive' (Ortega, 2013), as exclusively about linguistic development and the cognitive processes leading to it. Two statements made by Gass in her 1998 article make this case clearly. In reference to the SLA side of her diagram, Gass notes how in one of her studies (Varonis & Gass, 1985), participants '*were* learners inasmuch as these individuals were students at the English Language Institute of the University of Michigan, where they were paying rather large sums of money to learn' (1998: 85; emphasis in the original). And in reference to the second language (SL) use side, she notes how 'many of the individuals in a workplace setting, for example, are not learners in the sense that is of interest to researchers in SLA ... [as] they do not evidence change in grammatical systems' (p. 84).

Finding support for claims of this type is notoriously difficult, and one might well wonder if being a student 'at the English Language Institute of the University of Michigan' and 'paying rather large sums of money to learn' is hard evidence that one is a learner and if using language in a workplace, presumably as opposed to in a language classroom, is evidence that one is not. Surely where a researcher stands on this issue depends on what view he or she takes of learning. If learning can take place only in contexts which everyone agrees are for learning and if activity qualifies as learning activity only when those deemed to be the learners recognize their activity as such, then it seems to me that we are indeed on slippery ground. For if information processing is on-going activity, moment to moment, as we make our way through life, then surely the potential to learn anything – from how to assemble a piece of furniture from a flatpack to learning a language – is always with us. Age and other factors may figure in how strong this potential is, but surely it is always there. And where there is potential for more learning, we can say that the process is not over. In short, the language learning process never ends as long as one has access to opportunities to use the target language. In response to Gass, Firth and Wagner (1998: 91) made this point quite eloquently, arguing that 'what constitutes "acquisition" is essentially unclear ... [as] we cannot be sure where "use" ends and "acquisition" begins ... [and] there is surely no easily distinguishable dividing line between psycholinguistics and sociolinguistics'.

As Jasone Cenoz and Durk Gorter suggest in the introduction to this volume, the students who appear in Chapters 2 to 9 can be placed on a continuum as regards the kind of language-mediated activity that they are engaged in, from 'becoming multilingual' to 'being multilingual'. This continuum is different from the learner vs. user dichotomy, although it does make a similar differentiation when it comes to what is being done with multilingual resources. In the case of becoming a multilingual, the focus is on actions taken by teachers and students which facilitate further language development (from grammatical to discursive competence), such as the use of scaffolding as a teaching strategy or the use of translation as a learning strategy, and in this sense there is a clear SLA angle on matters. As Cenoz and Gorter note, this is more clearly the case in Luk and Lin's account of Hong Kong secondary school students moving from Chinese-medium instruction to English-medium instruction; Ballinger's account of teachers' and students' bilingual (English and French) strategies and translanguaging practices in a language arts class in Montreal; and Arteagoitia and Howard's study of how Latino middle-school students in the United States are able to use their knowledge of Spanish, and specifically Spanish–English cognates, in the development of English language reading skills. There is also a clear 'becoming multilingual' element in the three chapters by Levine, Kramsch and Huffmaster, and Fuller, focusing on Americans on a study-abroad programme in Germany, the study of German at an American university and German and international students at an English-medium American school in Germany, respectively, even if in these cases there are also more explicit positionings of students as being multilingual in their language-mediated practices. Finally, the complementary school context in Britain – Creese, Blackledge and Takhi focusing on a Panjabi school in Birmingham and Li Wei focusing on Chinese schools in London – and the bilingual school context in the United States – Garcia, Flores and Woodley focusing on a Spanish–English school in New York – seem to provide more examples of being multilingual, that is, for more self-conscious affiliations to ethnolinguistic identities via practices such as translanguaging.

But is a distinction between becoming multilingual and being multilingual really possible? Cenoz and Gorter are careful to emphasize that what they propose is a continuum and not a dichotomous either/or proposition. Still, it is worthwhile to try to pick apart this continuum, and in the next section I aim to do so by examining an example of ambiguous bilingual practices: ambiguous in that it is not clear exactly where they are situated on the becoming multilingual/being multilingual continuum, even if they can be discussed in terms of it.

11.2 Learning and using; becoming and being multilingual

In a series of publications (e.g. Block, 2006, 2007a, 2007b, 2008), I have written about Carlos, a Colombian man I met in London in 2003, who was my principal informant in a small-scale study of Spanish-speaking Latinos which I carried out in 2003–2004. Carlos was well educated but, because of his relatively limited English-speaking skills, he worked in a series of jobs which required far less of him than the job as a university lecturer which he had held in Colombia. Despite this experience of downward mobility, Carlos did not seem particularly concerned about improving his English, and he was able to maintain a middle-class standard of living and lifestyle, which was mediated primarily in Spanish.[1] Indeed, my interpretation of Carlos's life, based on recordings of his interactions at home and in the workplace as well as in face-to-face interviews in which we talked about these interactions, was that he affiliated to a transnational Spanish-speaking community which was primarily middle class and comfortable with the regular use of Spanish in London (or anywhere else in the world). When I have written about Carlos, I have tended to position him as an English language user, in Gass's terms, and as being multilingual, in Cenoz and Gorter's terms and, in doing so, I have not considered his interactions as learning experiences and as part of the process of becoming multilingual (specifically, becoming a Spanish–English bilingual). Here I shall cast a different eye on Carlos's activity in English, examining how his English language use might be seen as English language learning and how being multilingual goes hand in hand with an on-going process of becoming multilingual. My starting point is a conversation which took place in a canteen at work. Carlos (C) is having lunch with his wife (K) and three of her work colleagues (F, P, M). The conversation has moved to the topic of soups and the following exchange takes place. (The transcription conventions used in this and other examples follow those listed in the Appendix unless otherwise stated.)

Conversation 1:   Over lunch with K's colleagues in late 2003

```
 1  C:   but in Bogota it's different / it's another soup with uhh
         vegetables=
 2  K:   =which one? /
 3  C:   uhhh (3) how do you call it? /
 4  F:   vegetable soup <laughing> / (2)
 5  K:   why don't you say it in Spanish? /
 6  C:   I can't remember in Spanish / I've got that thing in my head
         [ehrm
 7  P:   [you focus on the taste and you've forgotten the name
         <laughing> /
 8  K:   a vegetable soup /
 9  C:   yes / but with=
10  K:   =with **avena** {oat}? /
11  C:   with avena / and little chickens in the soup /
12  K:   ahh yeah / yeah / yeah / from Bogotá /
13  C:   from Bogotá / yes (3)
14  C:   and for kernal ((xxx)) /
15  K:   and with cream=
16  C:   =with cream / yes=
17  K:   =and sweetcorn
18  C:   =sweetcorn
19  M:   with **avena** / it's oats /
20  C:   yes /
21  M:   but it's never heard of / putting oats in a soup /
22  C:   yes / we make a lot of kind of soup with oats (.5)
23  M:   very interesting
         ...
```

This conversation takes place in a naturalistic setting, and therefore it is an example of second language use, in Gass's terms, and being multilingual in Cenoz and Gorter's terms. However, it also contains within it characteristic features of classroom discourse in terms of how teachers and more knowledgeable interlocutors accompany learners as they attempt to communicate in a target language. From the beginning of this exchange, K acts as a monitor, and indeed scaffolder, of Carlos's speech. She first of all pushes Carlos to be more precise in turn 2, and when he cannot find the word for *avena* in English, she tells him to say it in Spanish in turn 5. When he says that he cannot remember the word in Spanish, but then carries on regardless, K provides 'avena' in turn 10, although curiously enough, with no translation into English for the other three participants in the conversation. However, this move serves to free Carlos from his impasse and the recipe continues.

In the next part of the conversation, K comes into the conversation in the wake of Carlos's turns, showing understanding in turn 12 and then adding recipe ingredients in turns 15 and 17. In both cases, the words are repeated by Carlos, who also attempts to emulate K's pronunciation (turns 16 and 18). He thus engages in imitation and repetition, which sociocultural theory researchers (e.g. DiCamilla & Antón, 1997) and theorists (e.g. Lantolf, 2006) have argued are a fundamental part of the mentor–mentee interaction and second language learning processes. By this time in the conversation, and after he repeats K's final intervention (the word 'sweetcorn' in turn 18), Carlos is on his own as he addresses M's query about 'avena'.

When I asked Carlos in an interview if he considered K to be acting as a kind of a mentor and guardian of his speech in this and other conversations in English, he responded as follows:

Interview excerpt 1

> yes / it's true that she / ehh (1) serves as my backup in conversations when (1.5) I know that she knows what I am trying to explain in English (1) because we have already talked about it / and (1) in that moment / ehh (2) the situation escapes me right? / I can't be specific (1) obviously K plays this part / K backs me up / and that may be by taking me through the medium / let's say in Spanish / or even in English / she tries to make it more specific as we go along / yes / that's right ...

> / sí / es indudable que ella / ehh (1) me sirve de refuerzo en conversaciones cuando (1.5) yo sé que ella conoce lo que yo estoy explicando en inglés (1) porque ya lo hemos hablado / y (1) en ese momento / ehh (2) la situación se me se me diluye no? / No logro precisar (1) claro K hace ese papel / K refuerza / y ya sea a través de llevarme por el medio / digamos en español / o aun en el inglés / trata de írmelo haciendo mas concreto / sí / es cierto ...

> (Carlos, 6/2/04)

When I asked Carlos if he saw this relationship with K as one of dependence, he said that he was conscious of how he used the support which she provided ('los apoyos que ella me ha dado'). However, when K was not present, for example when Carlos participated in conversations with his immediate workmates, events generally unfolded in a very different way. On these occasions, he was either ignored or ended up participating in conversations which he generally found too difficult to follow, given their fast pace and the fact that his colleagues spoke in heavy cockney accents which Carlos claimed to have difficulty understanding (see Block, 2006 for a detailed account of this phenomenon). However, on other occasions his work colleagues moved in the opposite direction, seemingly taking him for someone with very low English language skills who had to be talked to as if he were a child. Unlike his conversations involving K, these apparent attempts at mentoring and scaffolding did not have the desired effect, as we see in the following example. In it, Carlos is talking to his line manager about an office move that is scheduled for the same day and which will require the assistance of a group of workers who, despite being from a range of South American countries, were known by the shorthand term 'the Colombians'.

Conversation 2:   Gary and Carlos talking about an office move in late 2003

```
1   C:   what do you say about Ben? / he's not coming work /
2   G:   if he does not come into today? /
3   C:   yeah /
4   G:   do you know what to do with the Colombians / with the Colombian
         helpers we've got? / or do we have [outside
5   C:                                        [yes, Bob I [need to to do the
         Wheeler
6   G:                                                    [house moves
7   C:   Centre all right and (1) Ms Smith / she's [moving
8   G:                                              [yes she's got a couple
         of crates [upstairs
9   C:             [crates plus uhhh =
10  G:   = which is on this list here / this orange list / <unfolding piece of
         paper> /
11  C:   yeah /
12  G:   she's got / uhm <tearing paper> /ooops ((xxx)) / or this [colour
13  C:                                                            [yeah
14  G:   on her crates to know [where to go
15  C:                         [yeah ok
```

In contrast to the previous example, this exchange seems to work less well as a language learning experience for Carlos. The numerous overlaps point to the ways in which in terms of the content, Carlos already knows the script and indeed he is able to anticipate what Gary was going to tell him on several occasions (turns 5–10 and 13–16). Gary serves as a far less effective interlocutor than K in this case as, instead of lifting Carlos upwards on the way to achieving something, he talks down to him, using exaggerated pronunciation.

For example, in turn 2 we find the non-use of the contracted form 'does not', which would be expected, as well as the rising intonation of the utterance, which is characteristic of speech to small children (or people deemed to be slow). Thus, we have a situation in which Carlos is being talked down to and not as an equal conversational partner. Interestingly enough, Carlos saw his position vis-à-vis Gary, and on the job, in a slightly different light, as the following interview excerpt shows:

Interview excerpt 2

... and so I realised (.5) that coping with this vocabulary was easy / because it was very much limited to saying / you have to put this table over there / bring those chairs over here / and I carved out a space there (1) very interesting / because I ended up being the bridge with the rest of the Colombians / or with the Latinos who came to do work / I would talk to Gary / and he would tell me what needed to be done (1) and one time / I sat in on a meeting with Gary and some administrators (1) it was / well / I let them talk / and I was thinking about other things / and then Gary asked me something very precise about what they were talking about / right? / and I / uhn uhn / I wasn't very sure at that point (1) I came back at him with something like / but are you sure about what you said? / and so I managed to divert the conversation / you know? (1) and I realised that with just a couple of little things / I could go here and there / and no worries /

... y luego me di cuenta (.5) que manejar este vocabulario era fácil / porque era muy limitado a decir / tienes que poner esta mesa para allá / traer esas sillas para acá / y allí me hice un espacio (1) muy interesante / porque yo quedé como de puente con el resto de colombianos / o de latinos que venían a trabajar / yo hablaba con Gary / y el me decía lo que hay que hacer (1) y una vez / me senté en una reunión con Gary y unos administradores (1) yo lo pasé / bueno / yo les dejé que hablaran / y yo estaba pensando en otras cosas / y en un momento Gary me preguntó algo preciso sobre lo que estaban conversando / ¿ no? / y yo / uhn uhn / no estaba muy seguro entonces (1) yo le devolví algo así como / ¿ pero usted esta seguro de lo que dijo? / y ya la conversación logré des- viarla / ¿me entiendes? (1) y me di cuenta que / con un par de cositas /podia ir para allá para acá / y tranquilo /

Carlos, 6/2/04)

Here Carlos makes clear that he does not find the kinds of work-related conversations he has with his immediate work colleagues particularly challenging. He does not find it difficult to understand the details of an office move and the language which might be used to talk about such a move. In addition, he explains how when he encounters language that he does not understand – or in the case cited here, when he is not paying attention and is interrupted from his reverie – he has a repertoire of bluffing strategies to get him through potential communication breakdowns. However, a few minutes after telling me this story, Carlos revealed to me that Gary had actually asked him to supply the number of hours per week that he normally spent on office moves, a piece of information which only Carlos would have. Thus, in this case his bluffing response – 'Are you sure about what you said?' – no doubt came across as odd to Gary and the other people present at the meeting.

The upshot of this brief foray into the data that I collected from Carlos some ten years ago is that it is hard to classify on-going communication in a second or additional language as either becoming multilingual or being multilingual. In a sense, all instances of communication are about being multilingual once the individual is in a context in which he or she is asked or forced to communicate in a second or additional language. However, not all such instances of communication may be understood as becoming multilingual in terms of gains in language development or intentions in this direction, although they may be seen as being about becoming multilingual in a social-psychological sense, in which case there are direct links to notions of identity, integral to the being multilingual position.

11.3 Back to the chapters

So, how is this fuzziness in the being/becoming multilingual continuum dealt with in the different chapters in this volume? Space does not allow a thorough review of all of the main chapters in this volume, so I will focus on just two exemplary episodes, one from Chapter 3 (Ballinger) and the other from Chapter 8 (Creese et al.). However, what I have to say about the being/becoming multilingual continuum with regard to these two episodes applies across Chapters 2 to 9. As I have done with Carlos's data above, I will suggest that while the authors of the two chapters may have tended toward one or the other end of the continuum, it is possible to see how the individuals cited are working across it as they participate in communicative events.

Focusing on the learning strategies of students in an English/French bilingual language arts class in Montreal, Ballinger presents the following exchange involving two students working on a collaborative writing task (transcription conventions follow those used in Chapter 3):

Mohit and Stella

Mohit:　(Writing) Uh, *le poissonier*. Oh no. *Le* ...
Stella:　You wrote *'la'*.
Mohit:　*La* (mumbling).
Stella:　You don't ... It, it's a boy, Mohit. *C'est un gar!*
Mohit:　*La, le, la, le.*
Stella:　*Je sais parce que si c'est une fille ou un gar, c'est un gar!*
Mohit:　OK, you write it. I don't like it.

This exchange is ostensibly about a focus on form, but it is also about identity building: the on-going relationships between the two interlocutors, and their existing and emergent multilingual identities. Stella is acting as a mentor to Mohit, and there is definitely an orientation towards helping Mohit develop linguistically. Once she has identified article pronoun choice as the problem, Mohit engages in the kind of repetition for learning behaviour described by authors such as Lantolf (2006), repeating to himself in a low voice his article choices: '*La, le, la, le*'. However, as Ballinger explains, Stella's behaviour towards Mohit may be seen as face threatening as she takes no prisoners in the way that she deals with Mohit's confusion about French gender: '*Je sais parce que si c'est une fille ou un gar, c'est un gar!*' And it is in this sense that the exchange seems also to be about being multilingual, as Mohit tries to carve out a multilingual identity as a respected user of French in addition to the rest of his linguistic repertoire. Thus, while this brief discussion of French gender might be understood to be situated at the becoming multilingual end of the continuum, there is also some being multilingual behaviour going on in the way that Mohit asserts himself as a French user who can make choices: 'OK, you write it. I don't like it.'

In Chapter 8, Creese et al. focus on constructions of authenticity through translanguaging practices in a Panjabi complementary school in Birmingham (UK). They present the following excerpt from a lesson in which the teacher, Hema, is talking to students about translation (transcription conventions follow those used in Chapter 8):

Hema's translation story

I will share one thing with you. Last week I was doing a translation for somebody. Er, it was a gurdwara <*Sikh temple*> and there was a leaflet. A couple of lines only I had to translate for some, er babaji <*grandfather*>, like bazurgh <*elderly person*> yeah? Elderly person. Er and the word was 'community', yeah? And, I was doing the translation and I said 'samhudai' <*community*> yeah? Community means samhudai. He couldn't understand! Ah then I tried to make this word more easier. No! Then I was thinking 'hunh mein ehnoo ki dasaa?' *<what shall I tell him now?>* 'what shall I tell him now?' Then I said shall I say the word 'community'? I said 'community'. It was fine! [laughter] [He] did understand, because some words like, they are so familiar right? The people, the people living with those words, right? He easily understood what I'm talking about. 'Community haa puth, tu community kehna si, community kehna si menoo!' *<yes child, you should have said community, should have said community to me!>* I said ok. I was 'uncleji *<uncle>* I was doing word to word translation'. Ok? Some words they are more easier to understand if you say them in English. Ok?

Hema's story is ostensibly about the trials and tribulations of translation in the context of twenty-first-century Britain as a host country to Panjabi-speaking Sikhs, and it follows a fairly standard narrative structure, as described by researchers ranging from Labov and Waletzky (1967) to Riessman (2008). It also may be seen as an 'act of identity' (Le Page & Tabouret-Keller, 1985), 'as an index of the speaker's identity ... the enactment of different dimensions of identity, such as ethnicity, nationality, gender and social class' (Block, 2007b: 40). Specifically, the narrative works as a way of indexing Hema as a transnational who is from India but has lived in the UK for 16 years; as an individual integrated in the local Sikh community, which itself has multiple transnational dimensions; and as a skilled teacher, as someone who works in and knows her way around the British educational system (she worked as an assistant in the secondary school where the complementary school classes were held).

However, the narrative may also be seen as the construction of Hema as someone who continues to learn, who while being multilingual remains in the process of becoming multilingual. Thus, the story that she tells here is about how she learned, or in any case realized, that 'community' is an acceptable word in the Panjabi spoken in Britain today. It is also interesting to see how in her exchange with the older man in the *Gurdwara*, she, the teacher, did not teach her interlocutor that the word for 'community' in Panjabi is *Samhudai*; rather, in the exchange she took the deferential role of *the instructed* as regards the appropriacy of using the word 'community' when speaking Panjabi in Birmingham.

11.4 Conclusion

In this chapter, I have argued that being multilingual and becoming multilingual (and indeed, language use and language learning) emerge as distinguishable yet interrelated and interlinked phenomena. And as we see from the contributions to this volume, these phenomena occur in multilingual educational settings across a range of geographical locations, contexts and practices. In the same way that the concept of language in multilingualism studies has undergone transformations in recent years, from Vivian Cook's (1996) multicompetence model to Sinfree Makoni and Alastair Pennycook's (2007) questioning of the integrity of individual languages, so too what individuals are *doing* when they engage in multilingual practices (e.g. translanguaging) has come to be seen from multiple perspectives. And, as is the case as regards language in multilingualism, the simultaneity of being and becoming multilingual is out of sync with language policies in general, where unitary views of language and language practices predominate. The contributions to this volume certainly provide food for thought for those who are committed to mounting challenges to the status quo in multilingual policy and practice. Above all, we see here the seeds of change as regards practice, as phenomena like translanguaging begin to be seen as acceptable in multilingual classrooms. It will be interesting to see how matters unfold in this regard in the future and if such changes in classrooms make their way up to the policy level.

Appendix: Transcription conventions

A slash (/) shows the end of a chunk of talk
A question mark (?) indicates question intonation
Bold indicates that the word is said in Spanish
Pauses of less than one second are shown with a full stop inside brackets (.5)
Pauses of one second and longer are timed to the nearest second and the number of seconds is put in brackets (2)
[square brackets one on top of the other indicates the point where speakers overlap
An equals sign (=) at the end of one utterance and the start of the next speaker's utterance shows that there was no audible gap between speakers
Double brackets around x's ((xxx)) shows that the speaker's utterance is inaudible or can't be made out
<phrases or words in angled brackets> is an additional comment by the transcriber on what is happening at the time or the way in which something is said

Note

1. There was sufficient income in the household for this middle-class standard of living because Carlos and his wife, who is British, owned a house which they rented out, lived in rent-controlled accommodation, had savings in the bank and had regular income from the full-time jobs that they held.

References

Block, D. (2003). *The Social Turn in Second Language Acquisition*. Edinburgh: Edinburgh University Press.

Block, D. (2006). *Multilingual Identities in a Global City: London Stories*. London: Palgrave.

Block, D. (2007a). 'Socialising' second language acquisition. In Zhu Hua, P. Seedhouse, Li Wei and V. Cook (eds.), *Language Learning and Teaching as Social Interaction* (pp. 89–102). London: Palgrave.

Block, D. (2007b). *Second Language Identities*. London: Continuum.

Block, D. (2008). Spanish-speaking Latinos in London: community and language practices. *Journal of Language, Identity and Education*, 7(1), 5–21.

Cook, V. (1996). Competence and multi-competence. In G. Brown, K. Malmkjaer and J. Williams (eds.), *Performance and Competence in Second Language Acquisition* (pp. 57–69). Cambridge: Cambridge University Press.

DiCamilla, F. J. and Antón, M. (1997). The function of repetition in the collaborative discourse of L2 learners. *The Canadian Modern Language Review*, 53(4), 609–33.

Firth, A. and Wagner, J. (1997). On discourse, communication, and (some) fundamental concepts in SLA research'. *Modern Language Journal*, 81(3), 286–300.

Firth, A. and Wagner, J. (1998). SLA property: no trespassing! *Modern Language Journal*, 82(1), 91–4.

Gass, S. (1998). Apples and oranges: or why apples are not oranges and don't need to be. A response to Firth and Wagner. *Modern Language Journal*, 82(1), 83–90.

Gass, S. (2000). Changing views of language learning. In H. Trappes-Lomax (ed.), *Change and Continuity in Applied Linguistics: Proceedings from the Annual Meeting of the British Association of Applied Linguistics, 1999* (pp. 51–67). Clevedon: Multilingual Matters.

Labov, W. and Waletzky, J. (1967). Narrative analysis: oral versions of personal experience. In W. Labov (ed.), *Language in the Inner City: Studies in the Black English Vernacular* (pp. 354–96). Philadelphia: University of Pennsylvania Press.

Lantolf, J. (2006). Sociocultural theory and L2: state of the art. *Studies in Second Language Acquisition*, 28(1), 67–109.

LePage, R. B. and Tabouret-Keller, A. (1985). *Acts of Identity: Creole-Based Approaches to Language and Ethnicity*. Cambridge: Cambridge University Press.

Makoni, S. and Pennycook, A. (2007). Disinventing and reconstituting languages. In S. Makoni A. and Pennycook (eds.), *Disinventing and Reconstituting Languages* (pp. 1–41). Clevedon: Multilingual Matters.

Ortega, L. (2013). Ways forward for a bi/multilingual turn in SLA. In S. May (ed.), *The Multilingual Turn: Implications for SLA, TESOL and Bilingual Education* (pp. 32–53). New York: Routledge.

Riessman, C. K. (2008). *Narrative Methods for the Human Sciences*. London: Sage.

Varonis, E. and Gass, S. (1985). Non-native/non-native conversations: a model for negotiation of meaning, *Applied Linguistics*, 6(1), 71–90.

Index

Lightning Source UK Ltd.
Milton Keynes UK
UKOW07f1934090215

245956UK00002B/76/P